Stefan Heym's uncompromising stance made him un-popular with a succession of political regimes. The National Socialists, the CIA, and the East German secret police all held files on him. He was Hitler's youngest literary exile; McCarthyism was to drive him from the USA; and even in what appeared his natural home – the first socialist state on German soil – he was to become the country's leading dissident.

This study traces Heym's career principally by reference to his novels, journalism, and political essays. It considers all stages of his writing, and thus gives more attention than has been common to his earliest, and practically unknown, pieces of poetry, prose, and drama. All his novels are analysed, the major ones in depth, and there is particular focus on Heym's battles against Stalinism and censorship: the way in which his courageous defiance of a repressive regime inspired others and paved a way for the 'new' eastern literature of the eighties. Without Heym, literary opposition in the GDR could well have crumbled. No study of East German literature, or even East German history, can be complete without frequent reference to his achievements.

CAMBRIDGE STUDIES IN GERMAN

STEFAN HEYM

STEFAN HEYM

The perpetual dissident

PETER HUTCHINSON

Fellow of Trinity Hall,
University of Cambridge

CAMBRIDGE
UNIVERSITY PRESS

Published by the Press Syndicate of the University of Cambridge
The Pitt Building, Trumpington Street, Cambridge, CB2 1RP
40 West 20th Street, New York, NY 10011–4211, USA
10 Stamford Road, Oakleigh, Victoria 3166, Australia

First published 1992

Printed and bound in Great Britain by
Woolnough Bookbinding Ltd, Irthlingborough, Northamptonshire

A catalogue record for this book is available from the British Library

Library of Congress cataloguing in publication data
Hutchinson, Peter, 1944–
Stefan Heym: the perpetual dissident / Peter Hutchinson.
p.   cm. – (Cambridge studies in German)
Includes bibliographical references and index.
ISBN 0 521 40438 X
1. Heym, Stefan, 1913– .
2. Authors, German – 20th century – Biography
1. Title.   II Series.
PT2617.E948z68   1992
833′.914–dc20
[B]   91–851   CIP

ISBN 0 521 40438 x hardback

Contents

Acknowledgments

For their advice and encouragement, I should like to express my thanks to the General Editors of this series, Barry Nisbet and Martin Swales. The latter's specific comments were of particular value. I am also deeply grateful to Elisabeth Stopp for her reading of my first draft, and for her host of thoughtful suggestions. Kate Brett, at CUP, was a model of helpfulness. Most of all, though, I owe a debt to Stefan Heym himself. I undertook my first visit to Grünau in order to prepare a short article on self-translation, but the wide-ranging discussions of that initial encounter opened my eyes to the fascinating phenomenon of Heym the man, the politician, the writer. His life and achievement thus became a source of inspiration in themselves, and led me to recognise far more clearly the opportunities for successful literary dissent in the modern age. The decision to write a full study could only be taken, of course, against the background of happy family life and the pleasures of Fellowship at one of the friendliest Colleges in Cambridge.

CHAPTER I

Introduction

Stefan Heym was a rebel long before he reached the German Democratic Republic, but he proved to be that country's first, one of its most popular, and certainly one of its most successful dissidents. He was, typically, centrally involved in the journalistic pressure on the GDR government prior to its resignation, and he was one of the first to take a symbolic step through the Berlin Wall. Unlike many of his contemporaries, Heym did not allow himself to be either muzzled by censorship or to be harassed into exile in West Germany. He maintained his sharply critical position despite all dangers, and he completed no fewer than thirty-six years of open, serious disagreement with the government and its official bodies. No study of East German literature, or even East German history, is complete without substantial reference to his achievements.

Given the wide range of activities in which Heym has been involved, there is no difficulty in finding a succession of adjectives to describe his personality. The most obvious, in an approximate order of celebrity are: courageous, shrewd, versatile, indefatigable, committed, outspoken, single-minded. As the list suggests, Heym does not choose easy options, and he has never relied on others for support. He has therefore had to struggle, simply in order to survive, at virtually every stage of his career.

Heym has proved remarkably uncomfortable a person to the regimes under which he has lived, and he has been a form of outsider in every society in which he has existed: the Weimar Republic, the Third Reich, the USA, and the GDR. His early revolt against National Socialism resulted in teenage exile. Yet

I

Heym's enforced travels had positive consequences. His writing was to benefit considerably from his experience of widely differing political systems, life styles, reading habits, and tastes. In addition, exile brought linguistic advantages. The need to compose in a language other than his own ultimately led to Heym becoming one of the most distinguished self-translators of our age. He translated virtually all his own novels, which have consequently appeared in at least two languages. The majority have been translated into many other tongues, ranging from Russian, Polish, Czech and Hungarian, to Chinese, Greek and Tamil.

It would be a mistake, however, to concentrate exclusively on Heym's work as a novelist when attempting to assess his achievement. Although his greatest works have been in the form of fiction, his investigative journalism has made him accessible to readers on a much wider scale, and his journalistic activity has nourished and inspired much of his fictional composition. This study will consequently devote much space to the relationship between Heym's active political life and his writing. It has, of course, been his journalism which has often placed him so firmly and so regularly at the centre of political events, with his reformist zeal repeatedly contributing to the early development of the German Democratic Republic. Like most successful journalists, Heym had to show considerable courage in his preparedness to investigate and to publish, and in some respects it is remarkable that he was never imprisoned for his candour. He has stood against what he felt to be unacceptable in a succession of different societies (the militarism of the National Socialists, US imperialism, East German Stalinism and dogmatism), and in his fiction he has repeatedly used the figure of the struggling intellectual as a focus for broad inquiries into the nature of truth, and into the influence and corruption of power. He has repeatedly asked uncomfortable questions, using his own brand of practical, commonsense socialism as an ideal, and as a result he has enjoyed tremendous popular support. His personal bravery has been a key factor in encouraging other East German dissidents to resist the demands of the government and the censorship office, thus paving the way for the 'new' GDR literature of the eighties. This study will pay much attention to the calculated risks which Heym regularly took, one of the most dangerous of which resulted in a nationally significant paragraph in the penal code, the so-called 'Lex Heym'.

Critics have found it difficult to classify Heym, partly as a result of his exceptional linguistic ability. For a period he was avoided by West German critics, for although he was attractive as a gifted and dissident East German, he nevertheless wrote in English, defended the concept of socialism, and did not conform to any clear patterns in eastern development. He was obviously shunned by East German critics, since for a number of years his writing was effectively banned in their country; and even when he was allowed publication, critics could never be sure when he might again fall from favour. Yet he was also avoided by English-language critics, because his work did not follow any English or American traditions, and most of it had to be related to the German scene. Consequently, despite the fact that his novels have always received widespread reviews, there have only been two books devoted to him. One of them a highly detailed study of his novel *Ahasver*, the other a fairly short, and rather inadequate survey of his life and work. The collapse of the GDR, and the unification of Germany, provide an ideal moment to assess Heym's political, as well as his literary, achievements.

Several of Heym's novels have been bestsellers, and it was also reckoned that his column in an East Berlin newspaper used to be a considerable bolster to sales of that paper. It would be wrong, however, to deduce from this that Heym in any way panders to the sensationalist or other needs of certain readers. His newspaper stories may regularly be concerned with controversial issues, and his novels with major events of our age, but Heym's approach is always reflective, dialectic, and historical. One of his main tasks – in whatever medium he has chosen – is to make his readers *think*. He is never satisfied with narrative alone. He sees his task as exploiting a story in order to force reflection on those aspects of his readers' lives which they may take for granted, on forces in history, on such key concepts as 'freedom', 'democracy', and 'socialism'. He is also very much concerned with the limits of political and moral freedom, and the way in which history may be seen to repeat itself.

Heym's interest in traditional liberal values stretches through the majority of his novels and is regularly associated with a common liberal dilemma: the question of compromise in the attainment of one's ideals. This is an issue with which Heym saw the East German government repeatedly confronted, but it was one he had raised in his earliest fiction and his position was thus well established long before he was to castigate that government for its inconsistency. For Heym, compromise is a clear indication of moral inadequacy. Nor is passive resistance a sufficient response. Repressed societies need those who are prepared to stand firm or to fight. Progress tends to be achieved only by martyrdom. Perhaps not surprisingly for one who has remained consistent to his own ideals, Heym's choice of martyr figures is itself consistent. His preferred central character is the embattled intellectual, who is sometimes uneasy in the role of campaigner for human or civil rights. But in those cases where such a figure fails to engage in the battle, the result is not only detrimental to the cause: the individual himself is undone. Bravery, even of the most modest form, will achieve far more than the most subtle of compromises. The reason for this is simple: the forces of reaction can never be trusted. The evil and the powerful are ruthless in seeking their own selfish aims, and they surround themselves with brutal henchmen and fearful sycophants.

All these characters tend to be male. Heym's females are almost invariably background figures, self-sacrificing, often denying themselves for their more self-centred, ambitious, and sexually easily distracted partners. Intellectually often more limited, they nevertheless possess far stronger intuitive gifts and emotional resources which play a key protective and supportive role.

Those aspects of Heym's writing which one tends to praise first are his clarity, his logic, his creation of character. He also has a discriminating eye for detail, and he can develop his themes through use of dramatic confrontation and vigorous dialogue. It often tends to be overlooked, but Heym is also a witty writer. It is not coincidental he should have chosen to write his MA dissertation on Heinrich Heine, and like his great forerunner, he has been a Jewish exile with a love–hate relationship to his homeland. Heym, like Heine, began as a poet, but he adapted himself to those areas in which his main strength lay, and where the age in which he lived could best be influenced. 'If Heine had lived today, then he would have been on television' Heym once jested in conversation, and television was in fact one of the most successful ways in which he tried to reach his East German audience. Unable to feature on the programmes in his own country, he regularly made himself available as a guest on West German channels. These channels were naturally received in the East, and in this way the author managed to reach a public to which he was otherwise denied access. Like Heine, then, Heym outwitted the censors, and he also took a particular delight in outwitting the party bureaucrats. His desire to reach his public is equally evident in the large number of interviews which he has given over the years. He was a favourite of western television producers, who found his forceful personality ideal for discussion programmes, particularly about the Third Reich and the future of Germany, and he was also popular with newspapers and literary critical journals. Heym was – and remains – in demand as an interviewee for two reasons. As a newspaper man himself, he knows what journalists need: he does not dodge questions, and he can combine the telling and witty anecdote with an underlying serious argument which may well have universal interest. In addition, Heym is remarkably well informed on all aspects of world events. He is an avid reader of newspapers, he has an excellent memory, he can formulate his thoughts quickly, even under pressure, and produce the ideal mixture of provocative statement, philosophical reflection, casual aperçu, cautious prediction, and literary insight – all this without padding, without cliché, without jargon.

In this study I intend to trace the development of Heym up to his most recent publications, giving more attention than usual to his earliest and practically unknown pieces of poetry, prose, and drama. I shall show how in the thinking and the methods of his youth we can detect the seeds of his mature approach, and how his presentation of ideas has been changed and sharpened in response to different political climates.

CHAPTER 2

The early years: revolt and exile

One is surprised by two features of Heym's earliest years as a professional writer: first, his youth, and second, his versatility. By the age of twenty-two he had published poetry, fiction, newspaper articles and reviews, and two of his dramas had been performed. He might well have wished a more gradual start to his career, but the choice was not his: as an exile from Nazi Germany, he was forced to write simply in order to survive. And to write, moreover, in anonymity. 'Stefan Heym' is one of several *noms de plume* under which his first pieces appeared.

Helmut Flieg was born in the industrial city of Chemnitz on 10 April 1913.[1] His father, Daniel, was married to the much younger Elsa, only daughter of a successful textile business-man, and a second child was born to the Fliegs in the spring of 1918. The whole family was Jewish, and Daniel worked for his father-in-law's company in an executive capacity. Throughout the boys' youth the Fliegs therefore enjoyed a sound financial existence, and for a period in the twenties, when the textile industry was flourishing, they moved to a large house in one of the more prestigious parts of the town. But depression affected them like others, and a return to the original flat proved necessary after a few years.

Heym's memoirs, *Nachruf*, gives us an idea of Helmut Flieg's youth and of those influences which shaped his adolescence. The impression is of a boy with a rich imagination, precocious and questioning; isolated from others through his intelligence, his family's comparative affluence, and his Jewish faith, a faith he found difficulty in accepting fully. Particular literary influences would appear to have been Schiller, and, among modern writers, Erich Kästner, Kurt Tucholsky, and Walter Mehring. Kästner himself was actually invited to read from his work in Chemnitz at the instigation (and organisation) of the young Flieg. The theatre flourished in the town at that point, and Flieg was fortunate enough to have several contacts among the actors. Indeed, he wrote a play himself during his school years, and this was actually staged in an amateur production by his Jewish contemporaries. Nothing has remained of any early experiments, however, and for literary purposes his career begins abruptly, and frighteningly, on 7 September 1931. On that day the local social-democratic newspaper, the *Chemnitzer Volksstimme*, published a poem simply entitled 'Exportgeschäft'. It is polemical and satirical, and furthermore, it attacks an aspect of German army policy which had been reported on the previous day – the decision by General von Seeckt to send instructors to Chiang Kai Shek's army in China. It was a bold move to publish such a poem at this point (the newspaper was actually banned in 1933), and even bolder for its author to couch his criticism in such openly scornful tones. The poem, in fact, derives its effects from a macabre imagery, which is used in a combination of arrogance and enthusiasm by a speaker who identifies himself with von Seeckt's cause.

Exportgeschäft

Wir exportieren!
Wir exportieren!
Wir machen Export in Offizieren!
Wir machen Export!
Wir machen Export!
Das Kriegsspiel ist ein gesunder Sport!
Die Herren exportieren deutsches Wesen
zu den Chinesen!
zu den Chinesen!

Gasinstrukteure,
Flammengranaten,
auf arme, kleine gelbe Soldaten –

denn davon wird die Welt genesen.
Hoffentlich
lohnt es sich!

China, ein schöner Machtbereich.
Da können sie schnorren und schreien.
Ein neuer Krieg –
sie kommen sogleich,
mit Taktik und Reglement und Plänen
Generale, Majore!
Als ob sie Hyänen der Leichenfelder seien.

Sie haben uns einen Krieg verloren.
Satt haben sie ihn noch nicht –
wie sie am Frieden der Völker bohren!
Aus Deutschland kommt das Licht!
Patrioten!
Zollfrei Fabrikanten von Toten!

Wir lehren Mord! Wir speien Mord!
Wir haben in Morden großen Export!
Ja!
Es freut sich das Kind, es freut sich die Frau.
Von Gas werden die Gesichter blau
Die Instruktionsoffiziere sind da.

Was tun wir denn Böses?
Wir vertreten doch nur die deutsche Kultur.[2]

Export business

We're exporting!
We're exporting!
And it's military officers we're transporting!
We're into export!
We're into export!
Playing war is a healthy sport!

The bosses are sending things Germanic, if you please,
To the Chinese!
To the Chinese!

Gas instructors,
Flame throwers,

At poor, small yellow soldiers –
The world will then get rid of disease.
Let's hope
It's got scope!

China, a splendid power sphere.
There they can scrounge and shout.
A new war –
They'll soon be here
With tactics and regulations and plans,
Generals, majors!
Like hyenas on corpse-fields, roaming about.

One war for us they went and lost,
But they're still hungry to fight –
They gnaw at peace at others' cost!
From Germany comes the light!
Patriots, you see!
Manufacturers of death – tax free!

It's murder we teach! Murder we spew!
Murder's our export, we do quite a few!
Clear?
The child is pleased, his mother too.
The gas is turning faces blue.
The officer instructors are here.

Anything wrong with what we do?
Just German culture is what we feature.

This represents an amazingly sarcastic challenge to authority, and a revolt against the author's comfortable bourgeois
existence and its preference for conservative values. The
ecstatic opening announcement takes us straight into the mind
of the speaker and conveys the delight of this 'patriot' at the
resurgence of Germany's military power. War, to him, is a
healthy game. The exclamatory tone attempts to diminish the
horrors which are referred to, as do several lines which are
presented in jocular form. 'Aus Deutschland kommt das Licht',
for example, with its inversion of traditional symbolism, or
'Zollfrei Fabrikanten von Toten', which takes delight in the

avoidance of taxes in the committing of murder and which contains a possible echo of Heine. The black humour aroused by such lines becomes more grotesque in the following stanza, however, 'Wir haben in Morden großen Export', or 'Von Gas werden die Gesichter blau': there is far less humour in this final example, and the impact would be stronger for a generation which actually knew the horrors of the First World War. As if in reaction to the unspoken question posed by this penultimate stanza, the speaker attempts to justify himself in the final two lines. The tone suddenly becomes muted. Surprised innocence ('denn') leads to semi-apologetic justification: the bold 'Wir lehren Mord' now gives way to the weakly explanatory 'doch nur', and the absurd euphemisms 'vertreten' and 'deutsche Kultur' produce the final unmasking of official policy through its own jargon.

We would not expect such a youthful poem to be without faults, especially since it was actually written during school hours! At points the rhythm is awkward and there are breaks in the speaker's perspective. His awareness of the army's past failings ('Sie haben uns einen Krieg verloren') is not consistent with his views elsewhere in the poem. (Such an ardent patriotic would adhere to the view that the army was not defeated but 'stabbed in the back' by the politicians who negotiated peace when the military was on the brink of victory.) Similarly, the 'arme, kleine gelbe Soldaten', which the reader is likely to accept in the figurative rather than the literal sense, suggests another change in viewpoint. The poet has not yet learnt the importance of consistency in perspective, even though his poem is as politically challenging as many other didactic pieces by established writers which were produced in the thirties.

Although 'Exportgeschäft' is traditionally claimed as Heym's first poem, the evidence suggests that it was preceded by a completely different type of work, the 'Melancholie vom 5. Stock', which appeared in the anthology *Um uns die Stadt* (Berlin, 1931).[3] The editors' introduction to this anthology is dated 'September 1931', so the poem was most probably in their hands before 'Exportgeschäft' had reached print. (Furthermore, the scene it describes is winter, suggesting composition as much as six months earlier.) And yet the tone, the imagery and the versification of this other contender for position of first publication are totally unlike those of its rival. This example of 'Großstadtlyrik' seems to lack all political awareness – the poet is more concerned with his own position in a frozen cityscape, seeing his sombre mood reflected above all in nature (snow, frost, cold) and its winter attack on the city:

Melancholie vom 5. Stock
Bahrtuchgleich lastet Schnee
auf traurig verbogenen Dächern.
Grauer Rauch aus schwanken Schloten
kräuselt in grauerem Nebel.
Totengräber Frost
greift mit eisig verknöcherten Fingern
zwischen die Ritzen dürftiger Fenster. –
Menschheit, zieh dir dein Federbett
über die blaugefrorenen Ohren!

Lichthöfe sind Schächte,
die tief ins Gedärm der Erde sich bohren.
Aber plötzlich ist Schluß. Aschenkästen.
Wär ich ein Kind, würd ich hinunterspucken –
vielleicht gefrör unterwegs die Spucke.
Nur ist die Kindlichkeit in mir
eingefroren . . .

Winter der Stadt ist gefängnishaft Monotonie –
dekadent – Kunsthonig –
Natur ist für andere Menschen geschaffen,
schwebend im Glück . . .

Menschheit, du Leiche, schlaf weiter!
Einen Kranz von kahlen Zweigen werd ich dir spenden,
hast es nicht besser verdient –
Rieselnder Schnee hüllt sanft dich ein.

Melancholy from the fifth floor
Snow lies like a coffin's pall
On sad, curved roofs.
Grey smoke, from unsteady chimneys

Curls upwards into even greyer fog.
Frost, the gravedigger,
gropes with his bony fingers of ice
between the cracks around meagre windows.
Humanity, pull your feather-beds
over your ears, frozen blue!

Light wells are shafts
which bore deep into the bowels of the earth.
But suddenly they stop. Dustbins.
If I were a child, I'd spit down them –
perhaps the spittle would freeze on its way.
But the childlike part of me
has turned to ice . . .

Winter in the city is prison-like monotony –
decadent – artificial honey –
Nature was created for other people,
hovering in happiness . . .

Humanity, you corpse, sleep on!
I will give you a wreath of bare twigs,
you don't deserve better –
Fluttering snow softly covers you in.

The poet ignores the panoramic vision which a fifth floor could provide, nor does snow symbolise the purity or beauty which it does for certain earlier German poets. Images of death predominate, and there is a quiet, resigned acceptance of this state of affairs – no call to humanity to change. Humanity fails to struggle against the grip of winter, and the poet himself seems trapped. Yet curiously, there is one stanza which suggests a different perspective: these 'other people' on whom nature smiles. They are unnamed, however: all that is clear is that the poet is excluded from them. Are they possibly the rich, who can escape this scene? The idea is undeveloped, and this line therefore remains uncertain. It also seems at odds with the general appeal to a dead 'humanity' in the following stanza.

The lines of this poem are in general slow-moving and deliberately unpleasant on the ear, particularly, in the opening stanza. Hard consonants and long vowels set the tone of the first four lines, while in lines 6 and 7 the shorter and more high-pitched vowels seek to convey the penetrating effect of the frost. In the second stanza there is another controlled use of sound, and here more particularly rhythm, to reflect the poet's spiralling downward gaze, which is suddenly brought to a halt. The following simple word works symbolically too, and these are some of the best lines in the poem. For the rest, though, the poetic achievement is less. Neither sound, rhythm, nor image arrests us, and there is a lack of direction. The elegiac conclusion is also not really satisfactory, raising questions which remain unanswered – rather like that raised in the penultimate stanza. (Why does mankind not deserve better?) There does not seem to be an underlying uniformity of vision in the poem.

Of these two first works, it was the political poem which was to have by far the more significant effect and to change Flieg's life. While 'Melancholie . . . ' remained virtually unknown, the *Chemnitzer Volksstimme* transformed the young sixth former into a celebrity, who had to face brutal opposition from those he had attacked.

In the early thirties, National Socialist sympathies were steadily rising in Chemnitz. Much of the ethos of the party rested on high respect for the soldiers of the previous war, and so a poem like 'Exportgeschäft', which lampooned not just soldiers, but officers, was bound to arouse considerable anger. Indeed, when the poem's authorship became known, Flieg was beaten up by fellow sixth formers at the Chemnizter Staatsgymnasium and he had to spend several days away from school. (Rising anti-semitism doubtless also played its part in this attack.) The school authorities reprimanded those who had attacked Flieg, but they nevertheless recommended that he leave school. His father valiantly complained to the Ministry in Dresden about this treatment, but before the Ministry could receive the full report it requested from the school, the case was discussed at two gatherings of the National Socialists. At the second of these there was an enormous attendance, and according to a newspaper report, several hundred people had to be turned away from the overflowing hall.[4] Here Flieg was viciously attacked by the leading speaker, who claimed not only that the author of such a poem be expelled, but that efforts be made to ensure he did not receive his high school leaving certificate anywhere in Germany. Another speaker emphasised National Socialist principles, the importance of 'stiffening the national backbone', and lamented that certain teachers were Social Democrats and were contaminating pupils with Marxist ideas. Ironically, one speech which aroused considerable response from the hearers came from the leader of the 'Chemnitzer Schülerbund' (an organisation of school pupils themselves): he called for a return to older German values and for leadership from the front-line soldiers of the last war. The meeting finally voted unanimously for Flieg's expulsion from school and his being denied the opportunity of obtaining his matriculating certificate elsewhere in Germany.

The Nazis were vociferous in 1931, but they did not yet have legal control. Although Flieg had to leave the Chemnitzer Staatsgymnasium, he could not be prevented from moving to Berlin and attending the Heinrich Schliemann-Schule for the final six months of his school career. There he obtained his final certificate, in March 1932, with the overall classification 'good' – a remarkable achievement in view of the psychological pressures to which he must have been subject.

Flieg's ambition was to become a journalist, and later in 1932 he began studying at the Humboldt University in Berlin. But his pursuits were practical as much as academic, and his first newspaper article appeared in *Berlin am Morgen* as soon as 24 July: 'Berliner Hofmusik. Erlebnisse eines musizierenden Erwerbslosentrupps'. The journalist reports his day's experience with a group of unemployed who tried to supplement their meagre unemployment benefit by busking in the inner courtyards of Berlin, and the piece is as significant as the first poems for an insight into interests and methods.

The choice of subject alone suggests the sympathies of the reporter, and the reporting style itself is personal and engaged. We have a detailed description of the worst courtyard, and we are constantly reminded of the pressures on the poor and the unemployed. The wealthy are seen to be mean, the poor generous. And if a part of the town has risen in social prestige, then it will have fallen in terms of human generosity. The tone is far from objective, and from the start the reporter's sympathies with the victims of recession are undisguised. Indeed, hints of a revolutionary mood are also revealed at both beginning and end. In the opening lines, the reporter reveals his intention of considering the lowest rung of the social scale and determining how long it will tolerate its condition. And the conclusion provides a partial answer to this question: the author warns that a yet unexpressed threat lies behind these harmless melodies being busked in hidden courtyards.

Already in his first newspaper report the style for which Heym was later to become famous is apparent. He is simple and direct, and his descriptions are brief but symbolic. He includes numerous conversations to give his piece immediacy. He is not only an investigative journalist, participating personally with the stories he records, but a *reflective* one. He is anxious to see the wider implications of a story, its part in a trend, its representative features. Although he will often generalise, his account is not a balanced or a dispassionate one. He seeks to persuade as much as to inform, and his information is therefore presented from a particular, socialist, point of view.

The first article is signed 'F-g'. Nazi co-ordination only worked well at local level at this point, but there was clearly no need to antagonise openly, nor yet to jeopardise the position of his family in Chemnitz. Most future publications were therefore published under a *nom de plume*, and a variety of names was used for the growing number of pieces which came from Flieg's pen. Poetry seems to have been his preferred medium at this stage, and we see several examples in the 'Feuilleton' of the *Sozialistische Arbeiter Zeitung* and in *Die Weltbühne*, the left-wing weekly which was edited by Carl von Ossietzky and which was banned as soon as Hitler came to power. In most of these the poet is still experimenting with form, and an uneasy effect is often produced as rhythm and sense are sacrificed to the demands of rhyme. The themes are fairly constant: there is a sense of unease, sometimes despair at social conditions, with occasional hints that a workers' revolution is imminent. The poems in the *SAZ* are in the first instance political and accusatory. Notably, they are all signed 'Melchior Douglas'. Those signed 'Helmut Flieg' are on the whole more reflective and more personal. Already at this stage the author seems to have been using different names for different styles – a process which is more marked in exile. It is now difficult to trace all the newspaper articles written in Berlin, but it seems more likely that a large number were produced. At all stages of his career, Heym has written almost compulsively.

Flieg had been in Berlin little over a year when the fraud of the Reichstag fire was perpetrated. This event, on the night of 27 February 1933, allowed Hitler to issue a decree on the following day which gave the government almost complete power to suspend basic personal and civil rights, and also to take authority in any of the separate states. Warrants were immediately issued for the arrest of major figures whom the Nazis wished to have removed, although it was not until after the notorious 'Enabling Act' of 23 March that the Nazis had a legal basis for their subsequent acts of terror and suppression. A warrant for Flieg's arrest was issued very soon after the Reichstag fire. The party in Chemnitz were still anxious to settle their score over the publication of 'Exportgeschäft' (the editor of the paper in which it had appeared was arrested and the paper itself was banned later in the year), and they came to his parents' house in Chemnitz for information on his whereabouts. Fortunately, Nazi co-ordination was still only effective at local level, and so Flieg's younger brother was able to travel to Berlin and warn him of the situation. The boys' father had been taken as a hostage, but their mother had consulted lawyers about his imprisonment, and she had been assured he could not be held indefinitely. They were right, and Daniel Flieg was released several weeks later. Like so many other German Jews in the thirties, however, he later committed suicide. His elder son left the country only hours after he had been warned, on 12 March 1933. At the age of nineteen, he was Germany's youngest literary exile.

Flieg decided his best chances for what he believed to be only temporary, and relatively brief, exile lay in Prague, to which a

number of Communists in Berlin and elsewhere in Germany
decided to escape. Austria, with its lack of a language barrier,
its many publishing houses, newspapers and journals was a
popular alternative, but there was one severe disadvantage:
the country was not well inclined towards left-wing parties,
and repression of the left grew worse as the thirties developed.
Czechoslovakia, with its liberal political climate was far more
attractive, and its capital could in addition boast an established German-speaking intellectual minority, from which
such famous figures as Franz Kafka, Franz Werfel, and Max
Brod had sprung. An important practical advantage for Flieg
was that he knew a relatively safe route into the country:
unable to risk an official border crossing when he was a wanted
man, he decided to make the journey illegally through a
section of the Silesian mountains. A distant uncle was a doctor
near here, and Flieg knew a ski resort which lay exactly on the
border between Silesia and Czechoslovakia. The numerous
tales about his 'skiing to freedom' are, however, erroneous: the
reality was far less dramatic, far more exhausting and painful.
After taking public transport as far as possible, he had to walk
the rest of the distance to the resort, reaching it without mishap
but with very painful feet. A party of Czech skiers were
spending the weekend there, and one of the bus drivers who
had brought them from Prague kindly agreed to give Flieg a
lift on the return journey. The Czech capital was thus reached
without mishap, and a telegram was sent to his mother to
indicate his safe arrival. The code name used, on impulse:
Stefan Heym.

   The refugee had practically no contacts in Prague, but one
of the very few had come through the legendary reporter Egon
Erwin Kisch, whom he had met at a writers' gathering towards
the end of 1932. Kisch's family was a large one, and 'Heym'
went to their house in Old Prague where he was kindly
received by the old mother. One of Kisch's brothers, a doctor
who later worked with the International Brigade in Spain,
bandaged his feet and saw to it that he had a bed for the night.
Through left-wing contacts he was then found a bed with some
Hungarians – themselves refugees – who had been in Prague a

little longer, and here he stayed for the following fortnight. After this period he settled in a room of his own and managed to establish an independent existence. He was, it should be noted, one of the few who did not claim financial support from any of the committees that were formed to help Germen refugees. To generate income he took up the profession for which he had been studying in Berlin, and began to write for the newspapers – especially the German-language ones like *Prager Tagblatt* and *Deutsche Zeitung Bohemia*, but also for Czech papers (his pieces were translated). Short stories and sketches also appeared, a handful of which are now available in the 'Werkausgabe'. These reveal the easy versatility of the author, who is as at home in the field of character sketch as he is in that of humorous, or bitter, anecdote. Poetry still seems to have been a popular medium for him, and the majority of his contributions to the *Neue Weltbühne* (which took over from the banned *Weltbühne* of Berlin, to which he had previously contributed) are in this genre. But we also find political glosses and book reviews. Most of his pieces written at this point are short, usually assertive, often declamatory. Heym was beginning to establish a reputation, and he seems to have been determined not to appear either timid or dull. The poems, still political and often satirical, reveal a marked advance on those of the Berlin period. There is much greater care evident in composition, with a far more confident use of rhythm and greater consistency of tone and perspective.

The literary figures who were attracted to Prague established their own circles and clubs. Some were named after such figures as Thomas Mann and Bertolt Brecht, and they gathered in the literary cafés of the city. Here, despite his youth (still only twenty/twenty-one), Heym seems to have mingled among such figures as Ernst Ottwalt, F. C. Weiskopf and Wieland Herzfelde, and to have been accepted as one of them. It was also here that he met his first collaborator, the Czech Hanuš Burger, 'Dramaturg' at the city's Deutsches Theater.

Heym and Burger were both young, ambitious, and daring, but both were without experience of writing plays. In discussion, they found they shared an enthusiasm for Mark Twain, and so they decided to adapt – freely, and to suit the prevailing political conditions – material from one of his most famous novels: *Tom Sawyer*. The resulting play – *Tom Sawyers großes Abenteuer. Nacht Motiven von Mark Twain*, written in the winter of 1934/5 – draws largely on the murder of Twain's Dr Robinson and the resulting framing of Muff Potter. But the adaptors make a major change by using an intelligent, honest, and likeable black man (clearly based on the figure of 'Jim' in *Huckleberry Finn*) rather than the stupid drunk Muff Potter. They consequently allow the emphasis of the work to fall on prejudice and racial persecution. The play is aimed principally at children and adolescents, and the spectacle, the comedy, and the depiction of injustice are geared to their level of feeling, understanding, and awareness of moral values. The tension is held very well to a visually compelling denoument, in which there is a natural, triumphant celebration of youthful courage and human sympathy. Direct ideological remarks are very few in number, and they emerge convincingly from their context. The strongest is Tom's sudden, climactic insight: 'Du – ich glaube; arme Neger and arme Weiße – das ist ganz dasselbe' ('Hey – I'm beginning to think: poor negroes and poor whites – they're just the same') (p. 28). A line to which the Nazis would clearly take strong exception.

The emergence of political significance is gradual, and its background is, ironically, a story of adventure and youthful friendship firmly in the light-hearted spirit of Twain. Writing in 1952, for an East German edition of the play, Heym recalled that the two authors had repeatedly asked themselves the question 'Wie würde Mark Twein sein Buch schreiben, lebte er heute?' ('How would Mark Twain have written his book if he'd been alive today?) (p. 62). This sense of obligation to the original author was seen again in Heym's reaction to the 1953 staging of the play in the GDR. For ideological reasons the producer wished to cut the passage where Tom and Huck steal from Aunt Polly's shop, and one of the first reviewers even raised doubts about the pedagogical implications of choosing 'positive heroes' who have such faults as lack of respect for adults![5] Heym's firm rejection of such blatant ideological intrusion into the spirit of his model is characteristic of his concern to depict reality as he finds it. Polemic may be prominent in his newspaper articles, but in his fiction and drama his representation is determined by aesthetic rather than political criteria. As he remarked shortly after the 1953 production, 'Man muß den Leser dazu bringen, sich mit einer oder mehreren Figuren zu identifizieren; mit Figuren, die Leitartikeln reden oder sich leitartikelhaft benehmen, kann man sich aber nicht identifizieren.' ('You need to put your reader into a position where he can identify with one or several characters; but no identification is possible with characters who speak or act like the leader article in a newspaper.')[6]

Heym did not stay in Prague long enough to see the successful staging of his *Tom Sawyer* (albeit in Czech translation, since the government, under pressure from the Nazi Party, refused permission for the German version to be staged). Early in 1935 he happened to be approached – almost by chance – in connection with a scholarship to the USA offered by the American Jewish university fraternity of Phi Sigma Delta. Intended for those whose education had been disrupted by the Nazi seizure of power, the scholarship covered fees and living expenses, although it did not extend to travel costs to and from the States. Heym was then still optimistic that Nazi control over Germany would not last many years longer, and that by the time he had completed his study a return to his home country would be possible. He therefore applied for the scholarship and was accepted. In the light of his persecution by the Nazis, his numerous publications, and his clear academic potential, he must have been an obvious choice. There was, however, the problem of financing his crossing of the Atlantic, which he managed by, among other things, promising articles on America to the papers to which he had already contributed in Prague. New York was reached via Switzerland and France, and Heym began to study German literature in the University of Chicago.

The teaching was stimulating. Leonard Bloomfield, one of the great names in Linguistics, was there, and the atmosphere of the Department was friendly and encouraging. Heym's

problem was to learn English rather than German, but he was
young, had an excellent memory, and was ambitious. He was
granted exemption from the preliminary courses, and he began
work on an MA dissertation. The topic: Heinrich Heine, in
particular his verse satire, *Atta Troll*. The choice was a natural
one. Like his nineteenth-century forbear, Heym was a Jewish
exile from Germany, a satirical poet, a journalist, a man with
tremendous energy and fighting spirit. And *Atta Troll*, a political satire, over which critics have often been divided, provides much scope for the discussion of Heine as a political
journalist, a man whose activities in such 'divided' fields as
political journalism and poetry could be seen to enrich – or
impoverish – each other. Heym's achievement – and plea – in
the dissertation, is for greater consideration of Heine's life in its
broad interaction with his age. Only in this way, he suggests,
can the poet's development be properly grasped. A second
point – and warning – which emerges forcefully is one which
Heym was later to level at students of his own work: the
reliance of critics on the work of others (p. 107). He points out
in particular the preparedness of Heine scholars to take over
unthinkingly the formulations and views of their predecessors,
which in the case of *Atta Troll* have led to the propagation of
misconceptions of Heine's understanding of 'Tendenz'. Only
by investigating the concept in relation to its age, he showed,
could full sense be made of Heine's usage and practice.

The versatile and workaholic Heym could not be content
with academic study alone, and despite his studies he found
time for numerous other activities. For example, a review of a
historical novel, Alfred Neumann's *Der neue Caesar*, was
published by *Neue Deutsche Blätter* in the 'Sonderheft Egon
Erwin Kisch' as early as June 1935 (and therefore possibly
written before he left for the USA, particularly since the May
issue was not published). This review, the longest in the issue,
already intimates Heym's view on a type of literature to which
he is to devote himself in later life. Here he emphasises the
freedom of the creative writer as opposed to the restricted
potential of the historian, but he also stresses the obligation of
the former to know the prevailing circumstances of the period

he depicts. He accuses Neumann in particular of failing to be aware of socio-economic factors in the rise of Napoleon, and of concentrating on individuals rather than giving equal weight to the circumstances in which they found themselves. This is no cheap attack, for in due course Heym's own historical novels were to be preceded by lengthy and detailed research on all aspects of the figures he was to depict.

Totally different in style and tone are the pieces promised to the Prague papers which paid Heym in advance so that he could buy his transatlantic ticket. For example, the eight articles on bewildering aspects of American life published in *Deutsche Zeitung Bohemia* under the pseudonym E. Kemp (stretching from 21 May 1935 to 2 November 1936). There are doubtless others, but the use of various pseudonyms (to protect his family) renders identification of them impossible. The name 'Stefan Heym' is, however, used consistently in *Die neue Welt-bühne*, in which eleven pieces (mainly poems) appear in the course of 1935–7. It is also used for all the pieces published in *Das Wort* (the journal for German exiles published in Moscow by Brecht, Lion Feuchtwanger and Willi Bredel), three of which deserve particular mention.

The first is the longest poem Heym ever wrote, and it is based on an event which took place on 14 August 1936 – the hanging of a black man for murder. The twenty stanzas deal largely with the feverish excitement of the townspeople of Owensboro, who anticipate the spectacle of a public hanging not with a sense of justice, but with sadistic delight. The black man's prayers, reflecting piety and repentance, are featured as a humane contrast to the ill-concealed, violent tendencies of the white mob, at least one of whose members is disturbingly blind to the immoral, racialist hatred which she is revealing. The moral viewpoint is created by constant shifts of perspective, moving between the mind of a harlot, that of the crowd, and that of the condemned man. The poet's own personality is suppressed: in contrast to the direct poems with unambiguous meaning written in Czechoslovakia, this is a work which reveals growing maturity in perspective.

The second important contribution to *Das Wort* is a short

play, the title of which prepares us for the continuing relevance
of its central scenes. *Gestern – Heute – Morgen* deals principally
with two key moments in American history. First, an encounter
between General Washingon and the Prussian Baron Steuben,
in which Steuben pledges himself to the General to fight for
freedom in America. Second, an encounter between Karl
Schurz (a German political exile after 1848) and Abraham
Lincoln, in which the former encourages the President to
abolish slavery forthwith and reads from a speech he intends to
deliver in the Cooper Union. In both scenes we have a German
exile who significantly influenced the course of American
history – Steuben became Washington's chief of staff and
transformed his army, Schurz paved the way for numerous
liberal developments. Heym leaves unstated what they actually achieved, this being self-evident to the likely audience, and
he presents these two encounters within the 'frame' of preparations for an anti-fascist 'German Day' in the States. Within
this frame the struggles of yesterday are seen to be simply those
of today in different guise – and the American future is seen to
be best served by the present-day German Americans fighting
the new enemy: National Socialism.

The play is a well-constructed work, which draws on historical documents (letters and speeches) for some of its force – a
technique to be repeated on numerous occasions in later works.
Its weaknesses lie in occasional woodenness of dialogue and in
the tenuous connection between the ideals of Steuben and
Schurz, and the actual problems currently facing German
Americans – as seen in the play. The conception of the whole is
certainly good, but the relationship between past and present
probably needs to be worked out in a longer space than a mere
eleven pages can allow. The argument of the final scene is
perhaps too condensed and too optimistic, although it is certainly as forceful as any 'agitprop' produced in the thirties.

Heym's third important contribution to *Das Wort* is a collection of four poems about the Spanish Civil War. These were
the last he was to publish, and they show even greater control
in this genre. The range of subject-matter is wide – from the
destruction of innocent victims, to the bragging of a German

fighter for Franco, to a song for the International Brigade (and actually sung by them, it seems). In these four pieces, Heym is constantly changing his perspective, his vocabulary, his tone, and yet this very 'restlessness' may perhaps betray his uncertainty as a poet. In this genre he never develops a distinctive style as he does in the novels, and his acute social conscience drives him away from lyric poetry. Yet the times and the circumstances in which he wrote were hardly favourable to his development as a poet. The constant need for income compelled him towards the more lucrative opportunities of journalism, and the newspaper style he developed allows him to display his versatility far more readily. In addition, the longer he stayed in America, the more he was likely to turn towards writing directly for those in that country – and to attempt this in verse would have been too severe a challenge. His first article in English seems to have appeared a mere twelve months after he reached the country: 'Youth in Hitler's Reich', which was featured in *Nation* for 27 June 1936.

In addition to this writing and various part-time jobs, other important matters had to be attended to. There was the conversion of his student visa into an immigration visa as the situation in Germany worsened, and then, a couple of years later, the rescue of his brother and mother to the USA through complex dealings with officialdom. Money was always a problem, but Heym survived financially, and one of his part-time jobs in fact led to full-time employment after he submitted his dissertation in December 1936. For some time he had helped with a small anti-fascist monthly which was published in Chicago and which bore the title *Volksfront*. The editor, Dr Erich von Schroetter, knew of Heym through the latter's activities with the German-American working class in Chicago (one of their clubs performed his second play, *Die Hinrichtung*) and he encouraged the young student to write for this paper. No trace remains of what was done here, but Heym obviously impressed, for shortly after completion of his MA he was invited to become chief editor of a weekly newspaper which was to be published in New York, *Deutsches Volksecho*. This, it was hoped, would achieve a large circulation among the German-speaking community.

Deutsches Volksecho effectively replaced the Communist weekly *Der Arbeiter*, the circulation of which had been dwindling and which ceased publication on 13 February 1937. The first issue of *DVE* appeared one week later, after *Arbeiter* readers had been encouraged to subscribe to the new paper. From the start, however, the policy which the editor adopted did not betray any features which made the newspaper clearly recognisable as an organ of Communist policy. Certainly, the paper was left-wing, but the very first issue emphasised the importance of a 'popular front'; it also presented itself as something for the German-American family, and for the American people as a whole.

The *Volksecho* had the sponsorship of two prominent German exiles, Kurt Rosenfeld (1877–1943), and Alfons Goldschmidt (1879–1940). The former had been a member of the Reichstag, and in 1931 he played a large part in the foundation of the 'Sozialistische Arbeiterpartei Deutschlands'. He was anxious to establish a broad anti-Nazi front among the American German exiles, and in this respect he differed from his colleague, Alfons Goldschmidt, who was more firmly Communist. The latter was an energetic and versatile man. He was also an economist, and it was under his financial guidance that the *Volksecho* appeared, even though his name only featured officially after 29 October 1938. It is unlikely Heym had met either of these figures while he was still in Germany, but he had been involved indirectly with both of them. Under the pseudonym of Melchior Douglas he had published poems in the official newspaper of the Sozialistische Arbeiterpartei (the *Sozialistische Arbeiterzeitung*), and he had also published in the Berlin *Die Weltbühne*, to which Goldschmidt had been economic adviser since 1918.

The twenty-four-year-old chief editor-elect came to Goldschmidt and Rosenfeld with ideas, with ideals, and above all with energy. He also had firm views on what made a newspaper attractive. The model for German-speaking Americans should not be the German press, but the American mass press: tabloid form, large headlines and pictures, especially on the front page, plenty of news, presented simply as 'news' and not commented upon (comment was for the editorial column only), information on sport – particularly baseball and boxing; there should also be something that appealed principally to women readers, and interviews, which really brought a newspaper to life. He even had ideas for a comic strip, with cartoons of Hitler and Goebbels. Unlike other German-language newspapers in America, his was to concern itself not only with events in Germany, but to take an active interest in American events too, particularly those in which exploitation of the working class was visible. An equally important aim of the newspaper, however, and this was where Rosenfeld and Goldschmidt were in complete support, was to expose Nazis and Nazi infiltration in the USA. One of the side products of this was a booklet in English, *Nazis in USA*, which actually led to the prosecution of some of those named, a point which is not given adequate recognition in most studies of Heym's accomplishments.

Together with an assistant editor, Martin Hall, and a small team of devoted assistants, Heym ran the paper without a break until 16 September 1939. And as chief editor, he was also chief contributor. His training for the profession of journalist was minimal – his 'study' in Berlin and a small number of published pieces – but his earliest contributions here reveal the qualities for which he was later to become famous. First and foremost, a sense of courage. At all stages of his career Heym has revealed remarkable bravery in his preparedness to stand against what he considered to be unacceptable. Personal safety rarely seems to have played a part in his decision whether or not to tackle a topic, and as a result his subject-matter has always been among the most controversial issues of his day. The firmness with which he grasps issues is likewise a hallmark of his method – both early and late. Innuendo and insinuation are to be found more in his fiction than in his journalism, where forthright statement and bold accusation are far more prevalent. The thrust of the argument is not weakened by the temptation to give two sides to the case and then proceed by argument to show the superiority of one of them. Rather, Heym concentrates on one side alone, weighting his evidence in such a way that the reader cannot but accept his point in the face of such overwhelming documentation. It seems futile to raise arguments when so much damning evidence has been produced. Heym could never have been a leader writer for an international, or traditional paper, where balanced argument must prevail. Nevertheless, it would be wrong to assume that he is not a reflective journalist. Both investigation and reflection are combined in his articles, although the investigative–denunciative is far stronger in the early period.

Another striking aspect of the *Volksecho* period is the versatility Heym reveals. The range of his subjects is the range of national and international events. Politics is his preferred subject, but culture features too, and the names of German literary emigrés writing for the *Volkescho* are among the most prestigious in the USA: Thomas Mann and Ludwig Renn, for example. The *Volkescho* was far from being the only German-language newspaper of the States: it had two major rivals. To get Thomas Mann to make Heym's paper the only one for which he gave interviews was therefore a considerable coup. It must be ascribed to Heym's energy, commitment, and a certain magnetic charm.

From a technical point of view, the articles themselves reveal the basic ingredients of sound journalistic practice. Heym never writes to a formula. There is variety of approach (denunciation can fall in either the first sentence or the last), clarity of development, avoidance of cliché, and a regular sense of drama. It is no coincidence that Heym's first novel (published in 1942) was a detective story. Throughout the *Volksecho* articles, there is often that sense of 'investigation' which we feel compelled to follow until all aspects of the story have been revealed.

Deutsches Volksecho, with its literal English sub-title, 'German People's Echo', begins auspiciously: telegrams with best wishes not only from Prague, but from Paris, Zurich, and Moscow. The chief editor, with what he later confesses as wishful thinking, gives the circulation of the new paper as 35,000. The contents reflect the initial plan: tabloid, news of crucial interest to German Americans, hard-hitting editorials, a strip cartoon

(The John Smiths), a sense of life in every one of its sixteen pages. By its final issue on 16 September 1939, however, the paper has shrunk to eight pages and is financially bankrupt. Why? It is hard to lay the blame on its chief editor, whose exceptional efforts kept the paper alive for so long. If there is a mistake he has made, then it is his consistent support for the Soviet Union, even throughout the period of the Moscow show trials. The non-aggression pact between Moscow and Berlin (signed 24 August 1939), between those he has glorified and those he has vilified, therefore comes as a cruel blow, and previous policy means that it must be defended. Such support must have lost the newspaper readers, but circulation had already fallen too far to justify much further life. Income came principally from sales of the actual newspapers, and there was, of course, a very small number of potential readers: German Americans. The longer these readers lived in the USA, the more likely their linguistic achievements would allow them to turn to the press of their adoptive country. Such a restricted, and falling, readership, could not attract many advertisers, and revenue from this quarter was limited and hard won. Small contributions from working men's clubs were the only other source of income. Another critical factor in the struggle to survive was the competition: from the New York *Aufbau*, a well-established weekly for the German-Jewish community; and most importantly, from the Social-Democratic paper *Neue Volks-Zeitung*, with its anti-Hitler *and* anti-Stalin policy. Already in his Chicago days Heym had attempted to persuade the latter to join forces with the *Volksfront*, and he had approached the editor, Gerhart Seger (former member of the Reichstag) as an emissary of the *Volksfront* – albeit under the assumed name of 'Hans Weber'. Seger had rejected the approach on that occasion just as he turned down the suggestion from the editor of the *Volksecho* that they combine forces and newspapers in a joint attack against Nazism. Seger was aware of Communist techniques of infiltration with the aim of take-over, and he refused to believe that the *Volksecho* was anything other than the old Communist *Arbeiter* in his new guise. He therefore became brutal in his rejection, and, recalling the visit paid to him by that collaborator of the Chicago *Volksfront*, he denounced that 'Hans Weber' as 'Hellmuth Fliegel' [sic], alias Stefan Heym. The denunciation must have received far wider publicity than that of his own paper, for 'Hellmuth Fliegel' was for years regularly given as the birth-name of Stefan Heym – not only in Britain, the USA and West Germany, but even in the GDR![7]

The attempt to unite with the official organ of the SPD in exile thus failed, and other efforts to broaden outlets of the *Volksecho* seem to have had equally little success. For example, on 1 and 8 January 1938, the title became *Deutsches Volksecho und Deutsch-Kanadische Volkszeitung*, but nothing seemed to come of the enterprise beyond a separate page of Canadian news in each of these issues, and periodic Canadian news thereafter. Not even the outstanding contribution of the *Volksecho* to German literature could safeguard against financial threat: to its readers, the names of the literary giants who appeared in it probably meant far less than they do to scholars of today: Thomas and Heinrich Mann, Bertolt Brecht, Ernst Bloch, Ludwig Renn, Max Brod, Arnold Zweig, Oskar Maria Graf. Contact with these must have been exhilarating for the editor and possibly inspirational in his own literary work. Neverthe-less, on 16 September 1939 the final issue was produced.[8] The chief editor was unemployed.

Heym first tried to obtain another job in journalism, writing for other papers as he did so. He published in the *New Republic* on 20 September 1939 and in the *New Masses* on 14 November 1939, but he could not find another full-time post. With his obviously left-wing tendencies and not yet total command of English, jobs in the mass-circulation dailies were clearly closed to him. In his typically resourceful way, though, he managed to create a job out of nothing: he offered his services to a printer, suggesting he would find new work for him on a commission basis. The cost to the printer himself would be nil, and if Heym were successful, the printer's turnover would obviously increase. The offer was accepted and the agent began a promising career, travelling constantly in search of customers, and sometimes landing sizeable orders. It was also around this time that he managed to complete the complex bureaucratic requirements for obtaining a visa for the rest of his family to emigrate. First for his brother, and then his mother. He was able to convince the authorities of his own financial security by organising a temporary loan from a wealthy sympathiser, but as the arrival of his brother approached, he needed to work harder in order to provide true security for him. Transferring his services to another printer, who paid better, was one means, and constant attempts to write for the stage were another. 'Deadline', about life in a newspaper editorial office was written early in 1940, and it was followed by a play about the 'clairvoyant' Hanussen, who had 'foreseen' the Reichstag fire and was found murdered shortly thereafter. *The Great Hanussen*, completed in 1941, at one point seemed to be heading for a successful Broadway performance – the famous actor Joseph Schildkraut had read the manuscript and was anxious to perform in the leading role. However, these hopes finally came to nothing, despite the activity of Max Pfeffer, a literary agent (an exile from Austria) whom Heym had engaged. Pfeffer was, nevertheless, to prove crucial in another respect: in encouraging Heym to write a novel, as he felt the market for fiction was less precarious than that for the stage. And this is what Heym did in a period of only three months in mid-1942. By working only half-time for his printer, he devoted the rest of his day entirely to writing, and within a short period managed to produce two specimen chapters. Psychologically, the rest of the writing was comparatively easy, since Pfeffer was able to get the major publisher Putnam's to accept the whole work on the basis of this evidence alone. The years of struggle for literary recognition and security were at last over: with the publication of his first novel Heym became a celebrity overnight.

CHAPTER 3

First novels: the Nazi enemy

Heym himself has described some of the circumstances under which he came to compose *Hostages*.[1] Although it was written in response to the American liking for detective stories, Heym wanted to write a detective story with a difference: he therefore decided on a plot in which the detective did *not* emerge as the victor. With his family's own experience of persecution in mind, he chose a Gestapo detective, set the story in Nazi-occupied Prague (a city of which he still had clear memories), and focussed on the resoluteness of the Czechs in fighting against tyrannical occupation forces. Such a plot gave scope for idealism, heroism, and also for a warning against National Socialism.

Traditional expectations of the thriller are not followed: the reader learns at an early stage that the dead man was not murdered but committed suicide, and we are provided throughout the text with much information the detective himself does not possess. We are thus placed above rather than behind this sinister Nazi, in terms of our knowledge and also morally. It is his investigation of his 'suspects' and their contacts which provides the framework of the novel, but the tension is provided by our emotional involvement with the Czech underground forces (one of whose members is a suspect), and the question of whether they will manage to blow up a supply of munitions destined for the eastern front. The author's principal interest is also his greatest achievement: the study of character, in particular, the investigation of human motivation. Two important themes which are to become central to the later works also emerge: that of freedom and that of truth. Heym is much concerned with the way these are suppressed by ruthless directives at all levels of Nazi command.

The novel takes us immediately into the Manes bar ('Parnass' in the German translation) where some German officers are drinking. One is sick, goes downstairs to the lavatory, and does not return. The lavatory attendant, Janoshik, a member of the Czech underground, is called upstairs to clear up the mess. He is disturbed to discover the officer is missing by the time he returns below, and he is forced to assume the man has left via a side door which leads to a jetty on the Moldau. The German officers take fright and call the Gestapo, who arrest all those left in the bar (only one, another member of the underground, has managed to slip out unnoticed); Reinhardt, the senior detective who takes charge of the case, decides these hostages will be shot unless the 'murderer' of the missing officer is found. The latter's body is soon afterwards taken from the Moldau and his pocket is found to contain a letter which suggests a disturbed state of mind; but Reinhardt, for a variety of reasons, maintains the fiction of murder and interrogates all the hostages as potential killers. Much of the action centres on the interaction of the five occupants of one cell and their attitudes as death approaches. One, a psychiatrist, documents the gradual breakdown of the others under stress; another, a wealthy and powerful Czech collaborator with the Nazis, pins all his hopes on his associates' achieving his release; a famous actor realises he can play one of the grandest roles of his life in 'confessing' the crime and in facing death with sublimity; the fourth, father of the child whom the actor believes to be his own, regrets what might have been; only the lavatory attendant, the underground agent, maintains his calmness and conceives a plan to return to his lavatory in order to leave a message for his underground contact. In the city itself, the girl whom the suicide loved becomes involved with the underground. Although she herself is arrested, the group she has met manages to broadcast an exposure of Reinhardt's murderous fraud. And almost simultaneously, the munitions supplies for the eastern front are successfully detonated, thanks to Janoshik's contact having managed to collect the crucial message. The novel is thus richly optimistic, at a time when the German conquest of Europe had reached its fullest extent.

Hostages was published on 16 October 1942. It was Heym's first bestseller and the publishers had such confidence that the first printing ran to 25,000 copies, the largest run they had ever produced for a first novel. A third printing was made within a fortnight. The *New York Times* reviewer described the book as the best novel he had read about life under the Nazis, 'with its thrilling suspense, its terrific excitement, its great dramatic power'.[2] He was also moved by the strong moral purpose. Other reviewers compared the author with such figures as Tolstoy, Gorky, Steinbeck, and Dostoyevsky.

The novel was written in three months, and part-time at that, yet the pressures under which the author worked may have been beneficial: the structure is taut; there is a minimum of (closely related) characters; and the dialogue and narrative are all clearly related to the development of the plot and the working out of central themes. The author's prime technical interest lies in the presentation of character, and a striking achievement of the work is the way the plot actually develops out of the analysis of human minds. The initial suicide of Glasenapp is, we see in retrospect, the inevitable consequence of his confusion, thwarted love, and inability to act as tough German officer; the arrest of the hostages is the natural reaction of the immature Gestapo underling who is so desperate to do what is proper in the eyes of his superiors and what will allow him to appear as master of those beneath him; the conflicts between the five hostages in one cell proceed directly from their own complexes and previous relationships. Significantly, the only points where our credulity is strained lie in those areas of plot where psychology is not used to provide a basis for the action, namely, in the events which precede the broadcast of a tape recording that exposes Reinhardt's deception. Here the narrative progresses rather as a thriller, and we find that realism, and particularly psychological realism, gives place to high drama and suspense. These sections are well handled, yet are somewhat at odds with the probing of the psyche which we find elsewhere. Another relative weakness is that psychology and drama combine with a 'love story', and here again, the sense of realism which so strengthens the bulk of the text is threatened by an almost idyllic encounter between a beautiful girl and a slightly idealised underground leader.

Features of the thriller and the love story have been criticised by certain reviewers as an attempt to appeal to the masses. Such criticism undervalues Heym's moral and political aims by imputing to him a largely financial interest. Accusations of this sort are unjust. In every major work from *Tom Sawyer* to *Schwarzenberg* there is a clear political purpose which takes precedence over financial considerations. (Indeed, in many works the political interest has repeatedly threatened the publishing success.) In *Hostages* Heym wished to continue the monitory work of the *Volksecho* on a broader, English-language canvas, and to expose Nazi brutality and the fascist mind. His combination of instruction and mass appeal is fully in the spirit of his model, Heinrich Heine, and the message was conveyed to a far broader audience than Heine could ever have reached in his times: even before publication, the film rights had been bought by Paramount.

Even if objections are raised to the more sensational parts of the novel, there was general agreement that the author's greatest gift lay in the presentation of characters from the most disparate walks of life. This ability continues throughout Heym's career, although his major interest lies in the presentation of men rather than women, and above all, of intellectuals under threat. (Many of these may reflect the fears of the threatened author himself, who has rarely known a sense of security.) In *Hostages*, the most successfully realised are Janoschik, the lavatory attendant, and Dr Wallerstein, the psychiatrist.

The notion that the American public would accept a lavatory attendant as hero seems faintly ridiculous; yet Heym carefully builds up his central figure into heroic stature by showing his capacity to outwit the Gestapo. The character has elements of the Schwejk made famous by Hašek (*The Good Soldier Schwejk*, 1912), that apparent simpleton whose loquacious musings on all possible rather than relevant implications of what is under discussion infuriate and confuse his interrogators. Schwejk is either very stupid or very cunning; his interrogators take him for the former, but the reader knows otherwise.

Heym himself acknowledged his debt to Hašek, but emphasised that he had reinterpreted his creation in the light of the Second World War. Would Schwejk have acted differently in modern times than in earlier ones? The belief that he would led Heym to the retention of a simple man of lower-class origin, but to expansion of the social and political dimension. Janoschik has always been socially aware and politically active, and his ability to act, to act the fool, and to dig up anecdotes of initially dubious validity and yet finally ingenious aptness, makes him into an important political force. His tendency to think in broad terms – of his country, of people of his kind, of those who had suffered in ages before him for the sake of freedom from oppression – generalises the importance of the struggle against the Nazis and allows him to gain symbolic stature. Ernst Otto has pointed out that the name Janosik occurs in Czech folksong and in numerous works of Slovak literature,[3] and Heym's choice of a name associated with the struggle against feudal oppression is unlikely to be a coincidence. Nor is the choice of the final cry from Janoschik's lips as he falls to his death: 'Pravda víteži' ('Truth will conquer'). These were the last words of Jan Hus, early-fifteenth-century fighter for Czech religious independence, and they are incorporated in the arms of the city of Prague.

These links with the Czech past are cryptic, of course, and essentially symbolic aspects of character. However, Heym seems to have felt as early as his first novel – and possibly his experiments on the stage were influential in this regard – that for a character to come to life a fully rounded picture was necessary. Janoschik emerges partly through his interaction with his cell mates, and partly through his conflict with the Gestapo. He is seen now through the eyes of others, now through his own speech and thoughts, now his own actions and gestures. The perspective from which the story is narrated is

third-person, but Janoschik, above all characters, is illumi-
nated from both inside and out.

In the presentation of the other occupants of the cell, Heym
uses the same method to a greater or lesser extent, the dominant mode varying according to the character in question. The
actor emerges more through gesture and his choice of sentimental language; the psychiatrist through his clinical, inter-
pretative approach to everything, including death; the collaborator through his ranting and repeated combinations of
threat and plea. With the Gestapo, however, the presentation
is different. Heym's obvious danger is a black/white division
between his two sides, and he guards against this by seeking to
show the threat under which the Gestapo too have to operate.
Even Reinhardt, the senior detective, is under threat from
Heydrich, the ultimate power in Prague, while he too is under
threat from Berlin.

One point Heym is anxious to make concerns the nature of
the fascist mind, and the peculiar pleasure which it derives
from seeing the effects of domination. One of the more repul-
sive scenes of the novel is to be found in the brothel episode, in
which Reinhardt, unable to arouse sufficient enthusiasm for
intercourse with one of the prostitutes, takes pleasure in seeing
his chauffeur have brutal intercourse with another. Reinhardt's sensations on this occasion are similar to those he
experiences after a successful, domineering interrogation and
after his later rape of the heroine. Heym suggests he is only
satisfied when acting with force, and he is therefore without a
sense of desire when faced with the willing charms of a prostitute. Indeed, the prostitute asks whether he wishes to whip her,
showing her acquaintance with the animalistic sense of sub-
jugation through brutality in which the Nazis are seen to revel.
This motif of sadistic domination, together with the image of
the frightened victim, is one which will recur in the majority of
Heym's later novels.

The immediate success of *Hostages* released Heym from his
job as printer's agent. He was suddenly much in demand as a
speaker and as a contributor to newspapers, and his financial
difficulties disappeared overnight. Paramount had bought the

rights before completion of the novel, and the film itself was produced in the following year. For the first time in his adult life, Heym was financially secure.

Yet success brought commitment of a different kind. Conscription to the army had not yet been necessary, since the first enquiries (in 1941) had established that Heym had a dependent relative – his mother. Although it was only in fact in their first days in the States that Heym had had to support her and his brother totally, to the authorities it was clear that his obligation to these relatives was now no longer dependent on his weekly wage. And so, in February 1943, Heym became a recruit. In the months before that he had worked almost as hard at a second novel as he had on his first: between lectures and publicity campaigns he wrote the manuscript of *No Turnpike Gates*, a novel of power struggles in America. Yet the publisher's reader rejected the work – mainly on stylistic, but possibly also on thematic grounds, since the image of American politics is cynical and the whole could be interpreted as an attack on certain living figures. Heym did not attempt to seek publication elsewhere. As was to be the case in the fifties, he took a conscious decision not to weaken his reputation by publishing a work which lacked the quality of his others.

Conscription meant the temporary severing of ties with New York, with his family, and in particular with Gertrude Gelbin, a widow with whom he had fallen in love during the composition of *Hostages*. A mature woman, a dozen years older than himself, her charm and beauty had captivated him at first sight, and the two had quickly established an intense relationship. The relationship extended to Heym's creative writing. Gertrude was employed by the film giant MGM, and she had much experience of editorial work. She could therefore make stylistic improvements to the emigré's English, and in due course discuss all other aspects of composition with him. Under the name of 'Valerie Stone' she published children's stories and articles on women's themes, and, until her death in 1969, she proved a constant source of inspiration and support.

Initial training for the army seemed haphazard, and it was some time before Heym reached the unit for which he was obviously best qualified. His first station was the large Camp Dix, where he quickly became involved in editing the Camp newspaper; but he was then transferred to Camp Crowder, a training unit for the Signal Corps. (It was here that he was sworn in as a US citizen.) There followed further transfer to Camp Ritchie, where the training became more specifically Military Intelligence, and it was here that he came into contact with many other European exiles, including his former collaborator from Prague, Hanuš Burger. 'Psychological warfare', weakening the enemy by attacking his mind, was the type of operation for which Heym was being prepared here, and more specific training (on writing leaflets and broadcasting) was conducted finally at Camp Sharpe, where he was taught by one of his future commanders, Hans Habe.

With his training complete, Heym was returned briefly to Camp Ritchie, and, knowing transportation to Europe was imminent, he proposed marriage to Gertrude. They were married, late in 1943, and by early 1944 Heym was on his way to England. Behind him he left half a manuscript, which he had managed to complete during the less hectic parts of his training. *Of Smiling Peace* was finished during his period in England, and it was published late in 1944 by Little, Brown and Company in Boston, and Skeffington and Son in London. Copies of the novel are now hard to obtain, and it is the only one of Heym's novels which has not been translated into German. There are probably two reasons for this: first, the style lacks the quality of his other novels; and second, the subject matter and many of the themes are dealt with in much greater depth (and much more skilfully) in his next novel, which was written under less pressure after the war.

In his first novel, Heym had used a background he knew well (Prague). In his second published novel, he used one that was completely unknown to him: North Africa. He compensated for this ignorance by reading and elementary research, and here we find the modest beginnings of what was later to be the intense preparations which were to precede every novel. At this point in time Heym also lacked first-hand knowledge of men

under fire, but here again his limited research allowed him to
produce a detailed and convincing depiction of men's reaction
to bombardment. A parallel case can be drawn with Stephen
Crane, whose *Red Badge of Courage* (1895) was read by Heym in
the very early stages of composition. Crane wrote of a youth in
the Civil War whose introduction to battle is violent and
bloody. Crane too had never seen men in action, but the
strength of his book lies in the forceful depiction of fighting and
the analysis of a young mind maturing under great stress. In
both authors there is an intensity created by constant action
and encounter (both novels are short), violence and brutality
are common (and not just in these two works), and there is a
concern with disturbing detail (of pain and death). The
humour tends to be grim, and there is also much cyncial
observation. Yet the two authors share an interest in the poor
and the unfortunate, in glimpses of those in some ways
'cheated' by life, in the moral support or the failings of others in
an as yet untried regiment, and in what actually constitutes
'courage'.

Like the majority of Heym's novels, *Of Smiling Peace* has
several aims: it is a tale of suspense and intrigue, aimed at
holding the reader's attention through its constant changes
between small groups of rival factions; a celebration of Allied
victory; and a booster for American morale (significantly, an
Armed Services edition was produced shortly afterwards). It is
also an investigation of the political, moral, and ideological
problems which face the restoration of order in a liberated
colony, a partial explanation of what the American soldier was
– or should have been – fighting for, and an exposé of the fascist
mentality.

The novel begins with the landing of Allied forces in French
North Africa, and it follows the progress of one soldier in
particular – Bert Wolff, an American Intelligence Officer who
had fought in Spain and who is totally committed to overcom-
ing Nazism. His principal adversary is the German General
Staff Officer Major von Liszt, who avoids capture as the
Americans take the German 'Armistice Commission' with
which the supporters of Vichy France have been collaborating.
Wolff's pursuit of Liszt is interspersed with numerous minor

adventures involving several characters connected with the American forces, Liszt's mistress and her other admirers, and a brutal French Foreign Legion commander, Monaitre. Liszt hopes to counter-attack the Americans through Nazi forces in collaboration with Monaitre's troops, but he is thwarted by the vigilance and determination of individual Americans. With a strong sense of poetic justice, the novel concludes with the capture of Liszt, the assassination of Monaitre, and the marriage of the beautiful mistress to a man of whom Liszt heartily disapproves.

The structure of the work was doubtless determined by the difficulties of composition. The plot dwells on a small number of characters for rarely more than a dozen pages, then shifts to another group who are usually removed in space, but not in time. The strands occasionally overlap, but only come together properly in the final chapter. Such a method of writing would suit the irregular life style of a recruit for whom lengthy deliberation and careful planning were hardly possible, but such a procedure also carries risks: occasionally the time scale is inaccurate, the geography is unclear, there is excessive use of coincidence in drawing the strands together. In the thinking behind the book, however, Heym remains much more constant, and his central theme is one which he will explore in numerous later novels, especially *The Crusaders*: to what extent can one co-operate with forces which previously supported fascism without prejudicing one's own ideals?

The motto to the novel contains the first reference to this problem:

> Play fast and loose with faith? so jest with heaven,
> Make such unconstant children of ourselves
> As now again to snatch our palm from palm,
> Unswear faith sworn, and on the marriage bed
> Of smiling peace to march a bloody host,
> And make a riot on the gentle brow
> Of true sincerity?
>
> *King John*, act III, scene I

King Philip is here protesting that one must be constant in one's beliefs and that it would be immoral to break with the principles which have just led to 'peace'. Such a temptation to abandon one's ideals faces the Americans as they occupy Algiers. The lack of law and order and the corruption which they encounter will take considerable time to eradicate if proper, democratic procedures are to be adhered to. In the meanwhile, the war has to continue, for there is a serious threat from reinforced Nazi troops along the coast. The simplest, and from a military point of view the wisest, course of action is to collaborate with those who have power and influence in these parts. But such figures are corrupt. To deal with them would be to negate one of the ideals for which one has supposedly fought. Monaitre may guarantee 'law and order' in return for what appear to be small compromises (in particular the demand not to liberate political prisoners or to re-establish political liberties), but these are ideals about which the Americans have gone to war. The American commander, Colonel Wintringham, finds himself torn:

To his own dismay, he found that the very fact that he had not immediately thrown Monaitre out on his ear constituted a compromise. Perhaps, one would have to go much farther on the road to expediency. What mattered most was American lives. And American lives could be saved best if the troops could advance quickly, unhampered by disturbances in the country. (p. 56)

Heym presents this dilemma not from the viewpoint of the idealist, Bert Wolff (whose belief in democracy had earlier led him to fight in Spain), but through the uncertain mind of a liberal who is also a practical and realistic commander, well aware of his responsibility for soldiers' lives as much as for political ideals. In the end Wintringham decides to procrastinate, a decision which proves to be wise when Monaitre's corruption is soon exposed. Yet the temptation to compromise was strong, and higher powers might well have approved such a solution.

The historical events upon which the novel is loosely based were rather different, and this is the first of Heym's 'historical' novels in which small changes are made in order to raise questions about past policies (and in his later works, to raise questions about future ones). The author follows the broad events of Operation 'Torch' to occupy North Africa, and he also has the historical General Nehring as the Nazi commander along the coast. Where he deviates is in choosing the figure of 'Monaitre' instead of Admiral François Darlan, a leading figure of the Vichy government who happened to be in Algiers at the time of the Allies' landings. It was with him, in fact, that the Allies concluded an armistice in November 1942. But Darlan, a grand intriguer and fiercely anti-British, had angered many Frenchmen through his speeches and his collaboration with the Nazis, and he was assassinated on Christmas Eve of the same year. This act gained very wide publicity. Heym is too balanced a thinker and writer to give only one side of his presentation of the negotiation with Monaitre/Darlan. Although he shows that collaboration with such as him was both unwise and immoral, he also suggests how attractive the choice of such a figure was from a military point of view. But he suggests throughout the novel that such decisions were possible through a general lack of clarity in the Americans' war aims. Another example of this is Wintringham's decision to place Monaitre under house arrest, which arises from fortuitous evidence rather than ideological conviction, and several of the American soldiers are seen to be equally unclear of their reasons for fighting. The few figures with firm views tend to be the cynics and egoists, who see the war as a struggle for power, or for creating profits for big business. Only Bert Wolff, clearly modelled on the author himself, recognises the danger of this policy, and yet his hopes for a new world in which the wishes of the 'people' will triumph seem a little naive. That the fascist personality extends beyond the boundaries of the Third Reich is clear to the reader from the figure of Monaitre, and the implications of this are explored more fully in *The Crusaders*. But already by the end of this earlier novel, the optimism of its title has been severely undermined.

After a few months of the relative peace of an English spring, Heym landed in Normandy only a few days after D-Day itself (6 June 1944). For the rest of the war in Europe he was close to the front, interrogating prisoners, writing leaflets, broadcasting by means of loudspeakers to enemy positions, and also writing

full-scale radio programmes. He was attached to what was
called a Mobile Radio Broadcasting company, and the diverse
activities, the constant improvising, the internal squabbles,
and the regular danger of such units, are very well conveyed in
the novel of these expereiences, *The Crusaders*.

A leaflet or a broadcast can obviously only be one of numerous factors which determine the reaction of an enemy. Individuals, villages, towns, and even fortresses, surrender principally because they feel their cause is lost, and the role which
propaganda will play is most likely to be in the *timing* of that
surrender. Although we cannot be certain of the role which
Heym's propaganda played in the war, some evidence of its
importance can be glimpsed in one incident where considerable loss of life was avoided and the invasion of Europe was
accelerated. The occasion came early in the Normandy campaign, in August 1944. The guns on the island of Cézembre,
which protected the harbour of St Malo, needed to be silenced
in order to allow the Allies another harbour in addition to
Cherbourg. The need was urgent, but the island was almost
impregnable. The garrison was well supplied with ammunition
and food, and all attempts to persuade them to give themselves
up had failed. Then Heym's leaflet was dropped: it was short,
imaginative, aggressive. Although it was very much in the
Allies' interests for the island to surrender, there was no hint of
a plea in Heym's words. He briefly suggested that the soldiers
recall their days as recruits and their attempts at target practice. What were the *feelings* of a target, Heym mused. The
garrison would have ample opportunity to find out, he suggested, for they were now 'living targets' who would soon be
completely wiped out if they did not bring reason to the few
officers who might think there was a sense of honour attached
to dying in this way. A final neat touch was to print this
statement on paper with the concentric rings of a target
proper. By the following day the garrison had overpowered its
officers and surrendered.

Heym's war activities were journalistic in a wide sense, and
some of his most impressive work was for the broadcasts for
Radio Luxemburg. These covered a period of several months

in 1944–5, and involved the writing of scripts which were intended to inform the enemy of recent Allied progress and thus weaken morale. Some of the best of these have now been published as *Reden an den Feind*. Here too Heym's imaginative powers are regularly evident in the conception of his sketches, and in the regular innuendo: many of these broadcasts are aimed at reducing the average soldier's confidence in his leaders – not just at the highest level, but more particularly those with whom he is in direct contact. Here, and in many of the leaflets, the author is drawing on information obtained from prisoners he has interrogated, on their unease and doubts about the war, their view of their leaders, and their opinions on the nature of their opposition. From a psychological point of view, these leaflets and broadcasts were finely conceived, and probably led to the granting of Heym's application for a 'front newspaper' in the German language, which appeared regularly after 14 August and which was dropped over the German lines. This paper, the *Frontpost*, contained longer articles of a more informative nature, and was inspired by the fact that the German soldiers themselves were regularly without information on the general situation. Three months later, on 5 November, it was followed by the smaller *Feldpost*, which was shot over the German lines, and therefore more likely to reach its immediate targets.

We can never know the effect of such propaganda, but we can gauge its importance by recalling the priority it was given (three thousand million leaflets were dropped over Germany by the American forces), and we can also judge it in terms of the quality of its argument. It is based on a firm knowledge of the German mind, of its preconceived ideas about Americans, of the propaganda to which it has been exposed in Germany, and of its day-to-day worries. A victor is clearly speaking in these pieces: one who is tough-minded, confident, who can afford to understate, and who has a number of morale-withering pet themes: the superiority of the Americans not necessarily in their ability to fight, but in terms of equipment and numbers of men; the importance to the Americans of preserving their own troops – equipment is dispensable, but not lives (in contrast to the German approach, which encourages standing to the last man); and above all, the *truth* of what the American leaflets contain. The importance of a 'strategy of truth' was widely accepted among the Allies, and the choice of a quotation from Ernst Moritz Arndt as a 'motto' for the *Frontpost* must surely have been approved by Sergeant Heym: 'Der Starke braucht die Wahrheit nicht zu fürchten' ('The strong man need not fear the truth'). The choice was actually that of Hans Habe, the commander of the unit (and later successful novelist), but these words obviously take us back to the Prague coat of arms.

Throughout the war in Europe, Heym was in perpetual danger. Working close to the front carried the obvious risk of capture in the event of German counter-attack. Although such attacks were unlikely to be common, there was, of course, the famous German advance in the Battle of the Bulge, and in this Heym was centrally involved.

At this point the 2nd Mobile Radio Broadcasting company was engaged in transmissions from the powerful Radio Luxemburg, an important station because of its established name, its potential for anti-Nazi broadcasts, and not least, its success as a psychological weapon for the Allies. It was an obvious target of enemy attack. To be captured was more serious a proposition for Heym than for most other American soldiers: quite apart from his position in military intelligence, he was not only Jewish, but also a political refugee fighting against the country which had forced him into exile. To fall into the hands of the enemy would have led to interrogation by the SS and almost certain death. It was therefore an act of considerable bravery to stay at the transmitter as the enemy's advance continued and the capture of Luxemburg began to seem likely. To have taken over that transmitter would have represented a major psychological victory for the enemy, but they were repelled just before they were able to do so. Sergeant Heym, who had stayed at his post throughout, received the Bronze Star for bravery. The remarks of his superior, Hans Habe, as the medal was awarded, are telling: 'You truly deserved it, for you stayed though you were frightened.'[4]

As the end of hostilities approached, the thinking of Heym's superiors turned away from psychological warfare towards education. There was now a need in liberated Germany for authoritative sources of information, for proper exposure of Nazi war crimes, and for encouragement to rebuild a shattered society. Newspapers were required, to be issued under the authority of the occupying powers, and they needed to be written in German by figures who were acceptable to the military authorities. No position could have been more suitable for the ex-editor of the anti-Nazi paper, *Deutsches Volksecho*, and for the first months after the war he was engaged in setting up what was to be the most successful paper of the American Zone of Occupation: *Die neue Zeitung*, which was based in Munich and which was to raise its circulation from 500,000 to 1.5 million in only three months. Here too Hans Habe was Heym's superior, and the two seem to have worked well together for the first two months of the paper's operation (it was published weekly). Heym was political editor, and in this capacity he covered the first part of the Lüneberg War Trials. Contributions from him appear in the paper (and also in others under American control, such as the *Ruhr-Zeitung*, of which he was officially listed as 'Editor') until 4 November, when Heym and Habe had a serious disagreement. Asked to write an anti-Soviet leader for the paper, Heym refused.[5] Shortly after this he returned to the States and was discharged. A dissatisfying conclusion to an army career which was otherwise full of success.

The Crusaders was the first of Heym's novels that he was to write at relative leisure, and with the enormous attention to detail, to character development, and gradual revelation of plot and theme which are evident in all the works that follow. A work of this magnitude (some 300,000 words, but the version initially submitted was much longer) requires careful planning, and especially time. Heym worked on the novel for three years, in fact, but its success justified that labour: four printings were made within three weeks of publication, and over two million copies of the work (in English and in many other languages) have been produced to date. None of his later publications has yet reached such popularity, although several of them are better written. Ironically, the success of the novel in the USA may in part be attributable to the cautious procedures of publishers. Although Heym signed a contract with Little, Brown and Company when he came out of the war, there was some uncertainty in the book trade as to whether the time was yet ripe for war novels. Looking back to the First World War, and the success of Remarque's *All Quiet on the Western Front* some ten years after the fighting, the publishers feared three years might be too short a time span. They therefore produced a limited edition of 500 copies, which they sent to leading critics and booksellers in order to obtain a reaction. So favourable was the first response that a brochure was made out of quotations from these first readers – this was sent out as advance publicity, which meant the novel was guaranteed favourable orders from the bookshops. On the other hand, this operation did delay publication by several months, and as a result *The Crusaders* was not the first major war novel to appear in America. It was preceded (albeit only briefly) by Norman Mailer's *The Naked and the Dead*, and Irwin Shaw's *The Young Lions*. Nevertheless, competition with these did not prejudice either sales or the critical reception. Most contemporary reviewers were enthusiastic, and in his 1969 survey of American novels of the fighting, Joseph Waldmeir could still describe the work 'by almost any measurement, one of the strongest novels to come out of the second World War'.[6]

Heym draws extensively on his experience of the Normandy invasion and his work in psychological warfare. He projects himself into two characters in a Mobile Radio Broadcasting company: Sergeant Bing, a young German Jew who has fled from the Nazis and is now returning with the US army; and Lieutenant Yates, an idealistic, but at times half-hearted, Assistant Professor of German at an American university. Both are seeking something in the course of the American advance into Germany: Bing the true nature of the country he had to flee, and Yates, almost unwittingly, the true aims for which the Americans are fighting. Few of the latter are seen to have any of the ideals which inspired their forefathers, and corruption is rife at all levels of the army. The victors are not interested in fully eradicating Nazism from Germany, but in establishing an order in which capitalism can again flourish. Yet Nazism *has* to be eradicated: Bing's sad experiences as he returns to his native village, close to a concentration camp, prove that many Germans have learnt nothing from defeat and that de-Nazification is a vital task. This should be one of the aims of the 'Crusade'.

The novel does not conclude with the end of the fighting in Europe: in order to bring out certain similarities between war and peace, Heym extends the plot to show the occupation forces seeking to administrate Germany. In this section of the book, just as in *Of Smiling Peace*, Heym shows that one cannot build a new society by forging practical compromises and using ex-Nazis to regain control. Making use of the Nazis is, of course, the quickest way to establish order, and 'order' is what the ambitious General Farrish is determined to obtain in his section of Germany. But Farrish's 'victory' for efficiency is bought at a cost. Just as his military successes were achieved at the expense of the highest casualty figures for any general during the war, his part of occupied Germany runs best because he has completely disregarded the task of de-Nazification. The occupation should have genuine objectives, but they are obscured, if not defeated, by trying to achieve efficiency at political and moral cost, and with the aim, furthermore, of self-aggrandisement in the American media. Farrish's rejection of 'democracy' in both war and peace is shown to be a failing typical of his countrymen, and a poor example to those Germans who are trying to find a new political idemnity.

Heym's sceptical view of both victors and vanquished is tempered by his depiction of isolated idealists and by the handful of Soviet soldiers who are glimpsed in the novel: their firmness of purpose stands in contrast to the uncertainty of most Americans, who shrewdly combine their 'ideals' with business acumen. At the same time, a certain sympathy for Communism is built up through the aggressive and ill-founded anti-Communism of the more unsavoury Americans. The latter's increasing use of such words as 'Crusaders', 'liberty', and 'democracy' serves mainly to reveal their abuse of these concepts. They are simply a form of camouflage for self-seeking, free enterprise, and control by the powerful.

Contemporary reviewers were divided on who the hero of this novel might be: some plumped for Bing, although the majority chose Yates. Both are figures who command our sympathy and in whose development we take considerable interest, but it is clear Heym wishes us to identify more with the character who develops into a true 'Crusader' for human decency and truth.

The novel opens with Bing, and he initially emerges as a figure superior to Yates through his youthful idealism and courage; as the plot develops, however, Bing becomes pessimistic and depressed, and when the American forces enter Germany, he becomes uncertain of himself. The return to his native town fills him not with satisfaction, but with unease, and an impetuous sexual adventure here results in his narrowly escaping capture. He fears his lust has led to the death of comrades in this town, and worse, that such action proves he is no better than those he is conquering. His own death is partly attributable to the apathy and sense of guilt which now descends upon him. Yates, on the other hand, develops from an indecisive and slightly self-satisfied, if amiable and kind-hearted academic, into a reliable leader who is politically and morally mature. Heym takes great care in showing Yates's growth to this position. At home in the States he had kept silent over the Spanish Civil War in order to protect his university post. But by acting in such a way, Yates was denying his true self – a point brought out by the warts which so embarrass him and which are clearly psychological in origin. His refusal to stand up for principles is attacked by his wife, who is a recurrent reminder of his failure on this count; he feels shamed by Bing, the exiled German who seems the only American soldier to have any firm belief in ancient American ideals; and he is given an example by the honesty of his superior, Colonel DeWitt. He is also inspired by the courage and self-sacrificing nobility of the hard fighting man Captain Troy, whose sense of responsibility for his men never ceases; and by a young French girl, with whom he falls in love and through whom he learns to renounce his own desires for the sake of a nobler goal. But Yates is changed equally by the negative forces with which he comes into contact. His willingness to compromise is steadily reduced by his humane reaction to the evil practices of the Americans around him and to the Nazis whom he has to interrogate. In the end, he commits himself fully to his belief and begins to fight for what he believes in, regardless of the cost. The disappearance of his warts is symbolic, reflecting his acceptance of responsibility.

One of the points made, but not fully developed, in *Of Smiling Peace*, is that the enemy is not alone in having his share of tyrants. As an unnamed soldier puts it in that novel: 'There's more than one Hitler in the world, and not only in Germany' (p. 65). He is referring, of course, to his own experiences in the USA. From the beginning of *The Crusaders*, Heym is developing this same point with reference to all levels of the American army. His choice of a psychological warfare group allows him to do this with comparative ease, for all ranks are featured, and they need to collaborate closely. There is also the opportunity to accord a fair amount of space to the activities of the hard-headed, blustering General Farrish, who is obviously modelled on General Patton. Through this microcosm the author is able to present one of the best overviews of the American war in Europe.

The central question of American war aims is raised at the start of the book. The histrionic General wishes to celebrate American Independence Day (4 July) with an attack of 48 rounds from 48 guns (each gun/shell representing one of the 48 States). Once this bombardment is over, leaflets will be fired at the enemy, explaining what 4 July means to the Americans, why they are fighting, why the enemy has no chance, and why surrender is the only sensible course of action. There are numerous technical objections to such a plan, but these are surmountable with hard work. The awkward part of the problem, it transpires, is explaining what the Americans are actually fighting *for*. Yates is stuck for an easy answer:

He could not say that what we are fighting for was a maze of motives, some clear, some hidden, some idealistic, some selfish, some political, some economic, and that one would have to write a book instead of a leaflet; and that even then, the issue would be anything but straight. (pp. 13–14)

In retrospect, this passage proves to be an instance of self-commentary by the author. As the book progresses, the 'maze of motives' to which he refers is rigorously analysed. By the end, the 'selfish', 'political' and 'economic' have proved more dominant than either Yates or the reader had expected. If, during the fighting itself, the self-seeking was less obvious and instances of bravery and self-sacrifice were visible, in the new Germany under allied occupation, self-advancement and profits reign supreme. In this respect all ranks prove equal. The General continues to think of his image in the media of the States, with his eye on a senatorship at the least; middle-ranking officers issue licences to German businesses on condition 10 per cent of the profits come back to those issuing the licences. And at the lowest level, the exchange of food and cigarettes for cash or sexual favours continues. True, all black-market activities are illegal in the eyes of the military authorities, but discovery and 'punishment' are virtually meaningless. Just as the cook, Dondolo, is quite content to be sent back from the front to the Replacement Depot (for he can probably arrange transfer well away from the dangerous zone to a unit where illicit sale of army food is just as easy), Colonel Willoughby, with his more grand-scale deceits, is equally content to be sent back to Base Section – which will simply mean a quicker return to the States. Willoughby's interior monologue, jerkily reflecting his arrogant sense of superiority, makes plain his triumph:

They imagined they had won – Yates, DeWitt, the whole faction of Crusaders. But they hadn't. They couldn't win. They would never win. He had always been one jump ahead of them, in war and in peace. Yes, sir. (p. 646)

The novel may conclude on a partial victory for the 'Crusaders': through Yates's campaigning an industrial baron's mansion is made over to displaced persons. But the idealists' victory is largely symbolic. Although Yates has recognised the importance of accepting responsibility for political and social injustice, the author leaves the conclusion of the novel with a warning: the ideological struggle will continue back in the USA. Yates's fight has only just begun.

It is tempting to see Heym's presentation of fascist traits in his American soldiers as owing something to Max Picard's influential *Hitler in uns selbst* (1946), a study which suggested fascism was not specifically a *German* phenomenon, but one with roots in European culture as a whole. However, Heym had been aware of the fascist element in America well before the war. In *Deutsches Volksecho*, for example, he had regularly attacked examples of Nazism in the USA. There is a difference, however, between the elements of fascism evident in Americans and those we see in the Nazis. The 'little Hitlers' of America are egoistic individuals, but with one exception, they are neither evil nor even malicious. By contrast, the Nazis seem more organised, there is a policy behind their oppression, they believe in the superiority of their kind and their right to exploit those beneath them. The major proponent of their ideology, Obersturmbannführer Erich Pettinger (of the SS), exemplifies the fascist mentality as it has already been seen in Commissioner Reinhardt and Major von Liszt. The length of *The Crusaders* allows much more detailed investigation of such a man's motivation, his aims, his ruthlessness in all spheres, whether in his killing the enemy, killing members of his own side, or in exploiting women. Further, the National Socialist victory he foresees is an ideological, not a military one: even if their armies are defeated, Pettinger considers the Nazis will ultimately come to gain control over Germany and exploit where they wish. His greatest fear, like that of his commanding officer, is defeat by the Soviets. Egalitarianism, not American capitalism, represents the only true danger to National Socialism. If figures like General Farrish were to have their way (and we see that they usually do), Nazism would again flourish.

In *Hostages* the author presupposed his reader's rejection of Nazism as an evil force, and the same holds true for *Of Smiling*

Peace. But in *The Crusaders* Heym's aim has shifted. He is anxious to show National Socialism under the broader mantle of fascism, and to reveal its dangers for American society. Almost every feature of Nazism is to be seen in the portrayal of the Americans as a whole – including sadism and anti-Semitism – and it may be for this reason that its prime representative is fully discredited in so many spheres – military, ethical, sexual. Although Heym does not disparage individual Americans to anywhere near the same degree as he does Pettinger, the latter stands as a monitory archetype, against which the potential of certain Americans should be measured.

Several reviewers of *The Crusaders* expressed surprise that a novel which was so firmly ideological in its implications should be almost totally lacking in 'editorialising'. The surprise should rather be that an author with so active a career in investigative/denunciative journalism could distinguish so carefully between literature and polemic. In newspaper articles written during the composition of the novel, for example, his views are undisguised and forthright. In 'Die Probleme einer Besatzungsmacht' and 'But the Hitler legend isn't dead', the argument is sharp and at times angry. In the novel, however, this anger is expressed by means of character interaction and plot. The narrator himself comments only indirectly: any accusations come from the mouths of the vast array of characters themselves (some fifty significant figures) and such remarks are relatively few in number. Indeed, the reader's mind is controlled not by statements but rather by questions: by the musing of characters on what they encounter and on what they expect. And the implications we draw from these reflections are moral, political and ideological. Occasionally, too, they are military. The human failings depicted are reflected in the organisation of battle as much as they are in the rest of army life.

Heym has sometimes been accused of lacking elegance in his English style, and it is true there are occasional stylistical lapses in *The Crusaders* – although far fewer than in his previous two novels. Heym's own suggestion that his 'literary roots' may lie with, among others, Hemingway,[7] has doubtless encouraged critics to view him in the 'hasty journalist' tradition, but this is a judgement which must be rejected. Heym adapts his style to meet the demands of the situation and characters with whom he is concerned. *The Crusaders* is heavily conversational and each character's language tends to reflect his station; but in the narrative proper, much of the description is through the eyes of a particular character, and his mentality is reflected in the language, length of sentences, and imagery. Motivation is again a principal concern of the author, and there is a constant interest in the interaction between speakers, as each tries to understand the mind of the other.

Against the ruggedness of the prose which will reflect battle, or argument, there is also a more fluid movement in those sections of protracted intellectual reflection or discussion. We find this in particular with characters like Yates, Crerar, DeWitt, Yasha Bereskin, Willoughby. Such figures often make a particular moral or political observation, and their speech and interior monologue tends to be far more aphoristic, provocative through its very succinctness. An obvious example is the well-known reaction of Yasha, the White Russian industrialist, to the proposals of the American Major Willoughby:

> Yasha could not help being amazed at the American. What ability to blend a concern for the welfare of mankind with sound business practice! The Germans were orphans compared to it; they had covered their unashamed bullying and grabbing with love for the Fatherland – lately, they had dropped even that pretence. But the Americans really believed their own liberalism, at least this Major did. A healthy people. They had achieved the perfect amalgam of God, democracy and the interest rate. Too bad they were running up against the unashamed decadence of Europe. (p. 191)

One of the reasons Heym excels in presenting the interior monologue of intellectuals is that this mode allows full scope to his interest in psychology and character. From *The Crusaders* onwards, his presentation of intellectuals is consistently successful. It relies on a gradual revelation of character traits and background, and constant interaction of minds with contrary views. And in both the speeches and the interior monologues which are used to bring out this conflict, rhythm is controlled in order to reflect speed of thought and intensity of emotion. The aphoristic touches of which Heym is so fond are comfortably at home in prose such as this. The delightful summing up of American capitalism, for example ('they had achieved the perfect amalgam of God, democracy, and the interest rate'), seems wholly in place here. Passages of this sort also often tell us as much about the character who is expressing such ideas as they do about the character against whom he is reacting.

The attack on American capitalism which we see here might suggest that the novel would receive a hostile reception by the more conservative critics. Yet the reviews were consistently warm across the complete range of the press. *The New York Daily Worker*, for example, praised the novel as 'one of the most adult and memorable novels on any theme to be published in a long, long time',[8] while at the other end of the political spectrum *The New York Times* considered the novel was 'not only a good book but a brilliant one'.[9] The recurrent point of the (very large number of) reviews was that this was the best novel, in conception and execution, to emerge from World War II. Only one reviewer expressed true displeasure, and that was Malcolm Cowley in the *New Republic* (a left-wing journal to which Heym had actually contributed before the war).[10] Cowley emphasised the contrivance of the conclusion, the way in which evil is all too satisfyingly vanquished, and the generally cinematic aspects of the novel. In the latter respect Cowley was certainly right, and after the successful filming of *Hostages* Heym may well have worked with the possibility of film in mind. There are numerous scenes of grand confrontation, and there is considerable potential for spectacle. But the author's hopes in this direction were disappointed. Senator McCarthy's influence was beginning to be felt, and although at one stage it seemed likely that MGM would take on the script, political pressures intervened. Later, in the GDR, the project (totally restructured for filming by Heym and his wife) was again to be turned down – for rather different, but once again, political reasons. Heym's sense of having been betrayed on two occasions is well recorded in *Nachruf* (pp. 424–5; 536–8).

CHAPTER 4

Writing for causes: unpopular political statements

In the writing of Heym's first three novels, there had been a clear moral aim. In *Hostages*, portraying the evils of National Socialism; in *Of Smiling Peace* and *The Crusaders*, further depiction of the evils of fascism, but with the scope extended to evils in the American army and in a number of American individuals. For his fourth novel Heym was to choose a completely different topic and to make a much bolder and more provocative political statement. His unease with American politics and the American way of life led him not only to a formal rejection of capitalism, but to the literary endorsement of a socialist approach: in this case, the Communist 'takeover' in Prague, 1948, the first of several 'revolutions' to which Heym was later to devote complete novels (*Lenz*; *5 Tage im Juni*; *Schwarzenberg*). He was to justify this takeover as something not only necessary and beneficial, but also as a step towards 'freedom' – when seen, that is, in the words of the title, through the 'Eyes of Reason'.

Heym's interest in the 'Prague Coup', as it was for long referred to in the West, must in part have been inspired by the American government's vigorous denunciation of the Communists' rise to power. At the time it was interpreted by the West as a move on Stalin's part towards the conquest of Western Europe, and within a year the NATO alliance had been formed and the Cold War was well under way. Subsequent events in Czechoslovakia – the collapse of the economy, show trials, and the rise of the secret police – led the West to feel fully vindicated in its initial denunciation, but it is often conveniently forgotten that millions of Czechs (though

57

far fewer Slovaks) welcomed the Communist Party's accession
in the firm belief it would mean greater prosperity for the
working man. Living standards did actually rise until 1951, as
capitalist wealth was redistributed, but they fell afterwards as
heavy industry was built up and the central planning system
began to destroy the economy. For its initial period, however,
the government commanded widespread support and considerable hope.

Late in 1948 Heym and his wife left the USA for an extended
visit to Europe. They spent two periods in Czechoslovakia. The
first principally in the capital, and the second, after a visit to
Israel, more in the countryside. Heym specifically investigated
aspects of glass-making in the small town of Nový Bor, and
recorded people's memories and opinions of the preceding
February. Detailed notes were made in preparation for composition on return to the States. Writing thus began early in
1949, and the final manuscript was delivered in June 1950. It
was published by Little, Brown and Company (who had also
published *The Crusaders*) in February 1951, but their publicity
campaign fell far short of that for the earlier novel. The major
reason for this lay in American involvement in Korea, which
had grown dramatically in June 1950 with the outbreak of war
between North and South. Anti-Communist feelings were
already running high as a result of Senator McCarthy's spectacular condemnation of subversion in government departments,
and so any novel which approved a Communist rise to power
was quite likely to arouse widespread anger. The month which
preceded the novel's publication actually witnessed much
bloodshed in Korea as the United Nations forces (consisting
principally of US troops) repelled a major Communist offensive. The circumstances likely to affect the reception of Heym's
novel were therefore far from auspicious.

In his first novels Heym had been concerned with individuals, principally men, to whom our emotional response is
relatively straightforward. In this next work our reactions are
more complex: the conflict takes place chiefly between men
who are all respectable in their very different ways (hence one
of the working titles was actually 'Men of Good Will'). All

three of the key figures are Czech patriots, who want the best for their ravaged post-war country and for their people. All three are brothers, who have been exposed to many of the same formative influences, although they have rebelled against these in contrasting ways; and their view of what is best for their nation has been further shaped by their differing roles during the war years. Their duties during this period brought out qualities which had already been dormant in them, and which are now sharpened in Czechoslovakia of the years 1945–8. There is therefore considerable interest in character in this novel, and in the issues which these characters espouse. The most important of these is that of freedom, which is investigated from various viewpoints throughout the work. This ideal, we are led to recognise, must be interpreted not through the emotions, but rather through the eyes of reason. Such a view is reached only at the close of the novel, after we have been carefully shown the alternatives.

In its approach, then, this novel aims to challenge traditional attitudes. Its principal target in this respect is those who hold liberal views on freedom, but it is also critical of those who would wish to curtail freedom excessively in the interests of a political ideal. As a result, the novel failed to find ideological approval in either East or West. The positive presentation of Communism incensed certain American reviewers, one of whom actually suggested that anyone who reviewed the work favourably should be imprisoned! In the East too, though, there was unease. For the book contains ample criticism of rigid adherence to the party line (particularly on issues of personal freedom), and the presentation of capitalism, and of individual capitalists, is at points quite generous. Ironically, then, Heym's avoidance of a schematic presentation of issue and character ensured unease in both ideological camps, and this had devastating repercussions on sales. The issues which the book addresses consequently failed to reach the intended, large market, and as a literary achievement the novel also remained unappreciated. This was highly unfortunate, for in terms of character presentation *The Eyes of Reason* remains one of Heym's greatest successes.

As suggested, the plot unfolds very much through the inter-action of key figures. The three Benda brothers, Joseph, Karel, and Thomas, are each trying to come to terms with themselves after their experiences in the war. Joseph, managing director of the family glassworks, spent this period outside the country – in the Royal Air Force; Karel, a doctor, spent several years in a German concentration camp; and Thomas, a novelist and thinker, was exiled in the USA, where he acted as a spokesman for the Czech people. Joseph, uneasy with the left-wing ten-dencies in Czechoslovakia after the war, is anxious to maintain his hold over the glassworks, and he becomes a politician, gaining a seat for the conservative party. Karel's politics are quite diffferent, and his deep social conscience (largely created through the despair that his father's money was made through exploitation of others) leads him to dedicate himself to helping and caring for the workers. Thomas, unlike his brothers, is totally unsure of his direction. An indecisive liberal, he is full of self-pity and he is unable to settle to proper creative work. In the end he decides to write a general essay on 'freedom', and although we never see this essay in full, quotations from it are scattered throughout the novel. As will become more common for Heym, these quotations stand as a form of commentary on the action. They also provide a transparent form of self-commentary on the method of Stefan Heym himself.

Thomas is the first writer whom Heym was to depict in depth, and he is one who holds an exalted view of his own profession. He values in particular the independence of the artist and thinker, and praises the *oppositional* mind, which alone can create works which will outlast its generation. Indeed, he claims, there is strong historical evidence that when dissent is forbidden, or becomes unnecessary, the creative sti-mulus is choked or falls dormant. As he puts it in one of the typical homely images with which his essay is enlivened: ' ... opposition, criticism, revolt are like the leaven in the dough without which the bread would turn out flat and tasteless' (p. 259). This is one of the clearest instances of self-commen-tary and, equally, of self-justification in the novel, and it could stand as a motto for Heym's work as a whole. In virtually all his fiction, his doubts, even about what he believes in, are not concealed. He constantly provokes his readers into considering things in their *relative* value, the shortcomings of any ideal, the fact that we can never rest comfortable with any political system or any ideology. In this respect the comments of Karel, Thomas's brother, are another instance of self-commentary: 'He [Thomas] has a wonderful knack for making you doubt all the comfortable, long accepted commonplaces – and without preaching. The thing forces you to think for yourself. It's disturbing and stimulating and annoying, and there is some arrogance in it, too ... ' (p. 297). The final words here are, in all probability, to be taken as a form of mild self-critique. Heym is too honest a personality to deny the mild vanity of the successful creative writer.

Thomas's essay, of which only fragments are seen in the novel, would seem to owe some of its inspiration to Tolstoy's *War and Peace*, in particular chapters 8–12 of the Second Part of the Epilogue. Tolstoy is concerned here with forces in history,[1] a topic in which Heym had long been interested. (We glimpse his first comments on this issue in his review of *Der neue Caesar* (1935), and it is a subject which recurs throughout his entire work.) Thomas's focus is quite different to that of the Russian, but Heym acknowledges a debt to the latter in two ways: first, he draws the title of his novel from chapter 10 of Tolstoy's Epilogue and, second, he features four sentences from it as his motto. This particular quotation is important for a general understanding of the novel as a whole, and not just of Thomas's essay. In these lines Tolstoy presents the difficulty of seeing human action as subject only to necessity (without any element of free will), having previously shown the difficulty of seeing human action springing entirely from free will (without an element of necessity):

Man's free will differs from every other force in that man is directly conscious of it, but in the eyes of reason it in no way differs from any other force. The forces of gravitation, electricity, or chemical affinity are only distinguished from one another in that they are differently defined by reason. Just so, the force of man's free will is distinguished by reason from the other forces of nature only by the definition reason gives it. Freedom, apart from necessity, that is, apart from the laws of reason that define it, differs in no way from gravitation, or heat, or the force that makes things grow; for reason, it is only a momentary undefinable sensation of life.

In this chapter as a whole, Tolstoy is concerned with the nature of free will, and the degree of free will which is possible; Heym on the other hand takes the concept largely for granted and asks questions about the nature of freedom within society. He is more concerned with political and practical issues than with philosophical ones, and he illustrates the practical consequences of various 'types' of freedom through his choice of character – from capitalists with few moral scruples about exploitation of the workers (achieved through flashbacks to the old Peter Benda, a wily entrepreneur), to Communists whose total concern for their party line blinds them to all other possibilities (e.g. the publisher Villner, a partial caricature of the party dogmatist). Between such extremes a view of freedom is articulated which inclines further towards the socialist view than the capitalist. One which embraces notions of responsibility and obligation, yet which does not demand complete subordination to an ideology. Further, it is one which follows Tolstoy's suggestion that our approach to this concept should be rational and unemotional. Comparable views are advanced also in Thomas's essay, an essay which is rejected by his publishing house 'Because it offends everybody, subverts everything, and fits in none of the known grooves'. Another instance of self-commentary, and Thomas's retort to the above could equally be Heym's: 'But that is freedom!' (p. 264).

The concept of freedom dominates numerous discussions and is very much linked with plot developments in the novel, particularly (in its closing stages) with the Czech political crisis of 1948. That event, although still fresh in the minds of Heym's first readers, nowadays needs some clarification. Between 1945 and 1948 Czechoslovakia underwent considerable political and economic upheaval as the Communist Party, under its leader Klement Gottwald, gradually came to power. In the elections of 1946, the progress of which we follow in a country town, the Communists gained more seats than any other party

– but they did not have an overall majority to form a government. They formed instead a 'National Front', which incorporated figures from all parties but in which, of course, the Communists managed to play the leading role. Extensive nationalisation followed. This was seen by the bourgeoisie as an infringement of individual freedom, and in the novel it is vigorously attacked by some of those who have suffered. But Heym sets the indignation of those who have been ousted into perspective by gently emphasising the gains of the workers in the nationalised plants – not in terms of payment but, more importantly, in terms of their health. This improvement of the worker's lot, which we see in Part I of the novel, acts as a background, indeed, a yardstick, against which the Communists' 'takeover' at the end of Part II should be judged. Their 'seizure of power' is precipitated, ironically, by the resignation of numerous (non-Communist) cabinet ministers in protest at the Communists' policy. The former's hopes of bringing down the government have quite the opposite effect, however, and their action merely serves to strengthen the position of those remaining. Joseph Benda is trapped into fleeing, along with the leader of his party, and they reach Munich by hi-jacking a plane. The machinations of such reactionaries are seen as evidence of greed and selfishness, based solely on a materialist approach to life (Joseph and his wife take with them all their valuables, but have to leave behind their daughter). The takeover is consequently welcomed by those of the Benda family that remain. This is a victory for the type of freedom which the novel endorses, as well as one for 'reason'. It also represents an inversion of the earlier electoral success of Joseph, which was achieved through charm, apparent sincerity, brilliant timing, and emotional blackmail. Although he was outclassed in terms of the quality of his argument, the unemotional reasoning of his opponent lost to Joseph's superior psychological and tactical skill. But Joseph's manipulated triumph over the hearts of the voters (culminating in the provision of goulash soup for all attending the rally) proves a temporary one. Although he believes fervently in the type of political freedom which he advocates, this belief is seen to be founded largely on self-interest. The freedom from 'oppression and exploitation' which is postulated by his opponents, is shown by the progress of the novel to be a superior form of freedom. It too, however, is not without its disadvantages, for the novel endorses one of the great paradoxes of freedom: that certain aspects can only be preserved by suppressing others. Freedom of the multitude can only be attained through restricting the freedom of those who would exploit them.

One aspect of freedom which is commended through the very existence of the book is obviously that of the writer: his liberty to question, to doubt, and to challenge. But in keeping with the method of the novel, such freedom is itself probed from various points of view. The traditional, western attitude is expressed by the ultra-conservative American journalist, Elinor Simpson, who reacts with horror to the suggestion of state interference in the business of the arts. Against this, Communist Party members express their belief in the control of the printed word for the benefit of mankind as a whole.

The idea of state-controlled authorship, and its concomitant, state-organised censorship, is one which Heym has always vigorously opposed. Nevertheless, within this novel he reveals greater awareness than in any other that the control of artists can be important to governments at certain points of their existence. The ideal, of course, is not that people be *told* what to think, but that they reach by themselves the appropriate answers, and the Czech people as a whole are regarded as sufficiently mature to operate in this way. But Heym does not exclude the possibility of control in other circumstances. As already suggested, his general purport is that certain minor freedoms must be suppressed in order to maintain other, greater ones, and that the boundaries of freedom will need to be modified according to the prevailing historical situation. There is, however, a striking sentence in the novel which warns against the excesses of state control and which actually anticipated the source of failure in much GDR literature and propaganda of the fifties and sixties. This is the complaint of the schoolteacher turned socialist politician, Professor Stanek: 'Much of our literature is ineffectual because it supplies rules, formulas, programs – all correct, naturally; but it fails to provoke the reader into thinking for himself, into arriving by himself at the correct rules, formulas, programs' (p. 300). Heym's conviction of the futility of overtly didactic writing will be expressed more forcefully in some of his later essays.

There is another paradox of freedom which is revealed in the novel, and this one owes much to Tolstoy: it is that the higher a man stands on the social ladder, the less free his actions will be. In *War and Peace* Tolstoy had distinguished between a man's individual life and his 'elemental swarm-life', with the former providing a certain degree of freedom, but the latter constricting action through laws which are inevitable and which make men into unconscious instruments of historic forces. In *The Eyes of Reason* it is the figures of Joseph and Thomas who suggest this most clearly, with both becoming pawns as they rise above their local situations and become trapped in national issues. Only their brother, Karel, doing extensive medical good in a restricted area, can maintain his freedom to act independently and to revel in asserting it (such as his commandeering of medical equipment). Thomas lost his freedom, and with it his creative spirit, as he was drawn into his wartime position as 'spokesman' for the Czech nation. He never properly recovered. Joseph's largely satisfying life in the provinces is broken when he is elected to the National Assembly. At home he had control over a large glassworks and could make whatever changes he deemed appropriate – often humanitarian ones. In parliament he is totally controlled by his party. His need to bow to higher forces is demonstrated most clearly in his agreement to abandon the great humanitarian bill which he has come to see as his personal mission and personal contribution to Czech society. Ironically, he has to agree to its postponement only seconds before it would have been approved, and he has to abandon it in the interests of a very dubious 'higher' plan. Joseph's impotence here illustrates perfectly Tolstoy's views on the loss of freedom, and the moment is handled by Heym with great psychological and moral intensity.

This novel reveals further development in Heym's technique. Although his preference for a broad canvas continues, his scope is more restricted than in *The Crusaders*. The emphasis here is more on character development than plot (with particular attention to the way characters are converted to certain points of view or how they have become perverted from particular ideals), and the issues on which Heym focusses – the problems of the liberal intellectual in a rapidly changing world, the nature of 'freedom' – are much more fully presented than those of the earlier work, which is in the first instance a war novel and only in the second an investigation of the fascist personality and the problems of democracy. Heym's use of dialogue and description is also more subtle: there is far more conflict in the dialogue, and it is used more successfully as a method of indirect characterisation. There is greater use of *style indirect libre*, of sententious phrases, and there is greater variety of sentence construction. The structure of the novel as a whole shows greater balance than *The Crusaders*; the final section of the earlier novel, although vital to the ideological framework, was felt by some reviewers to represent an anticlimax after the sections devoted to war. In *The Eyes of Reason*, both the personal fate of the characters as well as the ideological implications of the whole novel reach their natural conclusion in the last chapter. Finally, the novel reveals Heym's ability to exploit his gifts in psychological analysis and description in the presentation of a complex web of historical, social, moral and philosophical issues. In no later novel does he achieve this so successfully.

Even before the hostile reception of *The Eyes of Reason*, Heym had serious doubts about whether he could continue to live in the USA. It was in 1949 that Senator McCarthy had begun his campaign of accusing – with little or no evidence – individuals in public office, or in the public gaze, of membership of the Communist Party, and Heym feared it might not be long before he too was accused. His wife was actually a member of the party, and denunciation of members by informers, and even by former party members, was becoming common. Given that the conclusion to *The Crusaders* had already aroused unease in right-wing circles, and that *The Eyes of Reason* would generate far more, it was likely that public vilification, and possible prosecution, would ensue sooner or later. The trial of the 'Hollywood Ten' (ten writers and directors who were imprisoned for refusing to divulge the names of their political associates) took place in 1950, and must have been a key factor which contributed to Heym's decision to leave America in the course of the following year. His destination, though, was uncertain, for there was no 'home' for him to return to. Prague was a possibility, and the two Heyms did spend time there in the course of their travels round Europe (which also took in France and Poland), but neither here nor elsewhere could they obtain a residence visa. Thoughts turned to Germany virtually as a last resort, for on both previous occasions on which Heym had left his mother country the circumstances had been hostile. His views on the German mentality – as seen in his novels – were not favourable, and his view of Western Germany, with its minimal attempts at de-Nazification, was contemptuous. He had not yet set foot in the Democratic Republic, which, like its western counterpart, was in 1951 barely two years old. However, as the Heyms moved around Europe, in ever more desperate attempts to find some sort of permanent residence, the GDR began to prove appealing. Here was, after all, the first established socialist state on German soil, in which such distinguished former exiles as Johannes R. Becher, Bertolt Brecht, and Anna Seghers were now prominent. In due course, therefore, after lengthy negotiation, Heym and his wife obtained a visa to reside in the country. They arrived at the turn of the year 1951–2, and by April 1953 Heym had irrevocably decided to make the GDR his home. On the 17th of that month he wrote his famous letter to President Eisenhower, in which he resigned his commission in the US Reserve Corps and returned the Bronze Star he had been awarded for bravery in the Battle of the Bulge. His reasons were that the American army was engaged in a war (in Korea) in which immoral methods were being used, and in which Nazi war criminals were serving.

These particular points were to be featured in two short stories that were written around this time, and other distressing

features of modern American society were to be highlighted in
several more.² In 'The Flea', for example, an ironic and
grotesque tale concerned with the development of insects for
military use; in 'Lem Kimble', which shows the inhumanity of
the war in Korea itself; and in the pointed title piece of the
collection in which these and several other stories are featured,
'The Cannibals'. In the latter Heym portrays the delight of an
elderly, poorly-paid man at the prospect of better work. But
this work is in a munitions factory which is reopening on
account of the war. The man reassures his wife he will soon
receive a telegram informing him of the job, and one does
indeed arrive – to inform him instead of the death of his son in
Korea.

These stories, published in a collection in 1953, are among
the most didactic, and the most bitter, Heym has written. They
expose aspects of a ruthless capitalism which thrives not simply
on the exploitation, but on the destruction of others, and there
are few individuals who are prepared to stand against the
numerous, and usually insidious forms of pressure which those
in power are prepared to wield. Those who do are victimised.
Although the content of these sombre tales is very different
from the earlier stories, their technique is much the same.
Despite their brevity, Heym maintains his interest in characters, and he has a firm penchant for repeated irony and a
concluding twist. Given the political content, such features
naturally sharpen the ideological implications.

It is not, however, short stories which provide the major
attack on American capitalism (and McCarthyism), but the
novel *Goldsborough*. As Heym has claimed with numerous other
works, he did not need to seek his material for this one: it arose
as a natural part of his life in the shape of three visitors who
came to his door, unannounced, early in 1950. The great
American miners' strike of 1949–50 was in progress, and two of
the miners had come from Pennsylvania to New York in order
to seek material support for their starving colleagues. A
contact, who had heard of Heym's sympathetic views on the
working class, had suggested they go to the great writer for
help, and this was immediately forthcoming. Heym not only

gave the miners help in New York, however; he travelled back to Pennsylvania with them and saw the conditions under which they were living. When the strike was over, he returned to the region, resided there to meet people and take notes, and went down a mine to get first-hand experience of working conditions. Since he was still engaged in a novel about Czechoslovakia, the novel which grew from these encounters was not completed for some time, and the manuscript was carried around Europe and into the GDR before final completion (December 1952). As the work had been begun in the USA, and the topic was American, the language of composition was naturally English. The novel was, however, first published in the GDR (in 1953), with a German translation following shortly thereafter. The English version first appeared in the USA in 1954.

The disrupted composition of *Goldsborough* can be seen to be reflected in the changing thematic focus of the novel. The first half is concerned chiefly with the strike, the men running it and those trying to frustrate it, but the second is devoted more to questions surrounding Communism, and especially the anti-Communist fervour which is being aroused in the USA. Although Americans' irrational fears over Communism had been a theme of Heym's work since *The Crusaders*, here the damage done by McCarthyism is given considerable prominence. Ironically, McCarthy's conduct was to be censured by the US Senate shortly after the novel was published in America, but the spirit of his campaign was to have extended consequences for the American reception of socialist writing.

The canvas of this novel is smaller than the preceding two. Most of the action is centred on the imaginary town of 'Goldsborough', an ironic name for a centre in which the majority of the inhabitants are poor and are dependent on the local coal mining company for their wages and houses. Their struggles to rise in life are perpetually frustrated by the control which the company exerts over all areas of small-town existence – not only does it fail to provide contracts, pensions, and safe conditions for its workers, but it also exerts considerable influence in the town administration, in the police force, and even in the judiciary. Progress only seems possible through immoral methods: by joining forces with the company and assisting in its exploitation of others. There are otherwise few prospects for the miners and their families, and their minor triumphs are repeatedly brought to earth by being seen in the context of their cheerless situation as a whole.

Goldsborough was begun within an American framework, and it is concerned exclusively with Americans. Most of its central figures are workers, and Heym was consequently developing a new form – there was no American tradition of 'worker novels', and although the figure of 'the worker' was soon to become important in the GDR, there were as then few in that country either (the obvious exception being Eduard Claudius's *Menschen an unsrer Seite* (1951)). Significantly, *Goldsborough* was for many years one of the few realistic presentations of the working man to appear in the GDR. Despite the exhortations to treat the problems of the working world in literature, East German writers regularly failed in this task. They either avoided the subject (preferring, for example, the war or other aspects of the Third Reich), or they presented workers and their surroundings in glamourised form. Heym's success is not only attributable to his skills as a novelist and his refusal to idealise the bleakness of manual labouring. It is in equal measure due to his thorough preparation for every novel. In this case it involved detailed study of working conditions, which combined with a natural interest and admiration for the working man – not only in his place of work, but also in his pursuits elsewhere.

The character at the centre of his novel is Carlisle Kennedy, a miner with a large family and numerous debts. It is he who is prepared to act as unofficial leader of a pit strike (when the official union leader, who is too concerned with his own live-lihood, fails to provide the necessary action), and his family life is as important a focus of the novel as is his life around the pit. As in the earlier novels, the author is much concerned with the psychology of his central figure – the motivation of a man who has struggled for years to achieve very little, whose family life is a constant series of arguments and dissatisfactions, and whose future seems very uncertain. Heym portrays the resilience of someone who refuses to capitulate under the system which oppresses him, and traces the attempts he makes to think things through for himself and for his workmates. In this respect he is akin to Janoschik of *Hostages*, whose slow mind doggedly works through his ideas. But the intellectual too finds a place in this novel, and as in all other works, it is an uncomfortable situation in which he finds himself. 'Doc' Hale, the dentist who could not complete a full dentistry course for lack of funds and who now works as a highly gifted dental mechanic, finds himself caught up in the miners' strike. He too becomes a victim of the ruthless pressure exerted by the local society and in the end has no option but to leave the town. Hale is not a member of the ruling class (and he is certainly not of their means), but neither is he one of the workers (although slightly above them in terms of social status and income). He lacks the camaraderie which binds the miners in their struggles, yet he also lacks the comforts which intellectual superiority usually brings. He is caught between two worlds, and his final farewell to the town has certain parallels with Heym's own departure from the USA.

The other central figure of this novel is Kennedy's daughter, Mickie. Although she was given undue prominence in a title which was used for later East German editions ('Goldsborough oder die Liebe der Miss Kennedy'), her role is subservient to those of the other central figures and her life offers a variation on theirs. Anxious to rise above her present position, and fearful that marriage to a miner will lead to an existence comparable to that of her own mother's, she compromises and, in the hope of reaching a finer existence in the big city, temporarily submits to an unscrupulous union official.

The subject-matter of *Goldsborough* demanded a different stylistic method from that of the earlier novels. Dialogue is far more significant here, with the plot developing to a large extent through interaction and confrontation. The miners' speech and their thought processes function at a more primitive level than those of most characters in *The Eyes of Reason*, and the places of work at which they are seen are portrayed from their point of view. The opening paragraph is typical of this style, and it also reflects the pessimistic attitude which pervades much of the novel:

The porch stairs were rotting away. Every time he set his foot on them he felt them give under his weight. He ought to do something about it. There was plenty of wood at the mine, and he could get it cheap. But the whole house was falling apart, and once he started making repairs there would be no end to it.

This dismal opening imagery, and the sense of hopelessness it conveys, is reflected in the syntax. These five sentences convey their information in a somewhat disjointed manner. The first three are short, with the first and third particularly simple. The fourth raises a sense of expectation, but that is crushed by the final one, in which the defeatism reveals itself in pathetic excuses. The simple development, the undemanding, collo-quial language, totally lacking in adornment, is characteristic of this work, which lives on a succession of short main clauses. The style reflects the activity and the personality of the partici-pants: it conveys above all a sense of frankness and bluntness.

The bleak surroundings of Kennedy's home recur elsewhere in the novel – in the drab surroundings of Goldsborough, its cheap bars, meeting places, and shops, in the darkness and dirtiness of the mine, and in the climate: the dominant impres-sion is of lowering clouds, dark skies, and of rain. Within the house, the atmosphere is likewise depressing: constant bicker-ing between Kennedy and his mother-in-law, squabbling between the children. The whole house is symbolic of the troubled and unfulfilled existence of the central figure, as of the miners as a whole. Although Kennedy feels he should do something about his situation, he feels so oppressed that he convinces himself all action would be futile. His decision to fight comes only after realisation that what little he does have might easily be taken from him.

One of Heym's concerns in this novel was that the official leaders of the strikers, at both local and national level, were not truly committed to the plight of their members. The leaders are part of the general corruption which the author sees throughout American society, and this accusation is one of the most troubling in the book. Not surprisingly, it caused some distress among socialist reviewers, but as with *The Eyes of Reason*, Heym was not prepared to compromise for the sake of any party line. Here he is suggesting that no major progress is possible, because the leaders are not campaigning for their own men. They are fighting to protect their own positions, and these are, ironically, dependent on the support of their opponents. The USA is depicted as a country in which too many men have their price, in which 'democracy' is a sham because supposedly democratic offices can be bought, and in which idealists are viewed with suspicion rather than admiration.

And yet, as in practically all Heym's novels, there is a faint note of optimism in the conclusion. This does not spring from the miners' 'victory' in their strike, for although they have technically won, they are in fact little better off than before. There have also been casualties among those who support them. Mickie, Kennedy's daughter, is pregnant by a young miner who has lost his life during the struggle. Hale, the intellectual, has been forced out of the town. But on the final pages we learn that Kennedy has decided to stand as a rival candidate for president of the local union, and the distinct possibility that he might succeed has alarmed one of the city clerk's henchmen. The full force of the opposition to Kennedy is revealed in the indignation of the city clerk that there might be difficulty in stopping Kennedy:

'You got the district organisation of your union!' Geoghan said cuttingly. 'You got my machine, and the press, and the radio, and the Catholic Church, and the FBI, and the courts, and every cop in Goldsborough County – and you shiver in your pants over a handful of dumb miners? What's the matter with you!'

With the sole exception of an individual member of the Catholic Church, all the above have acted against the miners in the course of the novel. The suggestion that such powerful establishment figures are not invincible is strengthened further by a postscript to the novel. Here the author recalls the moment he learnt of the outbreak of war in Korea, when he was actually drinking with a group of miners. Most of the men echoed the anti-Communist stance of the radio commentators, but one reminded them of the misleading information the media had given during the course of the recent strike, and he therefore counselled the others not to take over these opinions without questioning them. Through a reference to this man's set of teeth, it is made clear that he is the figure on whom the hero of the novel has been based; the postscript concludes with the author confidently suggesting that more will be heard of such men. Such drawing together of fact and fiction becomes more common in Heym's later works, where actual documents are introduced in order to strengthen the element of historical credibility.

As has been mentioned, *Goldsborough* was begun in the USA but completed in the GDR towards the end of 1952. With McCarthyism still intense, it was clear that the work's subject-matter would not appeal to a major publishing house in the USA. The novel was consequently first published in the GDR under the imprint 'Panther Books', a series of English-language volumes of which Heym himself was invited to be general editor, and one of the aims of which was to provide an outlet for American authors whose works had been proscribed by McCarthy. (With the appearance of an identical imprint in London, the title was later changed to 'Seven Seas' and the series was controlled by Heym's wife, Gertrude.) A German translation was obviously necessary, and this was the first major novel which Heym was to translate himself (*The Crusaders* and *The Eyes of Reason* having been tackled by professional translators, whose work had then been corrected by Heym). Instalments appeared in the *Neue Berliner Illustrierte*, and the standard of translation was impeccable. Most subsequent major works were translated by Heym, whether from English to German or German to English, thus making him the only major author capable of translating in both directions. His translation is characterised by total accuracy and frequently ingenious exploitation of the differing nature of the two languages. He is without doubt the most successful living ipso-translator of the German and English languages.[3]

In addition, though, this activity was to prove beneficial to Heym's methods of composition. From now on he worked with the knowledge that what he was writing – whether it be in

English or in German – would need to be translated into another language. Every sentence was therefore carefully weighed: would it flow equally well and equally clearly in the other tongue? Such considerations produced a clarity of style unusual for a German writer, and on completing a novel one of Heym's first, and relatively straightforward, tasks was to translate it. This exercise represented a partial relaxation after the demands of composition, but the habit had more serious aims. With the translations from German into English some of the motivation was undoubtedly political. In contrast to writers whose work was not known outside the GDR, Heym could maintain a life-long international status. This was to give him considerable standing among GDR cultural politicians, and to afford some protection against numerous – but by no means all – aspects of party harassment.

CHAPTER 5

Return to Germany: the struggles of the fifties

Heym's arrival in East Berlin is usually referred to as a 'return' to Germany, but the euphemism is misleading: he and his wife were essentially seeking political asylum there. No other European country – on either side of the Iron Curtain – had been prepared to allow them permament residence, and even the GDR had taken time to reach a decision. The reasons for hesitation may not now be obvious, especially since Heym had been a victim of National Socialism, a campaigner against fascism, and a successful novelist with indisputably left-wing sympathies. He had, however, been a US citizen, and an officer in the US army. In a period of intense anti-American feeling, which had been present since well before the Americans' breaking of the Berlin blockade (1948/9), any former association with the USA was viewed with considerable mistrust. This was to continue throughout the history of the Republic, and as late as 1979 memory of Heym's period in the USA was used in *Neues Deutschland* to heighten that paper's denunciation of him (14 May 1979). Asylum in 1951 was therefore far from straightforward, and the Heyms' visa may well have been granted only as a result of the energy and perseverance of benevolent intermediaries.

Ironically, although the GDR was not the Heym's first choice for exile, it was probably the most promising country to which they could have come at that stage in time. Traditionally, western critics have emphasised the negative features of the new state in its early years, and I shall turn to these aspects in due course. But for a socialist writer, and for creative socialist artists in general, the GDR represented a relative paradise. In contrast to the writer in the USA, for example, his GDR counterpart was highly esteemed as a central figure in the re-shaping of German minds after 'dehumanisation' during the Third Reich.[1] His task was to disseminate noble ideological ideals, encourage socialist reconstruction of the country, and create heroes who would stand as model figures, inspiring the reader to comparable feats or life styles. Writers were far from simple entertainers, then, but were invested with a political role. Given their importance, they were accorded the privileges of comparable leading political and intellectual figures, and so they enjoyed luxuries which were far beyond those of the general population. Notably, these included preferential treatment in food rations and in accommodation (and, after a difficult first year in spartan conditions, the Heyms in due course acquired a substantial residence in a pleasant suburb of Berlin). As far as writers' literary careers were concerned, state-controlled firms were eager to receive their manuscripts, and paid them handsome advances and generous royalties. Lucrative prizes were also to be won: notably the 'National Prizes', open to all in the arts, and which were allocated in gradations of 100,000, 50,000 and 25,000 marks, tax free (these were awarded to no fewer than eight writers in the first few years of their existence). Writers also enjoyed the support of a union (founded in 1952) which generally cared for their legal rights and minor privileges, and which also, as the years passed by, assisted its most loyal members (but not the critical ones) in such matters as obtaining a car without the customary waiting period of up to ten years, and organising travel outside the Republic – a privilege which aroused much envy among other groups.[2]

It was not only those involved with the arts who enjoyed substantial benefits, but intellectuals as a whole. The same document which announced the creation of National Prizes contained within its very first decree a remarkable evaluation of the intellectuals' position:

Alle Organe der demokratischen Verwaltung, die Leiter der volkseigenen Betriebe und der wissenschaftlichen und kulturellen Institute haben den Angehörigen der Intelligenz erhöhte Aufmerksamkeit zu widmen. Sie haben Maßnahmen zur praktischen Verbesserung der materiellen Lage und Arbeitsmöglichkeiten der Intelligenz unter Ausnutzung aller örtlichen Möglichkeiten zu treffen. Sie haben dafür Sorge zu tragen, daß die Intelligenz in großzügiger Weise und in breitem Umfange zum wirtschaftlichen und kulturellen Aufbau und im besonderen auch zur Entwicklung der Aktivistenbewegung in den volkseigenen Betrieben herangezogen wird...[3]

All organs of our democratic administration, those in charge of state-owned factories and scientific and cultural institutions, must pay increased attention to the needs of the intelligentsia. They must undertake measures towards the practical improvement of the material conditions of the intelligentsia and towards providing them with employment; all local possibilities must be employed to this end. They must see to it that the intelligentsia are drawn on a broad scale and in a more generous way into the economic and cultural process of rebuilding our country and especially also into the development of the activist movement.

This followed the Soviet model and was, of course, issued under the jurisdiction of the Soviet Military Administration (March 1949). Preferential treatment for the intelligentsia continued throughout the history of the Republic, especially for those who were also members of the party.

The relationship between writers and state was envisaged by the party as reciprocal: in return for this modern form of patronage the state expected support from its authors. And the nature of this support was made increasingly clear to writers, often through the medium of what became known as the 'cultural functionary' – senior members of the party, with a firm cultural background, unswerving commitment to socialist ideals, and considerable energy. The most prominent of these around the time of Heym's arrival were Alexander Abusch, Anton Ackermann, and Fritz Erpenbeck, and they enjoyed considerable power in all aspects of cultural control. Heavily influenced by Soviet models, they promulgated the concept of 'socialist realism' as the only appropriate method for contemporary German literature, and they denigrated all aspects of 'formalism' (the excessive concern with the 'form' of a work rather than with its subject-matter) and of 'cosmopolitanism' (reflection of imperialist, bourgeois, or generally western tendencies, reviled at that time more commonly in art and sculpture). Literature was to address itself principally to the realistic depiction of working people, the point of view adopted by the writer should be that of the working class, the individual cases depicted should be representative of general tendencies, and the completed work should portray the progress and triumph of socialism. This programme, with various modifications and additions, was to remain official cultural policy throughout the history of the Republic.

Although such an approach to literature might seem appropriate for a socialist writer, many felt unsettled and restricted when presented with a firm programme to which they were expected to conform. They felt further inhibited by the fact that although there was no official 'censorship', all manuscripts had to be submitted for scrutiny before a licence for their printing could be issued. Such a procedure could easily be justified against the background of the Third Reich, and it was indeed initially operated by the Allies in their respective Zones of Occupation. In the Soviet Zone all Nazi literature was removed from libraries shortly after the war (to be replaced mainly by classics of Russian and Soviet literature), and vigorous steps were taken to prevent the resurgence of any such material. Over and above this, however, the socialist state was anxious to provide a new literature which was not only uncontaminated by Nazi ways of thinking, by formalism, or by cosmopolitanism, but also one which extolled without reservation the GDR way of life. It was this latter point which was to provide so much aggravation for writers, for they were being urged to idealise a situation which every reader could recognise as being totally at odds with the depressing prevailing conditions. It was not only the encouragement to produce 'positive heroes' which disturbed writers, however, but the pressure to eradicate any minor detail which might possibly be misinterpreted by eastern readers or seized upon by the western 'enemies' as an example of eastern failure. Even such an eminent figure as Alfred Kantorowicz had difficulty in getting his play *Die Verbündeten* (briefly) performed, and the fact it reached the stage at all was, ironically, due to Soviet intervention (the Soviets were far more relaxed in their cultural policy than the new German leaders). Kantorowicz recorded in his diary the lengthy discussions he had to conduct before production was allowed.[4] The play dealt with the Maquis in France during the war, but it was criticised (among other things) for having an American among the resistance group, and for having that group listen to the BBC – rather than Radio Moscow, which was not always obtainable in France! Heym himself was criticised for comparable reasons during the preparations for staging his old *Tom Sawyer*. As was mentioned in chapter 2, he was involved in a serious discussion about whether Huckleberry Finn should be allowed to be seen stealing plums. His critics were apparently seriously worried that all schoolchildren who saw the play might follow this example.

These two illustrations bring out the unrealistic, narrow-minded and psychologically naive attitude which could only be advanced by functionaries lacking true artistic sensitivity; but they also bring out the desire of such functionaries to be of practical assistance. For writers were given considerable advice not simply on what was unacceptable in a text, but on how it might be ideologically modified, or even drastically altered. (It would seem to have been rare for a book to be turned down without discussion.) If a writer were to refuse to re-write, then the publishing house might well find some reason, possibly non-political, to turn down the manuscript. And if a proposal were refused by one house, then it would not be accepted by another in the all-state system. In order to spare themselves time and endless discussions, the practice of 'self-censorship' (i.e. recognising what would not be acceptable and deciding to omit or modify it) thus became important for many GDR writers, and this was at its most obvious in their simple avoidance of key moments in GDR history (notably, the events of 17 June 1953; the revelations following the Soviet Twentieth Party Congress in 1956). Over the years the process of obtaining permission to publish became more complex, and at times those responsible for granting it were quite unpredictable and irrational. By the end of the Republic the procedure was still formidably bureaucratic,[5] and the bulk of what was permitted bore little relation to the true demands of the reading public. But a number of writers successfully fought against these controls, and as a result produced the most important literary works to appear in the history of the Republic. The model for such figures, and their champion, was Stefan Heym.

Knowledge of prevailing cultural conditions is central to our understanding of what Heym fought against, and what he achieved, in the course of his career – particularly his early years in the GDR. And much of this was attained in material circumstances which were initially far from ideal. Parts of Berlin still lay in ruins, and the Heyms lived for over a year in a single room on the very outskirts of the city. There were financial and psychological problems, too. Royalties from the earlier novels were now much reduced, and it seemed most unlikely that income from the major work in progress, *Goldsborough*, could be substantial. There was delay in even getting a publishing house to take on *The Eyes of Reason* in German translation. Psychologically, too, the Heyms were initially without much sense of security. So many members of the circles in which they now moved had returned to Germany several years earlier and had either established themselves successfully in specific posts or were able to live off the earnings of a literature which suited the present cultural scene more readily than the independent writing of Heym. In addition, many of these had been in exile in the Soviet Union, and their loyalty to the GDR was therefore far less questionable than that of someone who had spent so much time in what was now regarded as the most hostile foreign power. Even worse, Heym had recently spent a period in Czechoslovakia, where the Slansky show trial (1952) was to cast a warning shadow over the whole Soviet bloc. The fact that eleven of the fourteen defendants in that trial were Jewish must have been deeply troubling for Heym, as must the fact that one of their supposed crimes was collaboration with foreign (western) powers. If Slansky, former General Secretary of the Czech Communist Party, could be executed for treason, there must surely be little hope for the free-thinking Heym and his USA-born wife. In the same year Heym was experiencing the rejection (by the GDR state film company) of the *Crusaders* film project, and political disagreements with the East Berlin press. A depressing background, which gave no inkling of the fact that Heym would soon emerge as the most popular journalist the Republic was ever to enjoy.

Heym had no desire to work exclusively as a novelist. Although he did consider himself principally a writer of fiction, he was also a newspaper writer with wide experience, and journalism was a profession from which he could derive a steadier form of income than from novels. Shortly after settling in Berlin, therefore, he began to write occasional pieces for newspapers. The first of these were for the *Tägliche Rundschau*, the Soviet-controlled paper of East Berlin, and a direct equivalent to the old *Neue Zeitung* on which Heym had worked in Munich. Heym managed to achieve a good relationship with those controlling the paper, but even though Soviet policy was less rigid than East German, he soon encountered political difficulties in connection with an article treating material which had been published in the West. In the open Berlin of 1952, access to western newspapers represented no particular difficulty to those living in the eastern part; but Soviet and East German policy was not to quote directly from anything which had appeared in the other half of the city, or, of course, of the nation. Such a short-sighted attitude towards quotation was to lead to Heym's well-publicised break with the newspaper world later in the fifties, but at this stage of his career his protests carried little weight. The same held true for his dealings with *Neues Deutschland*, the official organ of the Socialist Unity Party. They printed one of his stories, but rejected his translation of 'Lem Kimble' for reasons which could be deduced from the outline of cultural policy provided above. In stiff jargon, it was made clear that only the adulation of model heroes was worthy of being featured in a socialist newspaper, and if aspects of the West were to be portrayed, then a writer should depict only the insight of the misled into the fact they were being expoited. Heym's suggestion that the reader might be allowed to think for himself was ignored. In his memoirs, Heym quotes the letters exchanged between officialdom and himself on this issue (p. 550). Besides offering a comic illustration of a policy which was to alienate all but the dullest of readers, they establish that Heym's opposition to party cultural thinking was evident as early as 1952. Only a few months after settling in the GDR, then, he was again proving uncomfortable to those in power, and doing so in a way which was to endear him to the populace: frankly, without taboos, and with a sense of respect for the mind of the working man. Unlike the staff correspondents of the (state-controlled) press, he tried to establish a sense of communion between author and reader. This was uncommon in the GDR of the early fifties, when the attitude of those in power was often one of insensitive superiority.

The turning point for Heym came with 17 June 1953, the events of which have been recorded in all books on contemporary German history.[6] Those published in the West emphasise the *spontaneous* nature of the strikes and disturbances in East Berlin and other cities in the Republic. For them, the uprising was sparked off by the decree – and then the revocation of that decree – that the 'norms' of all workers were to be raised by 10 per cent; but, as western writers suggest, such a revolt against authority rested firmly on the basis of general dissatisfaction with living conditions in the Republic. Books published in the East have acknowledged some dissatisfaction and have recognised the unease over the situation with the 'norms', but they have laid major blame for the events on 'provocation' by the West Germans and their 'imperialist' allies.

The spontaneous nature of these events would seem to be confirmed by the consternation with which the governments of *both* German states reacted to the uprising, and after it had been quickly quelled by the arrival of Soviet tanks, there was a period in which widespread uncertainty prevailed – in both parts of the nation. It was at this point that Heym emerged as a spokesman for the common man, seizing the moment of uncertainty to write boldly and constructively and in the sort of language which was rarely seen in GDR newspapers. He completed six articles in quick succession (printed in *Vorwärts* and in the mass-circulation *Berliner Zeitung*; later collected into a mass-circulated brochure 'for discussion' by the Freier Deutscher Gewerkschaftsbund Bundesvorstand), and that these forceful pieces appeared at all can be attributed to several factors. First, that Heym defended the state (although he sharply criticised aspects of its policy); second, the uncertainty of those in charge of press censorship; third, a suspicion that lack of frankness was partly responsible for the present situation; and finally, that other writers were not prepared to commit themselves with such clarity. The party-liner Kuba [Kurt Barthel] wrote an appeal to the workers in which he claimed he was ashamed of them; over the course of the years it has earned some ridicule. Brecht also wrote a short and whimsical poem on the matter, which has been seen as typical of his generally shrewd and ambiguous behaviour in those years. With the sole exception of Erich Loest, every other writer failed to respond adequately. Loest, unfortunately, was later to be jailed for comparable outspokenness and supposed 'feindliche Gruppenbildung' ('creating oppositional groups').

These six articles were written in a slightly simpler style than Heym's usual contributions to newspapers, and they abound in personal anecdote introduced for the purpose of analogy: experiences in the USA, contacts with workers in the street, letters written to him, travels elsewhere in Europe. All are introduced to make basic points about the uprising and the lessons which can be learnt from it. Heym's position is stated bluntly on several occasions: the uprising was provoked from without, but provocation would not have succeeded if there had not been widespread and deep unease in the populace. Among the factors upon which Heym lays stress are the mistakes in party policy and party bureaucracy, and there is also criticism of the press for failing to reflect the genuine concerns of the workers. Nevertheless, Heym makes it abundantly clear that although mistakes have been made, the GDR can correct these, and that for all its faults, the country is far superior to Hitler's Germany and to that of Adenauer.

With these articles Heym was fully launched into GDR journalism. His image quickly became that of a figure crusading for frankness, someone determined to expose 'whitewashing' and to fight for the 'little man'. His contributions to newspapers in the mid-fifties were so popular that they were reprinted in two separate volumes: *Im Kopf – sauber. Schriften zum Tage* (1954), a collection of articles which had been published in the course of the preceding year, and *Offen gesagt. Neue Schriften zum Tage* (1957), which comprises his weekly columns in the Sunday editions of the mass-circulation *Berliner Zeitung*, 1955–7. Some of the best are reprinted in *Wege und Umwege*. The range of material covers all aspects of life in the GDR and also takes in criticism of West Germany.

There is no particular 'formula' for Heym's journalism, and so, like the rest of his life and his writing, it is remarkably difficult to classify – a feature of which he himself is particularly proud and which he maintains in his constant unpredictability. The range of subject-matter is wide, the approach is always urgent and energetic, Heym constantly writes with a sense of enthusiasm and a keen awareness of a reader. He does, in fact, tend to presuppose a particular type of reader: the average GDR worker, who feels misunderstood, ill-rewarded for his efforts, and abused by an officialdom which refuses to trust him and consistently withholds information. This, claims Heym in one of his most forthright articles, is one of the main reasons why the GDR press is so bad: the journalists are cut off from their readers, too dependent on instructions from above, and completely lacking in initiative; they thoughtlessly promulgate ridiculous untruths, perpetually glossing over the situation and therefore becoming untrustworthy on *all* matters; they do not report dramatic events for fear some of them might reflect badly on the Republic, but as a consequence leave such news for the West to exploit in its own political way. Heym further makes fun of using long and repetitive leader articles; of devising headlines as slogans; of claiming ridiculous trivia are representative of the Republic as a whole; and of employing the same, unimaginatively predictable epithets so that they become quite devoid of meaning. Finally, he accuses the 'official' newspapers (especially *Neues Deutschland*) of being boring in their entirety rather than in their official sections only – so spineless are GDR journalists in their approach to all matters, that even the review of books cannot rouse them to a personal opinion.[7]

In making such a dramatic broadside (in July 1953) Heym was by implication establishing a programme. He could now never allow himself to drop to the level of cliché, could never afford to be boring. But the challenge was realistic, for his advantages over fellow journalists were considerable. For example, he had never been able to rely on a captive audience, which was effectively the situation of his contemporaries (who therefore had little incentive to exert themselves). At *Deutsches Volksecho* Heym had needed to exercise constant versatility in the fight to retain readers. Life in New York had been hectic, totally different from the bored atmosphere of an East German editorial office, where the content of most of a 'news'paper was planned days, or even weeks in advance, where one's career was not to be jeopardised by expression of personal opinions, and where one was constantly aware of scrutiny from above. A second advantage had been Heym's training in psychological warfare, the repeated and painful experience of having to imagine himself into the situation of those for whom he was writing or broadcasting, and achieving this only after rigorous interrogation and discussion with captured enemy soldiers. One had the impression, by contrast, that certain East German journalists never actually spoke with the sort of person for whom they were supposedly writing. Heym was constantly among the people, listening to them and noting their grievances.

A third advantage, perverse though it may initially appear, was that Heym had had the good fortune *not* to be trained in an East German institute for journalists. The intellectual preparation of media personnel – and, after 1955, the 'training' of writers – was considered of great importance to the East German government, but the practical result of such schooling was the freezing of personal initiative and lifeless uniformity which characterised all the East German media: the press, radio, and television. Heym remained independent in all respects, bringing with him also his wide experience of other life styles and ways of thinking, together with his by now legendary courage.

Heym's constant 'freshness' is maintained not through his

choice of subject-matter, which is mainly everyday life in the GDR, but rather through the sense of personal engagement in what he is describing or discussing. There is a strongly auto-biographical element which prefers the personal pronoun and the personal anecdote, and above all a sense of irony. Light-heartedness was a very rare feature of the East German media, but Heym delights in satire and mild sarcasm. Whatever the tone, though, he is always seeking to reform or to improve. His ideals are not absolute: he is not a utopian, but a pragmatist who believes that in being awkward he really can achieve positive ends.

Heym will apparently pluck his subjects from nowhere. One article is simply entitled 'Nur ein Wort' ('Just a word') (20 January 1956, *Wege*, pp. 259–62). It does indeed concern itself with a single word, 'noch', but Heym subtly uses his realisation of the way this adverb was increasingly being used in the GDR in order to expose the general practice of whitewash and cliché, and to postulate instead a policy of plain language, honesty and commitment. The anecdote he introduces here has obvious relevance to his personal method. He recalls that at a recent conference the words of one worker had stood out on account of their unexpected directness: 'Dort wird', sagte er, 'zum Teil gearbeitet wie im Jahre 1800' ('Work in parts of our factory is carried out in the same way as it was in 1800') (p. 260). The remark had an immediate effect on all present. This would not have been the case if the speaker had indulged in 'Noch-Sprache' and expressed himself like a typical factory functionary: 'Es erweist sich als notwendig, die Modernisier-ung in unserem Betrieb noch weiter vorauszutreiben ...' ('it is proving necessary to forge ahead even further with the process of modernisation in our factory ...') (p. 260).

These articles are rich in crisply formulated warnings. In his attack on the press, for example, Heym points out a dangerous, but common, political pitfall:

Wer einmal schönfärbt, dem glaubt man nur schwer. (*Wege*, p. 211)

(Paper over the cracks just once, and your credibility rating will plummet.)

And in his recommendations for literature he warns against excessive didacticism and reminds artists of commercial realities they seem to have forgotten:

Von der Kunst wollen die Leute unterhalten werden. Dafür zahlen sie. (*Wege*, p. 221)

(People want to be entertained by art. That's what they pay for.)

The written word of a very different sort is attacked in another article, where Heym indulges in a complex joke at the expense of both Germanies. Here he comments on the contents of a (western) leaflet dropped over East Berlin on 1 May 1954:

Ich hatte mehr von drüben erwartet, westliche Qualität, sozusagen. (*Wege*, p. 227)

(I had been expecting more from over there. Western quality, as you might put it.)

The last example reveals Heym's delight in the unexpected, in anomalies, and, above all, in contradictions, and it is perhaps not surprising that his own writing should draw much strength from the general technique of inverting expectations. Heym loves surprising his readers, a respect in which he can be compared with Brecht.[8]

Heym's column was feared by functionaries to the same degree that it was enjoyed by the average worker, above all because it forced a reaction. Many features were the result of readers writing to Heym and asking him to publicise some irregularity or injustice, and he would regularly oblige. He thus helped shape the development of the Republic in a way no other journalist achieved, even on such incidental matters as pointing out the folly of rejecting jeans as a symptom of capitalism. Heym was not, however, a eulogist of the working man, and he was not afraid to make himself unpopular through uncompromising observations on the latter. In his two articles on the famous 'Nacherstedter Brief', for example (an open letter to East German writers from workers at a large plant in Nacherstedt, which called for a new approach to literary portrayal of 'the worker'), Heym suggested that there was a

distinct absence in reality of those positive features which the
authors of the letter wished to see featured in literature. The
real working man was often far from the ideal which was
emanating from Nacherstedt. Heym's second article on this
extended and wide controversy (which was given full coverage
in the GDR), contained two characteristic, sententious
remarks: 'Der Schriftsteller kann sich nicht verschließen die
Augen vor dem, was ist' ('Writers can't shut their eyes to what
they actually see'); and 'Die Schönfärberei jedoch ist einer der
Todfeinde des Sozialismus, und *der* Todfeind jeder echten
Literatur' ('Glossing over mistakes is one of the fatal enemies of
socialism, and *the* fatal enemy of all true literature').[9] Not even
the workers themselves were safe from Heym's strictures, in
other words, and it was this frankness in all matters which
made another aspect of his achievement possible: the encouragement to East Germans not to abandon their belief in socialism. Heym never ceased to defend the Republic and its ideology against West Germany and the evils of capitalism. For all
the eastern failings he ridiculed, he repeatedly expressed the
hope that the GDR would in due course become not only a
fairer and more peace-loving, but also a richer country than
the Federal Republic. Through his policy of openness and
apparent impartiality, this hope carried conviction.

The years 1953–7 mark the highest point that Heym was to
reach in the GDR as a regular contributor to newspapers
(although he was later to become far more widely known
through his novels and television appearances). He was given
various other assignments for the press, and these included
travelling to Moscow (to report for the *Tägliche Rundschau* on a
Congress of Soviet Writers in 1954) and travelling widely in
the USSR to produce reports on Soviet life and Soviet science
(he produced a rather idealistic view of conditions there in
Forschungsreise ins Herz der deutschen Arbeiterklasse (1953), and
Reise ins Land der unbegrenzten Möglichkeiten. Ein Bericht (1954);
also an equally idealistic view of scientific progress in *The
Cosmic Age. A Report* (1959)). All this work is carefully written,
but it is far from Heym's best. The tone, in particular, is rather
patronising. Heym is at his keenest only when in disagreement

with something or when thinking dialectically. Opportunities for a dissenting view were abundant in the GDR, of course, and the frankness of Heym's reporting, together with his justified criticism of blunders in (especially local) party policy, incurred frequent displeasure among senior party officials. This was doubtless increased by their knowledge that Heym's column was a major selling feature of the *Berliner Zeitung* Sunday edition. In 1957, therefore, after he had criticised the East German censorship of a document which had received widespread prominence in the West, he was urged to accept a form of censorship himself over what he wrote in his weekly features. Heym rejected this and preferred to give up the column rather than to be muzzled. (His integrity reminds us of the comparable action which brought to an end his work for the *Neue Zeitung*.) His contributions to newspapers are thenceforth less regular and more scattered.

There were advantages for Heym the novelist and short story writer in his giving up such a time-consuming activity as a weekly column (which generated much correspondence, all of which was personally answered). Work on a major novel had begun shortly after 17 June 1953, and the subject-matter was the substance of the uprising itself. First entitled 'A Day Marked X', this work was to engage Heym's attention for a full two decades until its publication in 1974. But the late fifties also witnessed publication of various short stories, ranging widely in content and tone. A number of these were collected in *Shadows and Lights*, which was first published in London in 1959, and which reached Germany, as *Schatten und Licht*, in the following year. (The language of composition was English, the translation into German in most cases being carried out by the author himself.) The sub-title of the German edition suggests the main focus for these pieces: 'Geschichten aus einem geteilten Lande'. Contemporary East Germany, with its Cold War attitudes, is the setting for almost all, but aspects of West German society are frequently introduced. One of the stories is set in the West, and most are concerned with negative aspects of western influence: attempts to encourage GDR intellectuals to defect, for example; black-market trade across East/West

Berlin; the nature of those seeking to return to the East after failing to make their way in the West. The narrative persona adopted is varied, but there is a constant concern for motivation and the fate of individuals (regularly tinged with a sad irony), together with a determination to show the moral superiority of the socialist way of life. The symbolic nature of 'shadows' and 'lights' soon becomes obvious.

These stories bear the clear stamp of the Cold War. West Germany is seen as the root of most evil: a place of violent anti-Communism, sexual immorality, love of money and power, unscrupulous methods to achieve questionable goals. The East, by contrast, is the land of hope, idealism, concern for others, a more just society for all. There is the occasional comment about poor living conditions in the East, but these are usually seen against the grander aims of that society. For example, a group of characters find themselves obliged to visit a provincial town at short notice. Their rooms are in 'das führende Hotel der Stadt' ('the town's leading hotel') (p. 104), which is then described in harsh terms: 'Das Hotel war viertklassig und roch dementsprechend' ('The hotel was fourthrate, and smelled accordingly') (p. 104). The condemnation of rural East Germany reaches an apparent peak in the following clause, but it is followed by a partial explanation: 'der frühere Besitzer war zusammen mit der Barmamsell nach dem Westen geflüchtet und hatte dem Arbeiter-und-Bauern-Staat seine Frau, seine Kinder und seine Schulden hinterlassen' ('together with the barmaid, the former owner had fled to the West and had left behind for the Workers' and Farmers' State his wife, his children, and his debts') (p. 104). No further excuses are offered for the state at this point, and, indeed, criticism actually increases as the apparent insensitivity of 'bureaucrats' becomes apparent. However, the conclusion encourages us to set such criticism into context. A western agent is exposed as being the instigator of an immoral plot to encourage a prominent eastern scientist to defect. One of the implications of this story – and it is repeated in practically all the others – is that had it not been for the West's repeated attempts at disruption, sabotage, and blackmail, the East would have prospered far more easily.

It is striking that East German critics should nevertheless have taken objection to these stories: not so much to their conclusions, but to the fact that they contain occasional criticism of Heym's own country. Wolfgang Joho, for example, a leading conservative critic of the fifties, deplored the manner in which aspects of West German propaganda against the East were featured in one story, through the mouth of an obvious opponent.[10] Joho's (unspoken) fear was clearly that waverers in the GDR might interpret this invective as well-founded, or justified criticism, and therefore as an incentive to flight. Such a view clearly betrays the continuing, Leninist, attitude to art, which demanded constant guidance of the reader and virtually presupposed an absence of moral sensibility. Heym, since 1952, had been presupposing intelligence in his audience, and insisting that it was counter-productive either to idealise characters and situations, or to omit what might be politically embarrassing. That principle is clearly followed in this collection.

Divided Germany of the fifties comprised two far less hospitable countries than were to be found in the seventies or eighties. The fifties was a period of heavy, and increasing emigration from East to West, and the propaganda war between the two parts of the nation was intense. Literature in the East reflected the attitudes of politicians, and some parts of *Schatten und Licht* do indeed mirror the antagonism and depth of suspicion between the two sides. Heym certainly did not succumb to the extremism – in retrospect, rather comical extremism – of various contemporary writers, although his image of the West was certainly uncompromising. This may be reflected in the fact that only two of these pieces were chosen for inclusion in the *Gesammelte Erzählungen*. His stories of the sixties are composed in a much more balanced and confident manner.

The evils of the West are also to be seen in the great novel on which Heym was working for much of the fifties, and for which the initial research alone took up a full twelve months. As with all his fiction, there was extensive planning, conversations with a good number of those who had been involved (from workers to ministers), re-reading of documents of the time, visiting of industrial plants. The topic was German, but the language of writing was English, and *A Day Marked X* was the first version of a book which was to become the most famous unpublished manuscript of post-war Germany. Writing began in 1954, but the constant interruptions from journalistic and other activities meant that composition was not complete until 1958.

The subject-matter of the novel was the strike, demonstrations, and ultimate quelling of all disturbances by Soviet troops in June 1953. As was suggested above, the spark to these events was provided by the government's decree that the 'norms' for industrial workers should be raised 10 per cent by 30 June (a 'norm' being the amount of work which the average worker could be expected to achieve in a certain time), but there were many underlying factors which made such a spark so decisive. These included a lower living standard than that prevailing in West Germany, a lack of consumer goods, and displeasure over various aspects of party policy. Heym refers to all these in the course of the novel, and in this respect he stands apart from other fiction on the subject. In general, the literature of East and West which has devoted itself to the uprising has followed the political interpretation of whichever part of the nation the writer happened to be a member, and has therefore given full emphasis to one political view only.[11] In addition, very few authors have considered the background to the events in any depth, and the only one to do so properly has in fact been Stefan Heym. As a result of his thorough research, and, indeed, his own experience of the day,[12] this novel stands apart from all others in its presentation of activities on both sides of the border and in advancing a view which, as it were, straddles the interpretations of East and West. According to Heym, this matches the private view of Otto Grotewohl, the then prime minister of the GDR: 'Die Lunte wurde vom Westen geliefert, aber der Zündstoff stammt von uns' ('The spark was provided by the West, but the tinder came from us').[13]

Heym knew that his general thesis, as well as many of his observations and points of analysis, would not be welcome to the leading party officials, whatever they might think in private. He deviated too much from the official standpoint. So rather than publish forthwith in an English-speaking country, he decided to test reaction in the GDR by translating the book into German and then sending cyclostyled copies to a wide variety of readers. (The translation, *Der Tag X*, follows the original English throughout, although it is perhaps freer than some of the other self-translations to which Heym has devoted himself.) Fifty copies were produced, privately in his own house, and Heym awaited the reaction with apprehension. The response was predictable. A number of eminent figures, who were, however, without major influence in the highest party circles, were troubled but impressed by the book, which they considered important for GDR self-understanding. But the views of the powerful figures were unanimously negative, and Heym's views were dismissed as erroneous and dangerous. With reluctance, the author decided not to seek publication abroad – either in West Germany or an English-speaking country – but to wait for better times in the GDR. This effectively meant waiting for the retirement of Walter Ulbricht.

Heym returned to his novel in the early seventies, shortly after the completion of *The King David Report* (Ulbricht having resigned in 1971). His attitude now was slightly different, and he claimed in an interview that he had learnt much since the first version.[14] The main shift in the novel's stance is indicated by the new title: *Five Days in June. A Day Marked X* employed a concept which had been formulated by certain members of the Federal Republic to denote the day of marching into East Germany in order to reclaim it – and the fact that such plans apparently existed was vigorously exploited by the East shortly after the events. But in his new title Heym sees events far more neutrally. True, he could possibly be echoing Trotsky's 'Five Days', one of the chapters in his *History of the Russian Revolution*, but if so, the echo is a distant one.

Heym's great hope was that the new volume would be published simultaneously in East and West, but his western publisher at the time, Kindler, decided against accepting the manuscript (presumably on account of possible political repercussions); the eastern publisher, Verlag Neues Leben, although initially willing, found it impossible to proceed as Honecker's early liberalism began to fade. Heym changed from Kindler to the Bertelsmann Verlag, who ran an excellent publicity campaign and published the novel in Munich in 1974. An English translation of this version appeared in 1977. It was not until 1989 that an edition was to appear in the GDR.

The first and final versions share numerous features. The story line is basically the same, but there are major stylistic improvements and a major change in content: the excision of an extensive sub-plot concerning a group of (American-financed) agents. The latter group is plotting the downfall of the GDR government and accepts (on instructions from Washington) the date of 17 June as 'Day X', the moment at which all their resources will be launched in an attempt to topple those in authority. In the final version western 'provocateurs' are still keenly in evidence, but the suggestion of major US backing has been removed.

The plot common to both versions centres on 'VEB Merkur', an industrial plant on the outskirts of East Berlin. Here the trade union chairman, Martin Witte, an honest, hard-working and commonsensical socialist, finds himself in conflict with higher powers over the call for a raising of the norms by 10 per cent. Witte, a worker himself for many years, and keenly in touch with the men he represents, warns against such a rise when the feelings of the workers are so firmly opposed to it. But his advice is ignored, and he is urged to resign his post. As the days develop, Witte is vindicated in his fear that the workers might rebel. Although he is initially relieved of his duties, he works hard to prevent a total strike in his own plant, and he acts courageously during the fighting at the centre of the city; by the conclusion of the novel he has been reinstated. Nevertheless, in the final version a 'Postlude' makes it clear that the party has learnt nothing from the uprising: instead of being left where he can serve his state best, among the workers whom he knows and who respect him, a year later Witte is removed from the plant and delegated to a party school for a year's course in 'theory'. Throughout the novel it has been made clear that 'theoretical' socialists, who are repeatedly seen to be lacking contact with grass roots, must accept a large amount of responsibility for the disturbances.

Witte's adversaries are both inside and outside the works. The party secretary, Banggartz, opposes him because Witte will not implement the call for a rise in the norms; a large number of workers resent him, because he nevertheless tries to get them to raise their norms voluntarily; and there are a few who oppose him because he represents the state which they are trying to overthrow (they are actually in the pay of western agents). Outside the works too, Witte faces difficulties – although he has supportive friends at the District Committee, those at the very top are insistent that his individualist attitude is destructive.

As the revised title emphasises, the plot extends over five days: (1) a short prelude on the 13th introducing the major character. (2) Approximately thirty pages on the 14th, in which the background and certain other key characters are introduced. (3) Approximately eighty-five pages on the 15th, as tension rises and the possibility of a strike looms larger. (4) Approximately 130 pages on the 16th, on which the workers, pushed by provocateurs, indicate their dissatisfaction more openly; in the city centre workers from other plants demonstrate in large numbers, as a result of which the demand for a raising of the norms is dropped; it becomes clear, however, that many workers are dissatisfied with more than just the norms. (5) Slightly less, approximately eighty-five pages, are devoted to the 17th itself: within VEB Merkur a large number of workers (driven on by agitators) stop work and march towards the centre of the city, where a certain amount of looting by other factions is taking place; the Soviet tanks move in to restore order, but not before Witte has managed to persuade many of his men to march back to work. As the page division makes clear, Heym's interest in the events of the 17th itself is subordinate to his concern for what preceded.

As in all Heym's novels, the number of major characters is large, and there is a key sub-plot. This concerns the efforts of western-paid agents to arouse dissent, provoke the strikes, and co-ordinate opposition with the ultimate aim of overthrowing the government. (In the first version the scale of this operation was large, and the involvement of the US in particular was central.) Spanning these plots, there is a characteristic 'love story' of a man caught between two women, and this brings together key figures from the two main strands of the action. It is here, however, that the element of coincidence is at its most striking, particularly when a third woman is introduced who also comes to span the two main threads of the action. The credibility of the plot is weakened by the relationships which are rapidly established or which themselves depend on earlier critical events and relationships.

On the other hand, the sense of veracity of primary events is strengthened by the 'documentary' technique of the novel, which serves to underpin the fiction by the regular insertion of previously published documents, broadcasts, and speeches. These range widely in origin and nature, and embrace both eastern and western sources (and there is clear balance here, in the selection of ten from the East, and ten from the West). All are subtly chosen, and their positioning within the novel shows that the author's central story line is based on published evidence. The nature of such evidence is, however, controversial, in that the sources are obviously (and inevitably) interested parties: official organs of the government of the GDR, for example, or the RIAS (an openly anti-GDR broadcasting station in West Berlin). Such documents, and particularly the officialese, euphemisms and understatement in which they are couched, stand in an ironic relationship to the events as related by Heym. None of the GDR official statements, for example, convey any of the drama, confusion, or fear which was the experience of most of the participants, and the dry account underlines one of Heym's principal themes: the administration's inability to be flexible, realistic, or humane. Quotations from western sources reveal an equally distasteful extreme – a passionate anti-communism which repeatedly distorts for its own political ends.

Through the choice of such quotations, Heym is attacking the folly of both East and West. But socialism itself is not one of

his targets: it is Stalinism which he is opposing here, and the
generalising way in which so many of his questions are phrased
suggests a wider target than solely GDR Stalinism of the early
fifties. A comparison of first and final versions brings out this
point. The first version is written along the lines of a contemporary account, more concerned with events and their direct
causes than with deeper, underlying problems and perennial
issues. The later version reads more like a historical novel, in
which cause and effect are depicted in a more complex way
and in which the author also has a clear concern for the
relevance of the past to the time of publication. The following
lines, for example, some of Witte's last ones in the novel,
indicate that wider interest in GDR history as a whole, and
raise a repeated theme of Heym's writing – the necessity to face
the mistakes of the past:

'Es wird viel von Schuld gesprochen werden in der nächsten Zeit',
sagte er, 'und manch einer wird sich verleiten lassen, die Schuld bei
anderen zu suchen. Aber wie viele werden vortreten und erklären: es
hat auch an mir gelegen, Genossen – und dann die Konsequenzen
ziehen? ... Das Schlimmste wäre, für das eigne Versagen den Feind
verantwortlich machen zu wollen. Wie mächtig wird dadurch der
Feind! ... Doch ist die Schuld nicht nur von heut und gestern. Auch
für die Arbeiterbewegung gilt, dass nur der sich der Zukunft zuwen-
den kann, der die Vergangenheit bewältigt hat...' (p. 360)

'There will be lots of talk in the near future about whose fault it was,'
he said, 'and quite a few will yield to the temptation of seeking the
fault outside themselves. I just wonder how many will have the guts
to step up and say: I, too, am to blame, Comrades – and then to draw
the consequences ... The worst thing for us would be to try to throw
the blame for our own incompetence and blunders on the enemy ...
In effect we'd be saying they're a bunch of supermen over there!
Though you'd have to search back farther than today or yesterday for
the origins of it all. It's as true for the working class movement as for
anyone else that only those can turn their face to the future who have
faced their past...' (*Five Days*, as rendered by Heym)

In his determination to round off the tale with a general
political message, Heym here falls victim to an obvious temptation of the historical novelist. He allows Witte the foresight of
what was to come, and the latter predicts with the very clichés

which were later to be used by politicians. Even allowing for
the fact that Witte is a trade union leader, his language at this
point sounds too much like that of an editorial to carry full
conviction, and even though the final aphoristic touch may not
be wholly out of character, it creates a moralistic air – something which Heym has always felt inappropriate in fiction. But
the key point here – that the enemy must not be made to seem
responsible for one's own mistakes – is one which Heym feels
bound to emphasise. It is a general point, which he has often
made elsewhere. It is *not* one which is applicable solely to the
failings after 17 June. For this reason it is false to assume that
the novel is concerned only with five days in the history of the
Republic. As Fritz Raddatz has put it, 'Dieser ist kein Roman
über den 17. Juni, sondern eine große prosavertarnte Studie
über Konflikte im Sozialismus' ('This is not a novel about 17
June, but a grand study of conflicts in socialism which has been
disguised in prose').[15]

A common technique of East German literature is more
prominent in *Five Days* than in any other work by Heym. This
is the method of paralleling characters' present actions with
comparable ones in the Third Reich (or, more generally,
simply allowing them to reflect on episodes from that period).
This applies both to sympathetic characters like Witte, whose
struggle against the Nazis is thus allowed to emerge, as well as
antipathetic figures like Heinz Hofer, son of Witte's landlady,
whose own activities (as well as those of his father) were on the
side of the Nazis. Besides acting as a means of characterisation,
such flashbacks and references serve to strengthen the ideological link which Heym creates between Third Reich and
Federal Republic. Personalities and politics are identical; the
western support of the uprising is consequently a continuation
of certain Nazi policies under a different guise. Anti-semitism
may have disappeared, but two other features are seen to
remain strong: the exploitation of the weak, and a vicious
desire to suppress Communism.

Such parallels are common enough in East German literature, but there is a further one which Heym makes much of in
this novel: the treatment of women in East and West/Third

Reich. Women, of course, acquired a status in the GDR which was possibly higher than that of any other country in the world, and Heym suggests the deference accorded them by GDR men. Western men are seen treating women very differently, regarding them rather as chattels or sex objects. The same holds true of men living in the East whose spiritual home is much more obviously the Federal Republic. The sole exception is the eastern worker Kallmann, whose harsh treatment of his wife is brought on by alcohol and is immediately regretted.

Heym has been criticised for excess in his depiction of contrasting attitudes in East and West. The charge would seem partially justified in the case of Heinz Hofer – ex-Nazi, ruthless anti-communist, immoral exploiter of both mother and wife, while Witte, too, has been regarded by some critics as too much of a 'positive hero'; in his earlier life he was a Communist fighting Nazism and he was prepared to be exploited for the sake of the party. His supposed weaknesses are essentially strengths – we learn, for example, of his earlier refusal to participate in a picket line alongside fascists (now recognised as a mistake by the party), and his refusal to accept that new norms should be implemented without discussion (which also turns out to be a sound decision). His attitude to women is likewise somewhat idealised, with political and social concerns playing a greater role in his mind than sexual ones.

Nevertheless, Witte is a credible figure, like all those in the novel, and the strength of their credibility rests in Heym's ability to take his reader inside the minds of his characters. This is a considerable achievement, for their number is large and the chapters are brief, perpetually switching over a wide range of localities. Further, we are plunged into each, usually by the suppression of an introductory temporal clause and by the avoidance of a capital letter. This partial disorientation provokes us into greater concentration on events and issues. Brief scenes and abrupt switches are the appropriate structural means of conveying the confusion experienced by all participants, and the reader is invited to share in this, being forced to enter the situation of those involved and to try and grasp the events and issues from their point of view. The tone of the narrative itself is essentially that of a 'report', with description terse and detail restricted; what brings us close to the characters are 'erlebte Rede' (*style indirect libre*), interior monologues, and a high percentage of dialogue which is consistently realistic. The drama of the final 'two days' in particular also heightens our participation, and for all the fact that we know the general outcome, Heym is able to heighten the suspense in individual issues. Again, though, there has been criticism of excess in this sphere: particularly of the fortuitous nature of certain events and the coincidences which bring Witte into contact with key western agents.[16] As was suggested above, the credibility of the plot is weakened by such features.

There is one aspect of the novel in which the author does not strain our credulity: the insertion of quotations from contemporary documents or radio reports. Heym has given much thought to the selection and positioning of these, and they play an important role in our understanding and interpretation of events. Ute Brandes has actually gone as far as to suggest that each is indispensable, and that the omission of a single one would change the sense of the whole book,[17] but such a claim is clearly far-fetched. Although most of the quotations do supply certain 'background' information, many of them provide details which we glean from the plot anyway. As to their actual function, this varies considerably. Some of them stress the background forces of which only a part can be portrayed in the novel proper – West German media pressure, for example. Many of them induce in the reader a form of critical stance towards the speaker or writer, for whatever is written/spoken can be judged by us with the benefit of hindsight – this is particularly so with respect to the cliché-ridden speeches by Ulbricht and Grotewohl, which show a pathetic failure to speak and to act in the way which is necessary. All of these quotations represent a stylistic contrast to their context, suddenly breaking the narrative and establishing a fully documentary tone. They remind us firmly of the historical framework.

In the first version, *Der Tag X*, Heym used only one quotation. This is repeated in *5 Tage*, and it stands at the beginning of the novel, almost as a form of motto:

Aus dem Statut der Sozialistischen Einheitspartei Deutschlands, angenommen auf deren IV. Parteitag im April 1954, Unterabschnitt 'Die Parteimitglieder, ihre Pflichten und Rechte', Absatz 2 (h)
Das Parteimitglied ist verpflichtet ... die Selbstkritik und Kritik von unten zu entwickeln, furchtlos Mängel in der Arbeit aufzudecken und sich für ihre Beseitigung einzusetzen; gegen Schönfärberei und die Neigung, sich an Erfolgen in der Arbeit zu berauschen, gegen jeden Versuch, die Kritik zu unterdrücken und sie durch Beschönigung und Lobhudelei zu ersetzen, anzukämpfen ...

From the Constitution of the Socialist Unity Party of Germany, as voted during its Fourth Party Congress in April 1954, Article entitled 'The Party Members, their Duties and Rights', Section 2, Paragraph h
It is the duty of the member of the party ... to develop self-cricitism and criticism from the ranks, to uncover without fear or favour shortcomings in the activities of the party and to help eliminate them; to struggle against gilding the truth and against the tendency of getting intoxicated with success, and to fight all attempts to suppress criticism or to gloss over criticism by apologies or false praise ... (*Five Days*, as rendered by Heym)

Such a motto could be interpreted in different ways. On the one hand, it might be possible to see the exhortation as an honest attempt to ensure events such as those described in the book did not recur. If all party members, at all levels, were to act in this way, then no disagreements between workers and party leaders would arise. But the date, 1954, is significant, and the quotation must anyway be seen in the light of GDR history up to the date of publication (1974). How often, in the years which followed 1954, was the party guilty of the features it lists here! The quotation, then, must act rather as an ironic prelude to the novel: it reveals at best blindness, at worst hypocrisy on the part of the party. On the part of the author, it may reflect either grim amusement, or a sense of despair.

CHAPTER 6

The uses of history: methods of the sixties

The party's opposition to *Der Tag X* was made clear to Heym by two recipients of the cyclostyled manuscript: Alfred Kurella (in charge of the Kommission für Fragen der Kultur beim Politbüro (Commission of the Politbureau responsible for Questions of Culture)) and Albert Norden (a member of the Politbüro itself).[1] The latter condemned the book in a letter, the former denounced it vigorously in person. Heym was tempted to believe the observation of his friend and neighbour Jan Petersen, that the recent award of a National Prize (Second Class) was intended as 'hush-money' to encourage him not to publish (*Nachruf*, p. 654). That, however, would seem unlikely. It was well known that Heym allowed nothing to stand in the way of what he wished to see in print, and the award of such a prize could only give him increased respectability. If he had wished, he could certainly have found a western publisher for the manuscript, but he decided to wait for easier political times, and to hope for joint publication in both parts of the nation.

In view of the difficulties presented by contemporary material, it seems only logical that Heym should have turned towards the past for his next novel, *Die Papiere des Andreas Lenz*. The subject he chose was revolution, and critics have been quick to suggest that in selecting the period 1848/9 he was trying to present a parallel to the situation presented in *Der Tag X*. This claim cannot be pursued too far. *Lenz* is certainly not a substitute for the former. True, certain speeches in the later novel carry relevance for the GDR, and the author undoubtedly wished their aptness to be savoured. But Heym was interested in revolt, revolution, strikes, and dissent well before the events of 1953, and when, in his later works, he uses the past to illuminate the present, there is little doubt about the parallels he is drawing and they tend to be extended. There are no anachronisms in *Lenz*, for example (in contrast to, say, *The Queen* or *The King David Report*), and its general relevance to the GDR is only oblique. The inspiration for the 1848 revolution was very different from that for the disturbances of 1953. 1848 had been instigated from within the state; according to Heym's view, 1953 had been organised from outside it.

Lenz was to be Heym's second-longest, and probably his most thoroughly researched novel. One reason for the time taken to complete it was the difficult nature of the subject: the revolutions of 1848/9 were complex in origin and without clear pattern in their development. Curiously, not only liberal and socialist, but also nationalist feelings were detectable in most parts of Europe at this point in time, and there were also strong underlying economic factors which lay behind most of the uprisings. After initial success in many areas, the 'revolutions' faded out and the concessions which had been won were withdrawn over the following two years. Lack of unity among the reformers, political inexperience, and the absence of a truly revolutionary spirit were the main failings of these movements, but what really broke them was the political and military strength of the conservative opposition. By the middle of 1849 all open dissent had been quelled.

Heym chose the revolution in Baden in the spring of 1849, where the fighting was probably the most intense of all German states, where freedom from previous rulers lasted for several months, and where the 'rebels' were the most numerous (possibly as many as half the male population of Baden became involved). The leadership here was a curious mixture, but more impressive than most: the brilliant lawyer Brentano, very much concerned with the art of the possible; the republican idealist Struve, often naive in his political judgement; the Polish patriot Mieroslawski, a flamboyant General who could not even speak German. There were also such figures as Johann Philipp Becker, a truly revolutionary thinker and fighter, and Friedrich Engels himself was actually involved in some of the action. Heym's aims in a novel of this scope were obviously manifold, but two features do stand out: first, the personalities of those involved, with particular concern for their motivation; and second, the reasons for their failure.

The plot opens in Rastatt, a fortress city, in the small German Grand Duchy of Baden. Dissatisfaction with the establishment is widespread, and it only takes some mouldy bread to spark off a soldiers' revolt against all aspects of army discipline. The troops are joined in their mutiny by the ordinary people of the town, and one of their first tasks is to free political prisoners – including Andreas Lenz, who has recently been roughly incarcerated for making inflammatory statements and for writing a popular revolutionary song. In other towns of Baden comparable uprisings are taking place, and the Grand Duke decides to flee. His senior army officers also escape in disarray, but as the plot develops, they are seen to regain their control. The troops who remain 'loyal' to them act mainly out of a sense of fear.

Heym is good at portraying the drama of revolution, but he proves equally skilful in depicting the less glamorous side to the succeeding period – the inaction and fruitless debate in which democratic arguments triumph at the expense of securing the revolution against the reactionaries. Here, as throughout the novel, Heym reveals the damaging political intrigue between the leaders of the revolution; and the equally unfortunate love intrigue between Lenz and the rivals for his affection: Lenore, elegant and intelligent daughter of the wealthy banker Einstein, and Josepha, poor, easy-living and passionate beauty. Lenore rejects the security of her family home to live with Lenz and act as nurse for the troops, while her father secretly pays to establish Josepha in a grand style so that she might win back her former lover.

The author has obvious pleasure in recreating the battles in which the revolutionaries engage (possibly as a result of his wartime experiences), and maps are inserted in the text to assist our appreciation of these (historical) encounters. The principal causes of the revolutionaries' defeats are lack of

military experience, poor command, and the entry of well-
trained Prussian soldiers. After losing the crucial battle of
Waghäusel the rebels divide into two groups. One reaches the
Swiss border; the other, with Lenz, takes refuge in Rastatt. The
latter finally surrender the fortress to the Prussians on condition they be allowed to go free, but the Prussians break their
word and begin to execute the leaders after summary trials.
Lenz, with help of friends and his former mistress Josepha,
manages to escape. We know from elsewhere in the text that he
and Lenore finally reach America.

In his concern for realism in characterisation, Heym has
produced one of the best researched novels on this period. In
excess of forty sources were used, a good number of them being
by the participants themselves or by contemporary historians.
Quotations from these are used at the beginning of most
chapters, partly to prepare us for the contents of that chapter
(and thus put us in a position from which we can judge the
decisions made), perhaps partly to strengthen the sense of
authenticity. After a while we recognise the tone and attitude
of the authors quoted: the reactionary Lt-Colonel Staroste, one
of the Prussian leaders sent to quell the insurgents, whose
idealisation of the Prussians and his scornful attitude towards
their opponents soon becomes transparent; the similarly
inclined Ludwig Häusser, Professor of History at Heidelberg,
eager to see the 'criminal' side of the revolution; on the other
hand, the calm reflections of Friedrich Engels, interested in
class forces and anxious to detect social origins and implications; the sad political and military recollections of Becker,
whose enthusiastic hopes for a wholly successful revolution are
still not dispelled; and the bitter life story of a common soldier,
written while he languishes in Bruchsal jail. In using material
from such diverse sources, the author is operating chiefly as a
historian, carefully outlining the political, military, and
economic factors which influence his characters, but he is also
much concerned to suggest general social and sexual forces,
striving for an authentic recreation of the characters in their
nineteenth-century milieu. The strength of the characterisation here springs in part from Heym's careful research. For

most figures he has operated like a biographer, attempting to draw a likeness which has a firm basis in the accounts by those characters' contemporaries. Imagination has clearly shaped their speeches, but gesture, physical features and temperament would seem to be authentic. The pace of this novel is relaxed, and so the individuals can emerge without authorial intervention – through their own speech, actions, and the plentiful observations of others.

Practically every character in this novel is based on historical evidence, but there is a striking exception: the hero, Andreas Lenz himself, is a complete invention on the part of the author. Many readers may be surprised by this, partly because so many other names are probably known from the history of the period, and partly because Heym takes such care to establish a realistic framework. The novel is supposedly based on the 'papers' left by Lenz at his death, which have been sent to the author by the widow of Lenz's grandson. These are inserted – with neatly realistic touches – among quotations from the other sources. This information is conveyed in a Prologue, in the course of which author and grandson encounter the grave of the original fighter (while the two of them are awaiting transportation to the battlefields of Europe in 1944). The grave is at Gettysburg, where Lenz had died fighting for Lincoln's army. Such a symbolic site serves a clear purpose: the fight for freedom in Germany in 1849 is linked with the fight for the freedom of the slaves in the American wars of 1862–5. And the death of the second-generation Lenz is linked with the fight against Nazism in Europe. (The technique is similar to that Heym had used in *Gestern – Heute – Morgen* many years before.) Against such a background we might expect the original Lenz to be an idealistic, and possibly idealised figure, but if this was a temptation to Heym, then it was resisted. The hero is politically somewhat immature, impetuous, not always reliable, and something of a libertine. A partial model may have been provided by the GDR songwriter Wolf Biermann, a personal friend of Heym's in the early sixties, and the link is provided by the fifteenth-century French ballad-writer François Villon. Biermann openly acknowledged

a debt to his wild predecessor, and one of his most famous early
pieces was the 'Ballade auf den Dichter François Villon'. Lenz
too is a Villon devotee, and on the first pages of the novel he
sings a stanza from the latter's 'Ballade de mercy'. Heym uses
his own translation here, not the famous one by K. L. Ammer
which was adapted by Brecht for a song in *Die Dreigroschenoper*.
Nevertheless, by employing such a well-known stanza, Heym
may be encouraging readers to see Lenz in a longer tradition of
iconoclastic youthful singers.

The failure of the revolution is traditionally ascribed to
various features, several of which have already been mentioned: lack of a clear goal, inexperience, too much respect for
democratic processes and not sufficient attention to the forces
of reaction which threatened – from both within and without.
These factors all feature within Heym's novel, but some are
emphasised far more than others. In particular, Heym stresses
the failure of the leaders, who are too half-hearted in their
policy and who try to keep open their options in case of a
return by the former rulers. Much is made of the failure to open
the Grand Duke's arsenal, for example, with consequent inability to provide sufficient weapons for the insurgents; recruits
have to practise rifle drill with broomsticks! Finance too is
handled timidly: the new leaders are not prepared to risk using
capital in case they are called to account should the Duke
return. Fear of this sort seems to determine the policy of several
key figures: they do not *believe* in the ultimate success of their
actions, and they therefore act with moderation in case they
may one day have to explain their activities to the counter-
revolutionary forces. Also, they are not revolutionaries in the
real sense of the word: they are afraid to use force in order to
consolidate their position. When they realise they must
authorise the equivalent of 'total war', they are too late.
Inhibited by their own democratic beliefs and their respect for
the law, they are reluctant to impose their will. Even some of
the most committed fighters feel this way. Lenz, for example, is
deeply troubled by the paradox that 'freedom' can only be
maintained by force. Becker, however, with experience elsewhere in Europe, recognises its necessity: 'I don't see any other

way for the defence of freedom but its curtailment. And may the curse of history come on our heads if we permit freedom to be curtailed by the wrong people, or in the wrong fields, or at the wrong time' (p. 180).

The problem of what constitutes 'freedom', explored so fully in *The Eyes of Reason*, is not exposed to the constant probing and questioning which were so important a structural technique in the earlier novel. 'Freedom' is here an important background issue, but probably not sufficiently prominent to justify the sub-title which appears in all West German editions ('Lenz oder die Freiheit'). The word itself is used sparingly, and the concept is seen in relation to other issues. The naive views of some of the insurgents are not the only ones on freedom that are advanced for consideration. An important counter-view is supplied, for example, by the hard-headed banker Einstein. Late in the novel, after the revolution has been defeated and he is seen to be vindicated in his cautious actions, he puts a conservative, relativising question: 'What is freedom? What is it to the poor labourer who doesn't know where his family's next meal is to come from? – an empty word' (p. 620). The capitalist Einstein develops his ideas not philosophically, but practically. He believes that most people's grand notions will disappear when they are earning money, and he interprets the concept in terms of general satisfaction with one's lot. He is not being disingenuous here, even though he has most to lose from revolutions, and Heym has chosen not to suppress this point of view:

'And after all that has been taken care of, freedom will still be nothing but a vague feeling of ease growing out of a more or less enforced adjustment to the conditions of the society under which you happen to live. For that, so much heartache and sacrifice?' (p. 620)

The sub-title of the West German edition ('Lenz oder die Freiheit') may give undue prominence to this theme, and passages such as this may consequently be highlighted. But the weight of the novel falls rather on the reasons for failure of the revolution rather than on the nature of freedom.

One of the reasons for this failure is that the freedom following

revolution is quite unlike that which many expected. And
Heym goes to some pains to make clear that the majority of
people are little better off under the revolutionary government.
The peasants are actually worse off, for their land, equipment
and livestock are now likely to be commandeered by either of
the two armies; and the chance of compensation, again from
either army, is slight. What most peasants find difficult to grasp
is that some of the methods of the new government are comparable to those of the old. Quoting Becker's *Geschichte der Süddeut-
schen Mai-Revolution* at the beginning of chapter 7, Heym draws
an exact parallel with the former leaders (p. 123). What the
people fail to realise is that a main function of any government
is to preserve itself – and the cost of self-preservation will
sometimes outweigh the preservation of previously held principles. One difference between the two regimes is that the older
relied on brutality to enforce its policies. The new one fails
because it cannot bring itself to do this – its leaders are
reluctant to resort to the extreme measures which are needed to
protect itself. Of course, Heym is only dealing with a brief
half-revolution, and the final vision of Lenz escaping to
America, together with the frame in which the story is set, do
provide a context of optimism. Nevertheless, as we know from
the novel which was born from the events which surround this
frame (*The Crusaders*), as also from that which immediately
preceded the writing of *Lenz* (*Five Days in June*): a full revolution would never be possible in Germany. There are too
many vested interests which prevent radical measures, and too
much half-heartedness.

Lenz was composed in English, and it was the last novel for
which Heym used a translator for the German version. On
account of delays with the English publishers, however, the
German edition reached print first: late in 1963. The English
volume followed early in 1964. The reviewer in the *Times
Literary Supplement* found some faults, particularly in the
characterisation (where he felt too little was left to our imagination), but he was generally warm in his assessment and
expressed admiration for the painstaking work which had gone
into the novel's composition.[2] In the GDR too, the response

was favourable. The chief editor of *Neue Deutsche Literatur*, official organ of the Writers' Union, reviewed the work himself, and his well-written article found much to admire in both the literary as well as the political sphere.[3] Heym, it seemed, was in favour, and the appearance of a West German edition in 1965 apparently provided further evidence of his widespread acceptability. In reality, though, Heym was *never* in 'favour' in the GDR. Suspicion over his plans for *Der Tag X* (which was increasingly referred to in the western press), and fear of his outspoken manner, assured continuing hostility from those in power.

Although the cultural politicians were probably relieved that Heym had written a historical novel rather than a contemporary tale, in one respect they were bound to be disappointed: their hopes were for a literature which sprang directly from the world of physical work, and since the spring of 1959 much politico-cultural activity has concentrated on encouraging writers to gain first-hand experience of the factory floor. A corollary had been efforts to help workers themselves to write about their lives at work, and as a result of this policy new talents had been discovered and fostered. (The best were sent on to the institute specially designed to train writers – the J. R. Becher Institut für Literatur in Leipzig.) The official launching of this grand scheme for both workers and writers had occurred in the industrial town of Bitterfeld, and the programme was later to become known officially as the 'Bitterfelder Weg'.[4] Ulbricht himself had delivered the main speech at the grand-scale conference which had been organised to explain its aims, and he took a personal interest in the response of writers to his call. He was consequently one of the first to lament the fact that so little of relevance was to appear from the pens of the professionals, despite the fact that considerable further encouragement was given at a conference a year after 'Bitterfeld' as well as at the 'II. Kulturkonferenz' in March 1963. True, a large number of short stories and poems were produced by workers, and the scheme undoubtedly raised the general response of workers to literary values; but little writing of real value was produced. The two well-known exceptions were Christa Wolf's *Der geteilte Himmel* and Erik Neutsch's *Spur der Steine*. The cultural politicians initially greeted both with mixed feelings, principally on account of their well supported criticism of various aspects of East German society.

Heym had a low opinion of the 'Bitterfelder Weg' (as also of the J. R. Becher Institute), and he was later to express scorn for its supposed achievements. He aroused bitterness by referring to certain debates created by the movement as 'Kontroversen ohne Kontroverse' and considered that there were far more pressing issues for widespread public discussion than, say, the fatherhood of an illegitimate child by an obscure party secretary (*Wege*, p. 292). To his mind the principal, undiscussed issue was the heritage of Stalin in the GDR, and shortly after the appearance of *Lenz* he was to publish the first of several articles which were to lead to a ban on all his publications in the Republic. All these pieces were concerned with the continuing and crippling effects of Stalinism, and the consequent need to discuss it freely within the GDR. The scars left by Stalinist methods was also the subject-matter of a novel, *The Architects*, which was written about this point but never published. Heym was the first to take a serious stand in this matter, and his campaign showed further evidence of his amazing courage in the face of potential prosecution and imprisonment.

Stalinism had been evident in almost the entire communist bloc for many years, but the GDR proved one of the last countries to abandon its methods. In the USSR, under Stalin himself, the means adopted to implement the policies of the Communist Party had been harsh, and regularly quite ruthless – taking no account of the individual in reaching ends which supposedly resulted in a better society as a whole. To the West, the most repugnant features were the general terrorisation of most of society into conformity, which was achieved through a secret police, with its immense powers of arrest, interrogation, torture, and even liquidation; the grand political 'show trials' in which defendants eagerly confessed their guilt (they had clearly been brainwashed or otherwise forced into 'confession'); and the slave labour camps for dissidents, many of whom might be guilty of only trivial offences, or even quite innocent of them. Other significant features were the suppression of contrary evidence in order to present a positive image in all aspects of life (this included the removal of certain persons' names from the history books); the vilification of the 'capitalist enemy'; and, as it was later to become known, the 'cult of personality', that concentration of power in a single figure whose adulation was controlled virtually by state directive. After the death of Stalin in 1953, and growing awareness of the ruthless abuses of his power, Khrushchev decided in 1956 to make an official break with the policies of the past. His 'Secret Speech' to the Soviet Twentieth Party Congress, with its enormous catalogue of Stalin's crimes, was widely leaked, and then published in full in the West.[5] The revelations were greeted with amazement, or mock amazement, by most of the other states in the Communist bloc. Even if there had been serious doubts about the secret police, Stalin himself had been regarded by many as the man whose armies had conquered Hitler. The position was now radically different. Khrushchev had formally denounced Stalin as militarily incompetent. And suddenly thousands of individuals who had been vilified, imprisoned, or even executed, were recognised as completely innocent. Some began to return from the slave labour camps, confirming the veracity of Khrushchev's statements. The perversions of justice verged on the incredible. The reliability of all previous Soviet records was in doubt, together with those of every other state which had pursued comparable policies. The leadership of the GDR, with its strong Stalinist inclinations, was particularly embarrassed. Practically every leading member of its Politbüro had risen to power under the reign of Stalin and thus shared guilt by association.

The GDR leadership did acknowledge the dangers of the 'personality cult', but only in terms of glorification of an individual rather than the concentration of power in a single source. In this sense the 'cult' was a relatively harmless issue with many historical antecedents, and it deflected attention from the implications of Khrushchev's other revelations and the need for the GDR to admit its own Stalinist practices.

Indeed, after some half-hearted attempts at de-Stalinisation (the rehabilitation of certain figures, wrongly accused, and the release of numerous others; a brief 'thaw' in the literary and literary critical scene), Ulbricht attempted to reassert Stalinist attitudes. It must be emphasised, of course, that these were essentially *attitudes*, and that the methods of the GDR government, and especially of its secret police, the Staatssicherheitsdienst ('Stasi'), never approached those which had existed in the USSR under Stalin. Nevertheless, Ulbricht responded to those urging a more liberal or democratic approach by imprisoning them on trumped-up charges (notably Wolfgang Harich, intellectual reformer) or removing them from their posts (Erich Wollweber, Head of State Security, Karl Schirdewan, Secretary of the Central Committee), exemplary acts of repression which were doubtless confirmed in his mind by the radical liberalisation movements in Poland, and, tragically, Hungary. Through forceful removal of opponents, Ulbricht successfully fought off – in typically Stalinist manner, although without executions – a threat to his style of leadership and his conception of socialism. He then began to intensify policies he had instigated earlier (notably in the collectivisation of the land). As for literature, there was obviously no encouragement for writers to investigate Stalinist errors of the past. As soon as July 1956 Alexander Abusch was claiming that already in 1953 the GDR had been beginning to overcome – albeit unwittingly – aspects of the 'personality cult'.[6] And by February 1957 he was belittling the ideological implications of the Twentieth Party Congress and calling for a 'geistige Offensive des Marxismus–Leninismus' ('intellectual offensive by Marxism–Leninism').[7] The GDR was thus firmly avoiding Khrushchev's path which culminated in Solzhenitsyn's *One Day in the Life of Ivan Denisovich* (the classic study of the Stalinist concentration camp, and which was published after the personal intervention of Khrushchev), and by 1959 all attention was directed towards Bitterfeld. Nor did the early sixties offer any shift in attitude, for Ulbricht's position was consolidated rather than weakened by the building of the Berlin Wall (1961). We find, therefore, that by March 1963, Kurt Hager (now the leading cultural functionary and unswerving supporter of Ulbricht) was effectively stating that the failings of the Stalinist era were to be ignored.[8] Speaking at a major gathering of members of the Politbüro, the Council of Ministers, and writers and artists, he explained that the GDR would not follow the Soviet example of publishing works which exposed the abuses of the past in the USSR. Instead, they would only allow works which placed their great Soviet ally in a favourable light. Hager made no suggestion that the GDR itself had any such perversions to expose, and he made reference only to the 'cult of personality'.

It was against such a denial of the past that Heym wrote his gravest indictment of Stalinism, *The Architects*. It is an uncompromising work and contains two particularly troubling allusions to figures who were then alive in the GDR: Wieland Herzfelde and Walter Ulbricht.

The plot is set shortly after Khrushchev has liberated some of those who have been falsely accused under Stalin. Daniel Wollin, arrested in Moscow in 1940, returns to East Germany and tries to take up his former career as an architect. He comes to stay with his old friend Arnold Sundstrom, for the two were initially together in Moscow exile. Unlike Wollin, Sundstrom came through that period without problems, and he is now one of the leading architects of the Republic, and a respected member of the party. Sundstrom has a very young wife, Julia, whom he initially fostered after the death of her parents – both of whom came to a distressing end after they were also accused of anti-communist activity. Julia's father, whose death the novel uses as a prelude, is shot while escaping from a convoy taking him and many other loyal communists back to Germany after the Hitler–Stalin pact.

As the plot develops, the perversions of the Stalin era are unfolded. It becomes clear that even in their own time various criminal acts by the state were sometimes recognised as such by those perpetrating them, but that various ideological arguments were employed to justify them. Such arguments are questioned, found to be unsustainable, inhumane, and in some respects comparable to those used by the Nazis. On another level, Sundstrom's grandest architectural scheme is seen to be derived from designs of Albert Speer, Hitler's favourite architect. Worst of all, though, Sundstrom is revealed to have been the figure who denounced not only Wollin, but also Julia's parents – out of fear and for self-advancement, not from the conviction they were guilty of any crime. By the end of the novel Julia has deserted her husband for Wollin, and the two of them join forces to submit an architectural plan for the centre-piece of the capital. Their submission is praised by the jury, but turned down in favour of that by a reliable conformist: Arnold Sundstrom.

The author does not wish Sundstrom to emerge as a total villain – he possesses certain human virtues and he does have a belief in socialism. But his egoism, ambition, fear, and inability to remain firm to personal principles allow him to furnish an excuse for every immoral action and to become the pawn in a political game. The horrors of exile in Moscow have been depicted in considerable detail by David Pike,[9] and Heym succeeds brilliantly in supplying the sort of arguments which must have been advanced at that time by certain exiles as they denounced innocent men. Sundstrom is in this respect a clearly representative figure.

If we turn to fact rather than fiction, we know that one of the German exiles who denounced a comrade was Wieland Herz-felde; he informed the authorities in Moscow that Ernst Ottwalt had received the same type of telegram on two different occasions.[10] As a result Ottwalt was interrogated and sent to Siberia on the charge of being a Nazi agent. He died in a camp in 1943. In 1956 he was declared to have been falsely accused. Another leading exile was Walter Ulbricht, who took an interest in Lotte Wendt after her husband Erich had been sent to a slave labour camp; in due course, Ulbricht married her.[11] Herzfelde's treachery is directly paralleled by Sund-strom's denunciation of Wollin (including the use of a tele-gram); and Ulbricht's marriage to Lotte Wendt is present behind Sundstrom's marriage to Julia.

The fact that Ulbricht had married the wife of a 'traitor' was well known, but no one had ever suggested that he had denounced her husband in order to do so. Nor, of course, does

The Architects make any direct connection between Sundstrom and Ulbricht, Herzfelde, or Henselmann, the then leading architect of the GDR – no work by Heym is a simple *roman à clef*. Further, it seems extremely unlikely that Ulbricht was involved in the denunciation of Wendt. The latter was arrested in 1936, when Ulbricht was in Paris. Collaborating on such a matter – at such a distance and in those years – would seem improbable. Further, Ulbricht did not arrive in Moscow until 1938, and could only have taken a proper interest in Lotte Wendt at that stage. Nevertheless, had the novel reached print, the montage in the figure of Sundstrom would have been quickly evident; it could have raised private and public questions about how those who had come through Moscow exile without scars had actually managed to do so.

In his memoirs, Heym recalls the verdict on *The Architects* sent to him by Desmond Flower (chairman of the London publishing house of Cassell's, which had published most of his earlier novels in England). Heym greatly respected Flower, and accepted his view that there were literary failings in the novel (*Nachruf*, p. 691). Yet Flower's comments seem unjust, particularly his view that the plot was predictable. Was Flower seeking to save Heym from the eastern vendetta which could well follow publication of the work in the West? Given Heym's point in the novel that Stalinism had not been eradicated from the GDR, Flower's opinion may well have been swayed by fears for the safety of his old, but dangerously courageous, friend.

From the literary point of view, it is regrettable that the manuscript remained unpublished, for this novel contains Heym's fullest, and most successful depiction of a female character. Critics have regularly found fault with Heym's women, suggesting they are either beautiful and passionate on the one hand, or intellectual and plain on the other. Julia is both intellectually and sexually motivated, and both her mind and her body are torn between mutually exclusive alternatives: between her sexual needs on the one hand, and her love of, and duty towards, her young child on the other. On the intellectual plane she is torn between her firm belief in socialism, and her sense of revulsion at the methods which were claimed to be necessary in its name. She is representative of that generation which was educated to revere Stalin and the country he led, and she is overwhelmed by the revelations following the Twentieth Party Congress. Her elders, Sundstrom and Wollin, are of the generation which has needed to learn how to live with different forms of split consciousness.

In the course of writing this novel, Heym's public attacks on Stalinism took increasingly sharper form. He considered them sufficiently important to feature all in *Wege und Umwege*, and they stretch over the period 1964–5.

The first of these is a short statement made at a film festival in Karlovy Vary (Czechoslovakia) in July 1964.[12] It underlines the importance of creative artists coming to grips with the conflicts created by Stalinism and the cult of personality, and it praises the film of Christa Wolf's *Der geteilte Himmel* as the first attempt 'wenigstens ein Zipfelchen des Teppichs zu lüften' (p. 345) ('to lift at least a tiny corner of the carpet'). Heym also calls for *realism* in writing, a plea he will regularly repeat over the years as he rejects the naïveté and ill-founded optimism of 'socialist realism'. A month later, while speaking to a congress of Slovakian writers in Táli, his pronouncements become more direct. The crisis of modern socialist writing is, he claims, a consequence of the fall of Stalinism and the demands it made on writers. He rejects the notion that the theory of socialist realism was conceived by the great figures in the early years of Communism – it is rather a patchwork of random remarks by Engels and Lenin. Writers have fortunately begun to reconsider the concept, and he urges them to continue this process and to write freely and honestly (pp. 346–7).

The speech is a mere page and a half in length, and by modern standards unexceptional in its attack (which is couched positively as a plea for new writing). But Heym's directness was quite unprecedented in such circles, and his comments were immediately given media publicity – much to the disgust of the GDR leadership. They took this, it would seem, as the final offence they would tolerate in the long list of politico-literary crimes of which Heym was guilty. As a result, a ban was extended over his literary activities: nothing by him was to be published; his speeches and readings were cancelled; his trips to the West were curtailed; study of his works was banned in the universities. It seemed he was well on the way to becoming the Stalinist 'unperson'.

Heym did not give in to this pressure in any way. He fought it vigorously.

In the following month he used an international colloquium of writers from the socialist countries as a means of gaining an audience. He had not been invited to the colloquium (held in East Berlin), but he simply walked in and, to the consternation of the delegates, delivered a brief and intriguingly entitled speech, 'Stalin verläßt den Raum'. The curious formulation came from an anecdote related to him by Ilja Ehrenburg: a film director responsible for one of those films which glorified Stalin had tried to illustrate the oppressive conditions under which he had had to work. His example had been unnerving. A script with a simple stage direction like 'Stalin leaves the room' would be submitted for approval and would be returned with an inclusion – in Stalin's own handwriting – '*The great* Stalin leaves the room'.

The anecdote has elements of the amusing, the pathetic, and the ridiculous, but Heym immediately turns to its horrific implications and the questions it raises in our minds about moral and political/philosophical issues. How could thousands of loyal Communists gradually submit to a situation which they recognised as evil and as being in conflict with all their ideals? How much of the thirty years of Stalinist misrule could be ascribed to the personality of Stalin, and how much to the pyramidic structure of Communist government (a structure established by its original authors)? How much could be attributed to Stalin's sober Marxist beliefs, and how much to his paranoia?

Such methodical probing of the roots and the organisation of Stalinism was far removed from the flamboyant and unreflective denunciations in which Khrushchev had indulged, and these issues had never been publicly couched in such a way in the socialist countries. The speaker's audience was gripped, and he continued to hold them with dramatic imagery and appeals to their conscience. The first section of the speech concluded by playing with the image of the title: for the sake of all the self-sacrificing revolutionaries of the past, the room which Stalin had vacated needed to be disinfected.

Heym then turned to an issue which must have stirred practically all his listeners – the difference between private feelings and public statements, the dangers of such hypocrisy, and the need for open discussion in order to overcome widespread cynicism. Progress could be made only by fearless dialogue, without taboos, and of basic issues – especially of the great conflict at the heart of socialism, that between 'revolutionary democracy' (which demands constant questioning of fundamental beliefs) and 'revolutionary discipline' (which demands unconditional obedience). There is, claims Heym, a craving for real discussion in the socialist countries, and he uses a paradoxical example to prove this. Debate is, he points out, intense on *trivial* matters; the reason for this is that discussion of more important issues is prevented by those in power. Here he includes his attack on Bitterfeld: there are *public* debates on such insignificant issues as a village mayor trying to force onto his local farmers an inappropriate type of byre (a reference to the widespread arguments provoked by Erwin Strittmatter's *Ole Bienkopp*)!

Heym rejects the well-known justification for allowing debate of only harmless matters, the old fear that talking about important issues could be exploited by the enemies of socialism. He considers such a policy to be self-defeating and a denial of the socialist revolution. 'Truth', his old watchword, may be painful, but must be endured in the interests of attaining the socialist ideal. There is nothing to fear about the ideal itself. Only the means of achieving it may be imperfect:

Wir dürfen die Schmerzen nicht fürchten, die es kostet, sich zur Wahrheit hindurchzufinden; die Wahrheit ist immer revolutionär; wo ihr untrüglicher Zeiger scheinbar gegen die Revolution ausschlägt, deutet er an, daß etwas fehlerhaft ist, nicht an der Idee der Revolution, wohl aber an der Art ihrer Durchführung. (*Wege*, p. 351)

We must not be afraid of the pain which it will cost us to find our way through to the truth; the truth is always revolutionary; where its infallible pointer apparently swings against the revolution, then it is signalling not that something is wrong with the idea of revolution, but rather with the way it has been implemented.

Heym concludes by urging a purification of socialism from the abuses of the past and the incompetence of the present, from the 'Rost- und Blutflecken der Stalin-Ära' ('the stains of rust and blood of the Stalin era'), and from the 'Schimmelpilz der Bürokratie' ('mould of bureaucracy'). He does not reject the grand ideals of the movement, but pleads for a rejuvenation of them, particularly for the sake of modern youth.

The impact of this compact and hard-hitting speech was tremendous, but Heym knew it would be and he was well prepared. He could satisfy all the requests for copies with which he was bombarded, retaining only one for Louis Aragon, editor of the French Communist journal *Lettres françaises*. Heym's expectation was that the article would be featured in France fairly swiftly, and he used the argument that it had in fact been first published by a French *Communist* journal when he had to defend himself during later interrogation. (He still believed this while writing his memoirs (see p. 638), but it was not in fact until July of 1965 that the piece appeared in France: in *Les Temps Modernes*.) One of the reasons for this interrogation was that the article had found its way into the West German *Die Zeit*, where it had naturally been given some prominence and been commented on very widely.

Heym's strategy was that of calculated risk. To accept the ban on publication and public speaking would have been literary suicide; to fight against it brought the possibility of prosecution and unpredictable consequences. Heym chose the latter course, and having made this decision, pursued it wholeheartedly. There is nothing conciliatory in any other speeches or articles made at this time, all of which had to appear outside the Republic. Heym was shrewd in his arguments, though, and he never suggested the socialist ideal was in any way flawed. All emphasis was put on the means by which it was being realised.

The final striking piece in this anti-Stalinist series was 'Die Langeweile von Minsk' ('The Boredom of Minsk'), an intriguingly entitled attack on the taboos of socialist writing. The inspiration for the title came from Brecht, who had told Heym in 1955 that the Soviet Union could again claim to have a true literature, when a novel published there began with words to the effect 'Minsk is one of the most boring cities in the world'. Brecht's hopes had been fulfilled in the last ten years, suggested Heym. The call for honesty and realism had been met in the Soviet Union.

After this playful introduction, with its typically serious implication, Heym goes on to insist on the importance of 'Wahrheit' ('truth'). He claims it is above all the responsibility of the writer to propagate the truth and, in dramatic, sweeping cadences, he claims an immense power for the written word, which can have considerable consequences for the development of mankind. Precisely because of his power, the writer has enjoyed honour and prizes on the one hand, or been subject to censorship on the other, and he has been influenced in his presentation of truth by the existence of taboos. But all writers must resist pressures, particularly those in the socialist countries. Here, alas, a whole range of taboos prevails, and these must be challenged – even if the grounds for the existence of some of them are readily understandable. Indeed, it is precisely for the reason that some colleagues do consider such taboos justified that these matters must be handled carefully in the campaign for truth and realism. The operation 'muß durchgeführt werden in der Überzeugung, daß die Grundmauern des Sozialismus fest sind, auch wenn das Gesims mitunter zu verschnörkelt ist und hier und da ein Stück Fassade immer wieder abbröckeln will' ('must be concluded in the conviction that the foundations of socialism are firm, even if the mouldings are occasionally too elaborate, and here and there a piece of the façade is constantly threatening to flake away') (p. 357). It is ironic, in view of the attack which Erich Honecker was soon to launch against Heym, that the first part of this statement bears a relationship to Honecker's own famous edict shortly after he came to power: 'Wenn man von der festen Position des Sozialismus ausgeht, kann es meines Erachtens auf dem Gebiet von Kunst und Literatur keine Tabus geben' ('Providing one sets out from the firm position of socialism, then in my opinion there can be no taboos in the field of art and literature' (Rüß, *Dokumente*, p. 287).

The final part of this article neatly exploits the attacks on West Germany, and, of course, on West German writers, which were so common a feature of the GDR in the fifties and sixties. Heym suggests there are greater difficulties for those in the West in their representation of truth, but that East Germans nevertheless expect their western colleagues will portray it fearlessly, without gloss, raising their voices against tyranny and for the rights of man, forgoing the rewards of conformity in order to serve the interests of the truth. In a brisk succession of blunt rhetorical questions, Heym demands to know whether socialist writers themselves match the expectations they have of their western colleagues. Only if the socialists practice what they preach will they feel justified in claiming any moral superiority.

It is not surprising 'Die Langeweile' quickly came to be one of Heym's most famous and most important articles. In its careful phrasing, light irony, precision of argument, and vigorous conclusions, it represented the most clearly focussed challenge to socialist writers which had ever been published by an East German writer. The irony, of course, is that it was not published in the GDR. Because of the ban, Heym had to seek first publication in *Kulturni Život* (an official party organ in Bratislava); publication in other official Communist journals quickly followed: in France, Italy, and Hungary. And then, with Heym's permission, came publication in *Die Zeit*.

There is, however, one publication in a GDR periodical during this period, and that is 'In höherem Auftrag' ('On orders from above'), a satirical short story which was printed in *Neue Deutsche Literatur* in November 1965. The responsibility for featuring this was that of Wolfgang Joho, chief editor of the journal, and his decision to include something by Heym, as well as (in the previous issue) an extract from an unpublished novel by Werner Bräunig, was soon to cost him his post.

The story is written in a light-hearted manner, even though the source of inspiration was a troubling one: the forced early retirement of a theatre critic for his refusal to conform to the party view.[13] Heym sets his plot in contemporary times and in the GDR, but he uses a heavily debunked Goethean framework (meeting between God and Mephistopheles) as an introduction to the dilemma. God wishes to save the socialist theatre critic Heinrich Faust from perdition (losing his job, penury for his wife and children), for Faust is foolishly refusing to comply with the demands of his editor for a eulogy of a bad play. The situation allows Heym to make several barbed remarks on GDR cultural policy and the practice of praising what was bad if it nevertheless pleased on ideological grounds. (And, of course, the corollary, especially applicable to the situation of Heym himself, of castigating works of high quality which failed to please on ideological grounds.) Thus we find the honest Faust claiming to his editor: 'Jedenfalls habe ich noch bei keinem der großen Klassiker ein Wort davon gefunden, daß der Wert eines literarischen Werks durch politische Entscheidungen bestimmt werden kann' ('However that may be, I haven't yet found a word in any of the great classics suggesting that the quality of a literary work can be determined by political decisions') (p. 100).

Faust is an exceptional figure for GDR literary criticism. Heym slips in the fact he is a former revolutionary who has been imprisoned under a different regime for his socialist beliefs, and he is prepared to resign rather than compromise in the interests of a peaceful existence. However, Mephisto, through exposing the unsocialist (sexual) weaknesses of the newspaper's editor, manages to bring the conflict to an easy solution: the editor will find another critic to write the necessary eulogy. This is a simple enough task since 'auf jeden Narren kommen bei uns zu Lande Gott sei Dank sechs gescheite Burschen' ('for every idiot in our country there are, thank God, six smart characters') (p. 104). Intelligence is thus acquainted with the ability to conform. Honesty is self-destructive. Faust is a playful variant of Heym's intellectual martyrs, without whose courageous interference the ideals of socialism would be slowly eradicated.

The publication of this story in *Neue Deutsche Literatur* was doubtless most gratifying for Heym. Despite writing much of his work in English and thus maintaining his reputation outside the GDR, the readers he wished to influence most were those in his own country. These could not be properly reached by features in the West German press, and besides, Heym was himself uneasy about using the media of capitalism for his cause. We should also note that East German authors in general very rarely used the West as an outlet for their material in those years. One of the reasons was western hostility towards them (the West had a clear preference for work by those who had escaped from the East and wished to denigrate aspects of life there). Another was that turning to a West German publishing house virtually represented a vote of no confidence in one's own state, even if it were a left-wing establishment in the West which accepted material that had been refused by a house in the East. It also required courage to publish 'abroad', since reprisals of some sort were likely. Nonetheless, such a situation did not deter three key figures from acting in this way in the course of 1965. One of them was Heym; another was Wolf Biermann (who placed his collection of angry songs, *Die Drahtharfe*, in West Berlin); and the third was Robert Havemann (who published in *Die Zeit* an essay with the ominous sub-title 'Warum ich Stalinist war und Anti-Stalinist wurde') ('Why I was a Stalinist and became an Anti-Stalinist').

Official wrath came in December of that year, at the famous Eleventh Plenary Session of the Central Committee of the SED. The main subject of this conference had originally been scheduled as the economic situation, but the suicide of Erich Apel, the leading government economist, forced a change. The cultural situation was obviously a fine alternative; there was much to attack and therefore to blame, and by this means attention could be diverted from elsewhere – from the economic position, for instance, where the GDR had just been forced into a highly unfavourable treaty with the Soviet Union.

The attack on the literary nonconformists was spearheaded by Erich Honecker, who was already seen as Ulbricht's likely successor. He began the famous third section of his speech with the usual extravagant clichés of those years, calling for a fight against 'das Alte und Rückständige aus der kapitalistischen Unkultur und Unmoral, wie sie in der amerikanischen Sex-Propaganda und der Verherrlichung des Banditentums zum Ausdruck kommen' ('the reactionary and outdated features of capitalist barbarity and immorality as they are featured in American sex-propaganda and the glorification of gangster-ism') (Schubbe, *Dokumente*, p. 1076). He then moved to the GDR, lamenting lapses of morality in aspects of broadcasting, film, and literature. He attacked the film of a novel by Manfred Bieler and a play by Heiner Müller, declared himself appalled by the ungrateful Wolf Biermann's attacks on the GDR, and suggested that Heym was using his appearances in the West to publicise his unpublished volume *Der Tag X*. The articles Heym had published in the West presented a false image of life in the GDR and the Soviet Union, and his conception of 'truth' was essentially a western one. Honecker prefaced his onslaught by suggesting it was workers themselves who took exception to Heym's attitudes, a point Heym was later to explode in grandly sarcastic manner:

Werktätige haben in Briefen gegen Stefan Heym Stellung genom-men, weil er zu den ständigen negativen Kritikern der Verhältnisse in der DDR gehört. Er ist offensichlich nicht bereit, Ratschläge, die ihm mehrfach gegeben worden sind, zu beachten. Er benutzt sein Auftreten in Westdeutschland zur Propagierung seines Romans 'Der Tag X', der wegen seiner völlig falschen Darstellung der Ereignisse des 17. Juni 1953 von den zuständigen Stellen nicht zugelassen werden konnte. Er schreibt Artikel für im Westen erscheinende Zeitschriften und Zeitungen, in denen er das Leben in der Sowjet-union und in der DDR falsch darstellt. Er gibt vor, nur der Wahrheit das Wort zu geben, womit er aber die westlich orientierte 'Wahrheit' meint. Die 'Wahrheit', die er verkündet, ist die Behauptung, daß nicht die Arbeiterklasse, sondern nur die Schriftsteller und Wissen-schaftler zur Führung der neuen Gesellschaft berufen seien. (Schubbe, *Dokumente*, p. 1078)

Workers have written letters in opposition to Stefan Heym because he belongs to the consistently negative critics of conditions in the GDR. He is obviously not prepared to heed suggestions which have repeatedly been made to him. He is making use of his appearances in

West Germany to publicise his novel 'Der Tag X', which could not be permitted by our authorities on account of its completely false presentation of the events of 17th June. He writes articles for newspapers and magazines which appear in the West and in which he presents a false image of life in the Soviet Union and the GDR. He claims that he only wishes to write the 'truth', but he means by this the western interpretation of that concept. The 'truth' which he proclaims is the claim that it is not the working class, but only writers and intellectuals who are competent to be leaders of our new society.

Honecker then attacked the extracts from an unpublished novel by Werner Bräunig which had appeared in *Neue Deutsche Literatur*, and he criticised the editors of *Junge Welt* and *Freie Welt* for comparable lapses in their standards. Finally, he deplored the broadcasting of 'Beat-Musik' by a GDR station. According to Honecker, this unsatisfactory cultural position was undermining the development of socialist youth, and it could be blamed on a number of factors; one of these was the 'philosophical scepticism' in certain intellectual circles which had failed to recognise the 'creative' aspects of the formal decisions at the Soviet Twentieth Party Congress! He made no reference to Stalin's 'secret speech'.

Honecker's 'solutions' were straightforward – for all to adhere to Marxism–Leninism, and for those in the Ministry of Culture and the Writers' Union to draw the necessary conclusions. In some cases, these 'conclusions' were drawn for them. In the following month, Hans Bentzien, Minister of Culture, lost his post. In February, so did his deputy, Günter Witt, despite his *Selbstkritik* ('self-criticism') at the conference. In February too, the executive of the Writers' Union published an *Erklärung* in which they accepted all the criticisms which had been levelled against writers at the Eleventh Session of the ZK. And the April issue of *Neue Deutsche Literatur* was the last to be edited by Wolfgang Joho.

Few protested. One exception was Christa Wolf, who bravely defended Werner Bräunig during the Eleventh Session. (She was heckled, and in due course not re-elected as a candidate-member of the Central Committee.) Another was Franz Fühmann, who resigned from the Writers' Union after they meekly accepted Honecker's criticism – which, as usual, had been endorsed by numerous other party-line politicians and writers who spoke at the Eleventh Session. And another, inevitably, was Stefan Heym. His protest was spectacular, and it functioned as an encouragement to all other writers who felt under pressure as a result of this return to the old dogmatism.

Before considering Heym's response, it is first necessary to explain a standard feature of socialist societies – 'self-criticism' – public admission of failings in official duties (usually for not adhering to party policy). In the case of important individuals, this was featured in the press and represented a minor version of the 'show trial'. Self-criticism always drew attention to the failings of the speaker rather than those of others (and certainly not those of the system), and it proved more common at times when progress was disappointing or scapegoats were necessary. (It was a regular feature of GDR life in the late fifties and sixties.) Through such an expression of failings, an individual could sometimes save himself or herself from dismissal, or at least ensure reinstatement elsewhere.

One can only assume that the Berlin branch of the Writers' Union expected Heym to perform like so many others had done when they invited him to address them in February 1966. The new Minister of Culture, Klaus Gysi was present, together with other prominent figures, and the aim of the meeting was to discuss (which effectively meant 'to welcome') the decisions reached at the Eleventh Session. Heym was invited to speak by the Secretary of the Union, who had privately urged him to admit some error – however small (*Nachruf*, p. 714); but such hopes were founded on a poor knowledge of the man who had consistently courted danger throughout his life.

Heym's speech to the branch was never published in the GDR, but it appears in *Wege und Umwege*. In it he systematically exposed the weaknesses, errors, and lies in Honecker's attack. The 'workers' who had supposedly taken exception to him were only two in number, and neither of them was a 'worker'. His supposed criticism of the GDR was a risible invention. Only a few months previously he had been commended for certain speeches in the West by none other than *Neues*

Deutschland! Newspapers in the West had reluctantly noted his shrewd and spirited defence of the GDR. He had not used the trips to publicise *Der Tag X* – he had simply answered questions about it. His articles published in the West were far from being devoted to a false depiction of the Soviet Union and the GDR, and since neither of them had appeared in his own country, Heym took the opportunity to quote from one of them. He concluded by pointing out that this piece, 'Die Langeweile von Minsk', which had aroused such protest, had appeared first in a Communist state and then in two Communist journals in the West before (much later) publication in *Die Zeit*. As for the odium surrounding that paper, he pointed out that *Die Zeit* had been asked, several months before, whether it would publish a long statement by Walter Ulbricht! [It had declined.] Heym thus exposed to total ridicule the contents of Honecker's attack. And he did so in lively and sarcastic language, which contrasted totally with the usual long-winded breast-beating apologies which were common on such occasions.

Although Heym had his facts absolutely correct and could not be faulted on any aspect of detail, he lived in a state which at that time paid scant regard to facts in achieving certain of its aims, and in which one could never be sure of the leadership's likely reactions. Heym's bravery is the more commendable in the light of a visit he received shortly before his self-defence. Walter Janka, former manager of the Aufbau Verlag and member of the so-called 'Harich-Gruppe', had visited him discreetly at home. Janka had been sentenced to five years of imprisonment in the fifties for his supposed counter-revolutionary activities, and he had spent just over four years in jail, in solitary confinement. He came, therefore, to give Heym advice on how to survive secret police interrogation and subsequent imprisonment. If Janka could be sentenced to five years for what he had (not) done, then the likely punishment for Heym would have been considerably greater.

The years following the Eleventh Plenary Session were meagre for Heym in terms of publications. His habit of contributing

occasional pieces to GDR newspapers and journals was frustrated by the ban, and constantly having to publish abroad
was disappointing to a man who felt a keen need for rapport
with readers in his own country. One exceptional publication
of this period was that of two fairy tales, 'Die Geschichte vom
Zwerg Casimir', and 'Cymbelinchen oder der Ernst des
Lebens'. Heym had signed a contract for a collection of four
such tales before the ban had become operational, and so the
publishers were under obligation to respond. But before they
would print the tales, changes were needed. Two of the four
were cut for fear they might be 'misinterpreted' (they were
printed at a later date), and the name of a mountain goat in
'Casimir' was changed from Lotte (Christian name of the wife
of Walter Ulbricht) to the more neutral Mathilde. These tales
are in part parodies of traditional tales and contain general
allegories with no clearly specific references to the GDR. They
were popular with slightly older children (the suggested age
group was from twelve upwards), and Heym was later to write
several more.

Heym had always considered himself to be a novelist in the
first instance, and so fiction was the field to which he again
turned in this difficult period. By composing, once again, in
English, he had his traditional overseas market to fall back on if
times should not improve in the GDR. The previous history of
the country did, however, suggest that a relative thaw might
develop at some point.

The subject-matter chosen for the next novel was the final
year in the life of Ferdinand Lassalle, and critics have identified a number of reasons for such a choice. Clearly, contemporary material was inadvisable. After the difficulties of the
Eleventh Session, the general atmosphere in the country, and
the problems caused by *Der Tag X*, historical subject-matter
ran far fewer risks of antagonising. The historical *Lenz*, for
example, had been published with relative ease, and nineteenth-century history had always been a source of considerable interest to Heym – stretching as far back as his review of
Neumann's *Der neue Caesar* of 1935, with its firm views on the
task of the historical novelist. Why Lasalle, though, rather than

Marx or Engels, whose lives had been touched on in *Lenz* and who might attract wider readership than that of a less significant and more controversial figure? Perhaps three reasons can be advanced.

First, Lassalle had been the founder of the Allgemeiner Deutscher Arbeiterverein, the first national workers' union, and he was responsible for creating a *working-class* organisation in which power was concentrated in a single figure. Yet even though his concern was the improvement of the working man, in particular through the secret and equal vote, his own policies were far from democratic and selfless. Indeed, the term 'dictator' seems the most appropriate one by which to describe him, and if we are to seek the origins of the 'cult of personality' in socialist societies – one-man dictatorship accompanied by glorification on state directive – then it is in the figure of Lassalle that we actually first encounter them. Origins of power, the dangers, the abuse of power, have always fascinated Heym, and so the choice of Lassalle was from this point of view a natural one. His career would allow exploration of certain questions which had been raised in 'Stalin'. In addition, though, Lassalle revealed another troubling aspect of any ideologically motivated group: how far is it possible to work with 'the enemy' in order to achieve aims which are in themselves progressive? Lassalle wrote a play which touched on this topic (*Franz von Sickingen*), and in the novel we see his own negotiations with Bismarck. For Lassalle, such dealings pose no problem. He is cheerfully prepared to compromise for the sake of 'progress', but we note that reasons of self-interest may also play an important role in this policy. The political image which emerges is thus not flattering. Compromise of this nature has always been distasteful to Heym, and it is condemned in both *The Crusaders* and *Of Smiling Peace*.

A second, less obvious, reason for the selection of Lassalle, lies far removed from the political arena, and it is one on which the author has proved quite frank in his memoirs. Here he admits to early fascination with this historical figure, and also to a sense of affinity. As he recalls it in a conversation with Klaus Gysi, the Minister of Culture:

Außerdem, aber das sagte er Gysi nicht und niemandem, spürte er im Charakter des Mannes Züge, und nicht immer schöne, die ihm den eigenen verwandt erschienen: die auffahrend eitle Art, geboren aus Unsicherheit; der Drang, sich in den Vordergrund zu spielen, und die Unfähigkeit, Niederlagen zu ertragen; die fast devote Ehrfurcht vor dem Alt-Etablierten und gleichzeitig das Ressentiment dagegen; und die aus sozialer Arroganz erwachsene sentimentale Haltung gegenüber den Armen und Unterdrückten, oder denen, die er dafür hielt.[14]

In addition, but this he kept from Gysi and all others, he felt there were certain features in the character of this man – and not always attractive ones – which seemed close to his own: his irascible and vain behaviour, born of a sense of insecurity; the urge to be in the limelight, and the inability to accept defeat; the almost servile respect for the ancient and established, and at the same time a resentfulness towards it; and, arising from social arrogance, his sentimental attitude towards the poor and the oppressed – or at least those whom he considered to be in that category.

One could comfortably add to this list: the bravery, at its clearest when the danger is at its most intense; the actual courting of danger in order to make a point of principle; the eloquence as a speaker, with the surprising rhetorical twists and ability to hold an audience; the magnetism as a personality, and the immense popularity, at all levels of society; the 'care of a lawyer and the imagination of an artist' (to quote the novel itself); the zest for hard work; and perhaps also the love of intelligent and beautiful women, together with Jewish ancestry. In his memoirs, Heym noted that critics had complained of an injustice to the figure of Lassalle, and he explained that self-identification had prevented him from casting his hero in too favourable a light. But equally, there may be aspects of self-criticism in his presentation of this brilliant, if slightly irascible and uncertain 'people's hero'.

There is a final reason for the selection of Lassalle, and it relates to the fact that so-called 'historical novels' are regularly as firmly connected with the age in which they are written as the age which they depict. If Heym were able to suggest that the difficulties surrounding Lassalle's organisation had their counterparts in contemporary GDR society, then the problems and paradoxes of the original 'Workers' Union' would obviously hold contemporary significance. And for a writer whose commitment to the present-day world is as firm as Heym's, this would be a natural expectation on the part of his readers.

Lassalle's final year witnessed not only his grotesque death in a farcical duel, but also his election to the presidency of the Workers' Union. Both events revealed the vain and flamboyant side of his personality. In the election, his extremism and love of histrionics worked to his advantage; in the events leading to the duel, they proved his undoing. Yet at no stage of his life was Lassalle capable of moderation, and at various points of the narrative Heym hints at the early background which led to this extremist life style. The concern here is to reveal the psychology of a megalomaniac, and also to show why such a figure was attractive to so many – politicians of left and right, intellectuals, workers, women.

The novel opens, in fact, not with Lassalle, but with the woman who was effectively to prove his downfall: Helen von Dönniges. Heym devotes much of the novel to her, her relationship with her grandmother, her parents, her social world. Her leisured, affluent society provides a contrast to the poverty of the other world which the novel explores. These aristocratic circles claim considerably more space than the others, though, and the hero also feels far more at home in them than in those to which he pledges his political support. It was with some justification that the dust cover designer of the first GDR edition chose to focus exclusively on the elegant costume of a nineteenth-century aristocrat (intending this to be seen as Lassalle, but not providing a face), an act which aroused considerable anger on the part of a prominent GDR reviewer, Werner Neubert. In his opinion, the concentration on this aspect of Lassalle's personality – in the novel as well as on the dust cover – represented a distortion of the great early socialist's achievement.[15]

The novel traces the development of Lassalle's relationship with Helen, which is part of his hectic life of studying, writing, lecturing, scheming, and defending himself and others in various courts. A good deal of space is devoted to his election to the presidency of the 'Arbeiterverein' ('Workers' Union') – the initial approaches to establish whether he is prepared to participate, his negotiations with the self-appointed committee, his insistence on absolute control, his final election. And then, of course, there is space for his travels in this capacity, his success with the masses, his rhetorical victories. Throughout, though, there is the spectre of ill health: headaches, throat pains, and those other small details which hint at (never-mentioned) syphilis. This is thus a medical as well as a psychological study, and one with total credibility. Whatever critics may have found fault with in this novel, it was certainly not the author's power of characterisation. Indeed, one suspects that certain East German reviewers were troubled by the very strength and credibility of the portrait, which was in conflict with the more idealistic one promulgated in the socialist countries.

The area in which Heym disturbs this image most troublingly is probably not in the parade of Lassalle's immoral private life. His sexual libertinism has always been acknowledged, but it has been seen in the context of the personality as a whole and in particular of his contribution to the development of German socialism. Personal weaknesses can always be explained; less pardonable, however, are political offences, and Heym reveals a major one in a pinnacle of Lassalle's socialist contribution: the constitution of the German Workers' Union, which established a type of model for later constitutions and practices. The concentration of power in a single individual is Lassalle's idea, but it is seen to be motivated not by political idealism – it seems born rather from a lust for power which masquerades as pragmatism. The present-day reader knows all too well the dangers of concentrating power in this way – its consequences in this century have been corruption, despotism, and the cult of personality; so to suggest that its origins were not pragmatic, and certainly not idealistic, strikes at a cherished notion of German socialism. It also poses questions about the continuing nature of autocratic government, in particular its present justification.

Heym shows how Lassalle's insistence on possessing near-dictatorial powers encountered some opposition, but also how the doubters capitulated as a result of bullying rhetoric and the fear that if the great man was not given his way, he would refuse to become president. The dignified arguments Lassalle used to the committee were, however, different from those which actually motivated him. These emerge in an interior monologue as he awaits the outcome of the election:

but the contradiction between the need for one-man rule and the need for democratic trappings was universal as long as people were what they were: a lot of contrary, uninformed, unthinking, egotistic louts who had to be forced to their own good and welfare. Democracy! . . . Democracy was the carrot you dangled before the donkey's nose; but the stick made him move. (pp. 60–1)

Heym's formulation has an obviously provocative touch for modern readers, believing as they must that people have developed from the 'contrary, uninformed, unthinking egotistic louts' whom Lassalle castigates here. The implication is surely that society has developed since this period, and that the measures appropriate to a different age are far from apt today. Heym's depiction of the situation thus represents a hidden questioning of those modern structures in which power remains invested in a single figure.

Lassalle's rejection of democracy is equally a rejection of individual liberty. His grand outward claims that freedom and authority have effectively been integrated in the Workers' Union are belied by his interior monologue. At certain points in the novel Lassalle's expressed views are seen as deliberate deception of his audience, while at others they are seen as self-delusion, so carried away is he by the spirit of his own rhetoric. The possibility of individual freedom, then, which has featured as a glorious ideal in the novels considered thus far, is again seen to be vain.

The publishing history of *Lassalle* is notorious. It was initially composed in English, and translated by the author into German. Cassell's in London and List in Munich expressed doubts, however, and although it was first warmly welcomed by the Aufbau Verlag in East Berlin, it was later turned down. Heym revised this English manuscript, therefore, chiefly stylistically, and translated again into German (the process was to take almost a year). On the revised version Cassell's were prepared to act, and the small Bechtle Verlag in Munich expressed readiness to do so. But before Heym received copies of the contract, he was summoned to the Büro für Urheberrechte, an East German office which officially controlled the publication of GDR manuscripts abroad. Although the aim of this agency was ostensibly to protect authors' interests, in reality it acted as a form of censorship office, which decided on whether or not manuscripts should be published abroad at all (particularly those which had not found a publisher in the GDR). The ridiculous position into which the Büro had got itself is wryly depicted in Heym's memoirs (pp. 732–6). The Büro, or their agents, had actually intercepted copies of the contract from Bechtle and were about to use these, together with a forged letter supposedly from the publishers, as evidence of the author's failure to apply to them before negotiating with a publishing house abroad. In due course Heym was fined 300 marks for the offence. This was the highest fine which could be imposed without going to court, an action which the Büro obviously wished to avoid, since this would provide the author with a useful platform for observations on literary freedom. However, Heym's complaint about the loss of registered international mail was to cost the GDR post office a much higher sum, and the story about the 'book they tried to ban' could do nothing but boost interest in Heym's works in the other part of the nation.

CHAPTER 7

The uses of literature: Defoe, and the Bible

Western observers have often wondered why Heym was never jailed for his attacks on so many aspects of GDR government. The answer lies in a powerful combination of circumstances. First, the fact that Heym is Jewish, and that he lived in a state which prided itself on having eradicated anti-semitism. It regularly contrasted this achievement with the supposed failure to do so in the Federal Republic, and made much of any anti-semitic outburst in the western part of the nation. Second, Heym had fought against National Socialism from as early as 1931. This should likewise be seen in the context of a state which regularly boasted that the Communist Party was the only one to offer full resistance to Hitler. The GDR drew considerable moral strength from this fact, and again contrasted itself constantly with what it declared to be the natural successor to the Third Reich: the Federal Republic. Finally, Heym had become too well known to imprison. His arrest would have caused an uproar in both parts of the nation. The same applied to his friends Robert Havemann and Wolf Biermann. These three were the most vocal and successful opponents of the political direction taken by the GDR, and they were all in some way regarded as popular heroes. They met periodically in the sixties, partly for pleasure, partly to discuss aspects of socialism and alternatives to current policies, and their gatherings were carefully monitored by the secret police. Havemann, like Heym, had been persecuted by Hitler, and he had in addition survived the Nazi death-cell. Biermann's father, a Communist, had perished under Hitler in Auschwitz. Havemann could easily have obtained distinguished posts in the Federal Republic, but he chose to remain in the East in order to argue for a better society there; Biermann had actually left the West in order to live in East Berlin; and Heym, of course, had left the USA. To imprison any one of these figures could thus be interpreted as a sign of partial self-condemnation by the state. All three were idealists who regularly declared their faith in socialism.[1]

Historical distance allows us to recognise the protective force of these circumstances without difficulty. In the sixties and seventies, however, this was far less evident, and all three figures were regularly warned against making statements which could be seen as detrimental to the GDR, they were denied publishing outlets in that country, and they were banned from travelling. They were followed, bugged, inter-rogated, and prosecuted. Despite this, their response was in every case courageous. Havemann made his interrogation the centre of a highly successful analysis of the GDR (*Fragen Antworten Fragen*, published, of course, in the West); Biermann ignored all calls for restraint, writing witty songs about contra-dictory aspects of life in the GDR and making his extensive bugging the topic of a highly popular 'ballad' ('Die Stasi-Ballade'); and Heym used the clumsy methods of the authori-ties as the subject-matter of his next significant works, *The Queen against Defoe* and *The King David Report*.

Of these three dissidents, Heym was by far the most careful and the most circumspect. Biermann was young and impetu-ous, and he was never able to gain an appropriate outlet for his talents in the GDR. His exile in 1976 came as a deep personal blow. Havemann was highly intelligent and experienced, but he was far too self-confident and he overestimated his strength against that of the party. He did not foresee the practical and psychological consequences of being removed from his univer-sity post, and he slowly lost the considerable public attention he had once commanded. Heym, however, proved artful and far-sighted. He expressed himself with enormous care on every subject on which he was questioned, whether by the eastern government ministries or the western media; he always claimed to be a loyal GDR subject; he vigorously exploited every loophole which was offered him by the state and its laws; and he also exploited to the full the opportunities offered by the media. This consciously hazardous policy of exposing himself at every available opportunity was, Heym later claimed, something he had learnt from the USA (*Nachruf*, p. 716). Whether his survival was indeed attributable to such tactics we shall never know, but he certainly triumphed repeatedly at the expense of the authorities, while less vigorous figures either capitulated and/or left the Republic (and one would here think of such prominent examples as Hartmut Lange, Manfred Bieler, Peter Huchel, Reiner Kunze, Sarah Kirsch, Günter Kunert, Jurek Becker, and Erich Loest, all of whom revealed bravery in their stance against the authorities, but who in the end decided that life under GDR socialism had become intolerable).

The Queen was written in a mere six weeks during the autumn of 1968, against the disturbing backcloth of Czech liberalism being crushed by Soviet intervention. The story itself depicts the attempt to victimise a prime representative of liberalism in early eighteenth-century England, and it offers a splendid example of Heym's imaginative use of historical camouflage. The method was high risk in that it is perfectly clear the main target of attack is the GDR, and yet by his close adherence to established fact Heym could claim this work was in the first instance a historical re-creation. He could also rely on that long-established crutch of the persecuted writer: proof of dissent must be furnished by the public prosecutor, and the latter can act only if he is prepared to explain the implications of a writer's narrative. Formal self-exposure of this nature was not relished by the legal organs of the GDR government, and writers were therefore curbed by insidious rather than formal or legal methods. Nevertheless, the major dissidents recognised that any of them could suddenly be selected as a public scapegoat. There would be little hope of a fair trial, and their punishment, like that devised for Daniel Defoe, would undoubtedly be exemplary.

The basic idea for *The Queen against Defoe* actually arose from bed-time rereading of an old favourite, *Robinson Crusoe*, and specifically of the long-ignored introduction on the career of its author. Defoe, it suddenly transpired, had not only created one of the greatest adventure stories of all time; like Heym, he had also embarked on a political career, and he had at one stage been put in the pillory for a particularly successful satire on the government of his age. To 'pillory' has an international metaphorical sense, and the situation of being subjected to attack without being able to defend oneself properly was something to which numerous GDR writers had been exposed in the recent past, Heym in particular. But further parallels between himself and Defoe became clear as Heym consulted the particular pamphlet for which the early eighteenth-century author had been condemned. Parallels with Heine must also have been noted, for Defoe had used one of the standard satirical methods of all time. In *The Shortest Way with the Dissenters* he had simply adopted the intolerant language and ideology of those he sought to ridicule, exaggerating only slightly the terms of the original argument. The measure of his success also proved his undoing, however. Although certain excesses in vocabulary clearly revealed the document as a spoof, it was actually taken seriously by a number of well-known right-wing contemporaries. Their displeasure at having been hoaxed naturally played its part in the ensuing prosecution of the author.

Heym took more from his source – and its historical circumstances – than many critics have realised. First, he took the actual story of how Defoe came to be arrested, prosecuted, and put in the pillory. Second, like Defoe, he devised the story as a spoof. He gave it a foreword in which he claimed he had been given the papers which were here reproduced by a descendant of one of the principal characters. (As in the case of the historical Defoe, Heym's spoof was in a sense *too* successful, and one of the first reviewers actually believed the 'papers' to be genuine!)[2] Third, he composed the main text in archaic English, following the language and cadences of *The Shortest Way*. Finally, he used the idea behind Defoe's method as that behind his own. Defoe had exaggerated language and ideas in order to make people realise the ridiculousness of them; Heym uses language for a comparable effect – to make his readers see the absurdity of the present-day equivalents. Heym suggested in his memoirs that Defoe's aim was to make his readers recognise 'mein Gott, *das* predigt und gebietet uns, *das* regiert uns gar? ('my God, those people are preaching to us and controlling us, *those* people are actually in power') (p. 749). Heym's objective is similar: to make the reader recognise the nature of modern forms of repression – their extremism, their lack of touch with the masses, their ultimate futility.

Daniel Defoe (1660?–1731) was a highly productive and versatile writer whose initial political sympathies were with the Whig cause and the Nonconfirmists, but he then served the Tories (as a direct political agent of the Minister Harley, who had him released from prison), until he later secretly betrayed them to the Whig government. Defoe attributed his political double-dealing to his temporary financial ruin and deep sense of injustice when prosecuted for *The Shortest Way*. Such mercenary vacillations on his part do cloud our image of him as a political idealist, but they are an aspect which Heym chooses to disregard in his text. He focusses exclusively on Defoe's career in 1702/3, when his idealism was seemingly at a peak. Heym's story is thus thoroughly optimistic. The writer is not only seen in a highly positive light, gloriously triumphing over the establishment, but we are also given a clear impression of the potential for literature to change the course of history. The selection of this episode may consequently be seen as a means of self-encouragement to Heym in a period of relative gloom over his own future as well as that of literature as a whole in the GDR. His identification with Defoe must have been strong: both were journalists, novelists, and persecuted political idealists with a keen sense of courage in the face of oppression.

The Queen against Defoe begins with the authorities recognising that something will have to be done about an anonymous pamphlet which seemingly approves the government position. Its author has taken the views of the High Tories to their logical conclusion, suggesting that the quickest way to eliminate religious dissent would be to exile the dissenters and to hang their preachers. Heym has his hero sum up the procedure quite simply: 'I saw that all I need do was fully to state the case of the establishment numskulls to have it drowned in ridicule' (p. 36). Although Defoe is vindicated by the popular reaction, it happens that he is here explaining his method to one of these very 'numskulls', the Earl of Nottingham, Secretary of State. Nottingham is indeed dull-witted and narrow-minded. He has no understanding of the literary mind, and he fears the power of the written word considerably more than 'the armies of France' (p. 13). He also finds it hard to accept that a single brain is behind the pamphlet, and he therefore suspects Defoe is at the centre of a plot to inspire a rebellion. In this respect he clearly resembles twentieth-century politicians of the eastern bloc. The writer is feared essentially for his ability to inspire revolution. Heym's readers would certainly see an echo here from the Hungarian uprising of 1956, in which literary figures played so prominent a part, and Heym was later to make an unambiguous allusion to that uprising in his novel *Collin*. In *The Queen*, however, his concerns are more general.

Defoe is dealt with according to the methods of his day: he and his family are threatened, and he is deceived into believing he will obtain clemency if he will agree to plead guilty. (Two further practices with clearly contemporary relevance.) To his dismay, he is sentenced to a period of imprisonment, fined heavily, and ordered to stand in the pillory on three successive days – a frightening prospect given that not only rotten fruit and vegetables are likely to be thrown at him, but also bricks and stones. Instead of pelting him, however, the mob honour him, garlanding him and using the opportunity to rail against the government. The Earl of Nottingham and his henchmen are humiliated, not least because they have planted a good number of paid agents in the crowd.

Heym allows the relevance of *The Queen* to the GDR of the late sixties to become apparent only slowly, and it is the ambiguity of his language which is just as significant here as are the parallels of situation. The first hint occurs on p. 12, when the narrator, a principal agent of the Earl of Nottingham, bemoans 'the deplorable circumstance that everything un-Christian and subversive is written so much more cleverly and effectively than the upright God-fearing tracts of the Established Church'. Although the context of Defoe's pamphlet is principally religious, the inclusion here of 'subversive' reminds us of its political implications; church and state are one, and to attack the church is to attack the state. But the possible parallel church/socialist party is sharpened by the suggestion that 'oppositional' writing is so much livelier than that composed in honour of the state. How regular a complaint it was in the GDR itself that party-line writing lacked character, while public attention was captured by such unorthodox and critical artists as Biermann, Kunze, and Heym. The so-called 'Lyrik-Debatte' of 1966 would still be active in the minds of many readers at this stage, even though the points made during it were only reformulations of basic positions. That debate, sparked off by the appearance of an anthology entitled *In diesem besseren Land*, brought into conflict the best poets of the Republic and the most reactionary of the critics. The editors of the anthology had taken the unprecedented step of including only poetry which they deemed of high merit, and had excluded all party-line writing by the established figures. The ensuing debate, in *Forum* (the intellectual journal of the 'Freie Deutsche Jugend'), illustrated only too clearly the resentment of the more distinguished poets at being told what, and how, to write.[3] The editor of *Forum*, Rudolf Bahro, was relieved of his post, but only after the 'damage' had been done; wide publicity had been given to the fact that the most gifted poets held views which were totally at odds with those of the establishment; and that these poets were far more entertaining to read than the dreary and unimaginative dogmatists who were promulgating the party line. Further, the two parties were separated not only on matters of aesthetics, but on the nature and function of society.

A second suggestion of a parallel emerges on the occasion of a public bookburning. Now official burning of undesirable literature has a lengthy history, but it is associated in Germany in particular with the Nazis' burning of books – particularly those by Jewish writers – in 1933. Defoe's *Shortest Way* certainly was burnt, but Heym's decision to include this episode (which adds nothing to the plot) was bound to be a telling one for

German readers. It implied an analogy which contemporary German governments would then have found particularly embarrassing.

The need to burn literature is another tacit admission of the power of the writer to influence the public, a firm belief of the socialist countries as a whole. Furthermore, as Heym once put it in an interview:

The restrictions prevalent in the socialist world tend to lend more weight to the words of a writer, especially when he says something that has not been said before or that is in contrast to official doctrine.[4]

The Queen contains a succession of hints about the power of the writer, ranging from an obvious reformulation of the pen being mightier than the sword ('we have entered upon an age in which ... a statesman can be toppled by a sharp pen as easily as by gunpowder', p. 17), to comic observations on the shame which might befall anyone who is associated with a free-thinking author (three dissenting ministers refused to pray with Defoe, 'although one of them some years ago did come to Newgate to pray with Mr Whitney before the latter's hanging; but Mr Whitney was a robber and a murderer and not a writer with a mind of his own' p. 44). Such remarks are relevant to any repressive government, but they have a particular application to the GDR of the late sixties. Ministers could then easily be toppled by the activity of writers, and association with certain of these could readily bring disfavour. Manfred Bieler, for example, recalled with delight that a minister lost his position as the result of a film based on one of his novels (Günter Witt in February 1966, on account of *Das Kaninchen bin ich*), and in his memoirs Heym talks of supporters having to visit him at night to avoid being seen. This is not to suggest, however, that *The Queen* is a *roman à clef* and that particular individuals are to be identified behind the Earl of Nottingham and his assistants. Equally, although Heym himself may be the most obvious figure behind the hero, Defoe is symbolic of dissident satirists from any age. Once the reader has recognised the irony, then every politico-literary observation holds implications. And although we may experience dismay at the con-

tinuing presence of primitive, early-eighteenth-century attitudes and practices, we also derive pleasure from the way in
which these political barbs are so naturally embedded in an
accurate historical framework.

The linking of Defoe's position with that of modern dissidents is achieved through choice of situation and ironic
language, but there are certain parallels which are strengthened – or, in fact, only established – in the German (self-)
translation. Here Heym is able to exploit different aspects of
linguistic ambiguity, and to link the story more specifically
with the GDR. The first instance of this sort occurs in the
opening page, and is to be found in the translation of Defoe's
title. The expectation might be 'Das kürzeste Verfahren mit
den Dissentern' (or perhaps 'Dissidenten' – both are used in
the literature on the subject), but Heym broadens the implications by choosing the completely different 'Abweichlern'.
Wahrig's *Deutsches Wörterbuch* of 1968 (the year of the composition of the tale) defines that word as follows:

Abweichler ⟨m. 3; bes. SBZ⟩ jmd, der eine andere Meinung vertritt als
die Partei.

Deviant (masc. Group 3 noun; especially Soviet Zone of occupation)
someone who takes a different view from that of the party.

A single German word, then, firmly alerts us to possible
GDR implications before the narrative itself has begun. (One
might also note, *en passant*, that even in 1968 a major West
German dictionary was still referring to the GDR as the 'SBZ'
('Sowjetische Besatzungszone Deutschlands'). This reflects the
widespread western view of the period that eastern writers
were still heavily influenced by Moscow and lived under
Stalinist literary conditions – a factor which doubtless contributed to the warm reception in the West for those who were
prepared to stand against the GDR authorities.)

Another small, but provocative, detail of the German text is
to be found in the designation of Mr Robert Stephens,
'Queen's Messenger in charge of matters of the press'. The
archaic formulation of the English is given a pointed twist in

Heym's translation: 'Mr Robert Stephens, den für Pressefragen zuständigen Boten der Königin'. Naturally, the 'Boten der Königin' has to match the historical context, but the formulation 'für Pressefragen zuständig' has clearly East German undertones. One notes in addition that there was no obvious corresponding figure in the free-enterprise England of the 1960s, but there clearly was in the GDR, where printing and the press were still strictly controlled by government. The historical situation, then, fits the GDR scene, but it is the choice of language which alerts us to it. In the same category is Defoe's rejection of the idea that 'jede nicht *amtlich gebilligte* Idee notwendig als Teil eines aufrührerischen Komplotts erscheint' (my italics: note that the idea of 'amtlich' ('officially') is not present in the original English: 'any idea not previously approved necessarily becomes part of a seditious plot'). As in all Heym's 'historical' works, parallels with the present are subtle; it is through ironic linguistic pointers that the author alerts the reader to his intentions.

As in the source, the narrative perspective is an unusual one: the situation is depicted by someone with whom any reasonable reader is *not* expected to identify. Heym had used such an approach before, especially in short stories where an antipathetic figure adopted an anti-communist or anti-humanist position. (In 'Der Floh', for example, and 'Mein verrückter Bruder'). In *The Queen* the central character is presented through his diaries, which quickly reveal him as sycophantic, prepared to bend whichever way is necessary to secure his own advancement, and consequently quite without moral scruple. The disturbing aspect of Josiah Creech is, however, that he holds considerable power and that he is prepared to use it without hesitation. Like such figures as Reinhardt, Liszt, Monaitre, Pettinger, he has a sadistic streak, and it is this which probably alienates him most from the reader. Yet Creech himself is dependent on the whims of others; as was seen with the figures just mentioned, and as will be seen in Heym's next novel, in any Stalinist situation power remains precarious. The modern implications of these observations are sharpened by their historical distance.

Several years earlier Heym had used a comparable historical framework to emphasise the precariousness of existence in a totalitarian system. In 'The Proper Approach', in which the title itself emphasises the theme of conformity, Heym relates the story of a Prussian minor civil servant who is anxious to please his masters through a combination of hard work, sycophancy, and a determination to outshine his colleagues. In his eagerness to ingratiate himself with those in power, he manages to 'solve' an apparent tax fraud, blinkering himself in the process to certain (barely hidden) implications. The fraud ultimately transpires to be condoned by the authorities, and Dressler's clandestine researches prove his undoing. What strikes us here, in a story quite unrelated to *The Queen*, is once again the ruthlessness of the minor power seekers (Dressler is quite pre-pared to accuse a friend in order to secure his own promotion); the fragile nature of power (Dressler, like Creech, is dismissed); and the apparent inscrutability of those in ultimate authority. There is also a troubling image here which finds counterparts in various other works. In 'The Proper Approach' it takes the form of the figure of authority stroking his beard before com-mitting himself to a decision: 'only von Bottwitz, still stroking his beard, seemed to have preserved some of his benevolence towards me' (pp. 97/8).

There is something decidedly unsettling about the fact that the character who wields most power is outwardly least troubled by the calamity. The simple act of stroking a beard thus acquires a certain mephistophelian quality, an act of sadistic playfulness. A comparable gesture of distraction, all the more ominous for its inappropriateness to the situation, is to be found after Josiah Creech's inability to decide which exactly is the 'right attitude' that should be adopted to Defoe's pamphlet. He refuses to commit himself, diplomatically concluding:

''Tis an awkward thing,' says I, 'to judge a matter without your superior's opinion.' (p. 10)

To which the response is enigmatic:

My Lord Nottingham toyed with his exceedingly long fingers but remained silent. (p. 11)

The dangerous face of power remains hidden: just as in *The King David Report* we find the first, and the last, encounters of the writer Ethan with King Solomon are tinged with comparble inscrutability. On the first occasion, the king distracts himself by fondling the noses of the cherubim carved on the chair in which he is sitting. On the final occasion, as Ethan waits to see whether his life will be spared, there is a moment of great tension after he declares himself 'not guilty' of the crimes with which he has been charged. Some of the powerful men present cannot conceal their emotions, but the King himself remains apparently unmoved:

There was silence. Benaiah ground his jaws, and Nathan looked at me anxiously, and the King toyed with the noses of the Cherubim. (p. 243)

Heym employs the same innocent verb ('toyed with') as he had for the description of Lord Nottingham. Yet the apparently harmless actions of the King are far more disconcerting than a direct display of feelings, and the gentleness of the action actually suggests a violence of thought behind it, which could spectacularly erupt at any moment.

Does such imagery have its origins in Heym's own experience of despotic behaviour in the GDR? One moment does in fact stand out as a clear example. Heym, summoned by Ulbricht, entered the innermost sanctum in some trepidation. But he was kept waiting while the most powerful man in the country did not come straight to the point, but began instead to eat an apple. Only then did he inform Heym that Wolfgang Harich (just arrested) had sat on the same chair as Heym several days before (*Nachruf*, p. 604). Unlike Harich, Creech, and Ethan, Heym emerged without damage.

Defoe shows considerable bravery in his attitude towards the establishment, but his actions are clearly dangerous. The popular support he enjoys is not something which he himself had expected, and the forces which oppose him are unlikely to allow him such a victory on a second occasion. In his next novel, then, Heym turns to a more cautious and more limited hero, but one whose preparedness to compromise is in fact necessitated by the far more repressive society in which he lives. Defoe's triumph, for all its splendour, is something of a 'naive' one; that of Ethan, in *The Kind David Report*, is more subtle and can only be seen as a posthumous victory. In his own lifetime, in fact, Ethan's actions represent a personal defeat. Yet Ethan's situation is more generally applicable to the life of an intellectual in a repressive state. Defoe, like Heym, is far rarer a figure.

The conditions which prevailed during the writing of *The King David Report* were some of the least propitious in the GDR's cultural history. Although 1968/9 did witness the publication of Christa Wolf's *Nachdenken über Christa T.*, the print run was very short (as were those of all volumes which were considered not perfectly suited to the emerging socialist society). In addition, the author was immediately attacked for writing such a novel, with the first review actually appearing before the book had been put on general sale.[5] At the 'VI. Schriftstellerkongress' in May of 1969, Christa Wolf was further denounced in the keynote address, and so too was Reiner Kunze for his latest volume of poetry, *Sensible Wege* (published in the West).[6] Publications that did find favour (and were given considerable official prominence) during these years were those like *Lyrik der DDR* (1970), an anthology compiled by Uwe Berger and Günter Deicke and devised as a counterpart to *In diesem besseren Land*. (The Berger/Deicke collection contained all the party-line poets whom the editors of the latter had chosen to ignore.) But the climate of these years can best be judged by recalling that such a volume as Hermann Kant's *Das Impressum*, highly positive in its view of the GDR and very mild in its criticism, was nevertheless kept from publication for over three years, reaching print only in 1972.[7] Against this background there was little likelihood of *The Queen* being published in the GDR; and the hopes for something as comparably ambiguous as *The King David Report* were equally meagre.

The writing of Heym's most complex novel took almost three years, and the initial stages were among the gloomiest of his life. Following the illness of his beloved wife Gertrude towards

the end of 1968, and her death early in 1969, Heym was lonely
and disconsolate. In one of his sleepless nights he turned for
consolation to the Bible – King James's Authorised Version, in
fact. His memoirs communicate well the excitement with
which he suddenly realised the power of the story of David,
and how he saw the seeds of his own version of it, one which
would convey the reality behind the fine words of the holy
source, and which would also come to terms with how the
original text might actually have been composed. Many other
authors had treated this particular tale, and some of them
Heym had read already, but he decided to bring out an issue
which no one had previously recognised as significant: the
contradictions which the story contains. He focusses on these
through well-founded speculations on how the account of King
David (in I and II Samuel and I Kings) could possibly have
come into being, and in so doing he raises the whole question of
biblical composition and of how the history of great men comes
to be written. Further, by means of linguistic pointers and neat
analogies, he establishes parallels between the society of
ancient Israel and that of following totalitarian regimes, in
particular those of the twentieth century. His novel is thus
political as much as it is biblical, and it is written in a style
which subtly parodies the language and cadences of the
Authorised Version. The German translation, which was completed after the English was composed but actually published
before it, just as successfully captures the rhythms and reso-
nances of Luther's Bible.[8] Heym was once again to prove that
'history has great relevance to our time'.[9]

Of the numerous other treatments of this biblical story, there
is one that is similar to Heym's in that it uses the figure of a
historian as the central character – Feuchtwanger's *Josephus*
trilogy, and in particular the final volume, *Der Tag wird
kommen*.[10] Heym, however, goes far beyond Feuchtwanger, for
he uses his novel to comment on its own function as a biblico-
historical work. Heym's concern is not only the high drama of
the Bible story, the contradictions it contains, and the parallels
with our own age, but also with the nature of the task the
historian may be instructed to perform, and how he must set

about it. Heym forces us to recognise the unreliability of any work that is written to a preconceived plan, and his novel exemplifies the wisdom of E. H. Carr's dictum: 'Study the historian before you begin to study the facts.'[11] By studying the historian, his aims and his restrictions, this novel becomes a study of historiography as much as a study of history. It acquires further depth by encapsulating within it the circumstances under which it actually came to be written. For the historian's difficulties in writing what he believes to be the truth reflect those of all writers who are obliged to follow any form of 'party line' and who can only hint at their meaning by indirect means. In particular, though, these difficulties reflect those of Stefan Heym himself in the period between 1965 and Honecker's accession to power in 1971.

The biblical David is something of an enigma: a poet and a singer of beautiful songs, but also the great leader who forged the tribes of Israel into a powerful nation. A seer, who felt himself chosen by, and in close communication with God, but also, if we read between the lines of the Bible, a double-dealing politician, a merciless warrior, at times an unscrupulous tyrant. As Heym forcefully brings out, the story which the Bible gives us was written for a particular purpose: it is not intended to be an objective account of David's rise, triumphs and various crimes. Although it mentions his weaknesses and sins against the Lord, it plays most of them down in order to give importance to other events. One of these is the return of the Ark to Jerusalem; the other is the accession of the man who followed David onto the throne: King Solomon. In the story of the accession itself, there are inconsistencies and thinly disguised suppressions, for the editors of the Bible story are clearly trying hard to stress the legitimacy of Solomon's succession and also the good fortune for the tribes of Israel that he should be their leader. For the modern reader, however, this presentation of the 'Wisest of Kings' is unsatisfactory, and scholars have for some time pointed out the unbalanced, partisan presentation of character which is to be found here. In line with modern scholarship, Heym depicts Solomon as a clever but brutal despot, who ruthlessly crushes his opponents and permits of no

view opposed to his own. In him are evident the other standard features of a totalitarian ruler: megalomania, cynicism,
and brutality.

Heym begins his novel by suggesting that Solomon, like all
rulers who have gained their position by underhand means, is
anxious to have his conduct vindicated. One of the best means
to this end is a definitive 'report', which will remove all
'contradiction and controversy' which so troubles the new
despot, and for which a commission – advised by an historian –
will be responsible. The historian who is commanded to tailor
the embarrassing facts to fit King Solomon's needs is Ethan of
Ezrah, author of Psalm 89 and about whom it is said (in 1
Kings 4:31) that he was one of the wisest men of Israel. He is
advised his history must be definitive, it must be wholly accurate, but at the same time it must make absolutely clear that
David was chosen to be King of Israel and that he chose
Solomon to be his successor. Yet on the very first pages of the
novel we discover that Solomon was *not* the obvious successor,
and that he was put on the throne by the machinations of his
mother, the backing of a private army, and the assistance of
some wily priests. So as the novel progresses, we find Ethan
being drawn in two opposing directions: as the servant of
Solomon, he is required to write a report which unambiguously confirms the legitimacy of the King's position; yet he is also
the servant of his conscience, which demands that he reveal
the truth. It is around this moral conflict that the novel may be
seen to turn, and the more Ethan discovers about David, the
more the terms of the conflict are sharpened. Ethan finally
finds himself isolated and trapped, precisely through the
knowledge he has attained. He can only extract himself by
some sort of factual or linguistic compromise. As a result, we
see Ethan, the official and respected historian, being forced to
evade what he has established to be the truth. A number of
items of information have to be suppressed, or carefully glossed
over, and it is in the reasons which are advanced for a 'dis-
creet' manipulation of such evidence that the second level of
the novel slowly becomes clear. The functioning of Old Israel
has much in common with the state in which a supposedly

glorious ideal is used to justify all means which may have to be adopted to achieve it.

This level of the novel might best be termed the 'political', and the principal parallel which Heym draws is the Soviet Union. Specifically Soviet references include an allusion to 'wonderful achievements' in the title which the report on David will carry (a standard Soviet term of the Stalin era for military and economic advances); the final branding of Ethan as an 'Unperson' (recalling some of Stalin's infamous legislation of the thirties); and the use of Trotsky's famous remark about the 'scrapheap of history'. King Solomon's mines provide a clear parallel to the Siberian slave labour camps; exemplary confessions and apparently impeccable witnesses to Stalinist 'show trials'; there is corruption and a black market, brutal suppression of all opposition (including regular purges), and a secret police; censorship is common to both regimes, as well as the recognition – and fear – of the power of the writer. Among the more humorous affinities between states which exist thousands of years apart are the 'state-owned' properties (which can be excellent or shoddy, depending on your influence and purse), and the renaming of streets (as the person after whom they are named falls from favour). This was more recurrent a feature of the German Democratic Republic (where the change was from 'Hitler' to 'Stalin' to 'Marx') than of the Soviet Union, and here the novel had clearer implications for Heym's own country.[12]

Nevertheless, the repeated and unambiguous references to the Soviet Union help to establish a major parallel of the novel – that of King David and Joseph Stalin.[13] The counterpointing does not end there. King Saul with Lenin, as well as Solomon with Khrushchev are the other, although far less important parts of the configuration, and in this respect it is worth noting that Khrushchev paralleled Solomon in producing a 'report' on his predecessor.[14] It would, however, be wrong to suggest that these parallels were worked out in any detail. Indeed, at points David may remind us more of the sanctified Lenin than of Stalin, and at others he may recall the iconoclastic Khrushchev. Such uncertainty is doubtless deliberate on Heym's part:

we are really dealing with a form of montage, rather than one-to-one allegorical equivalence.

What all four despots have in common is a desire to produce a definitive history of the recent past. This is a standard occupation of the single-party state, and Heym's own country had recently taken great pains to establish one for itself. The first call had come in 1955, from the Central Committee of the SED, and it was couched in the standard clichés of the age. The principal aims of historiography were seen to be: 'Durch gründliche wissenschaftliche Arbeiten und durch Verbreitung richtiger historischer Erkenntnisse den Massen unseres Volkes den Weg zum Sieg über seine Feinde, zu einem national geeinten, demokratischen und friedliebenden Deutschland zu weisen – darin besteht die Hauptaufgabe der deutschen Geschichtswissenschaft.'[15] ('By means of thorough scholarly investigations and by the dissemination of correct historical insights to show the mass of our people the way to victory over their opponents and to a national, unified, democratic and peace-loving Germany – that is the principal task for German historians.')

The bombastic terms of this grandiose programme can be regarded as typical of the numerous projects launched over the years with the aim of legitimising aspects of the GDR's status. Heym gently mocks these through the full, baroque-like title for the 'report' on which Ethan is engaged. Although this is intended to be awe-inspiring, practically every word embodies some ironic force: 'The One and Only True and Authoritative, Historically Correct and Officially Approved Report on the Amazing Rise, God-fearing Life, Heroic Deeds, and Wonderful Achievements of David the Son of Jesse, King of Judah for Seven Years and of both Judah and Israel for Thirty-three, Chosen of God, and Father of King Solomon' (p. 9).

There are other ironic parallels between states which existed thousands of years apart. For example, Ethan is not allowed to work alone but is a member of the 'commission' which is engaged in the report. That commission occasionally has to call upon the Wisest of Kings himself to address them on some problematic detail. Walter Ulbricht too was called upon to advise on tricky points in the preparation of East Germany's official history, as in his speech 'Über den Charakter der Novemberrevolution. Rede in der *Kommission* zur Vorbereitung der Thesen über die Novemberrevolution' [my italics] ('On the Nature of the November Revolution. Speech in the Commission appointed to prepare Theses on the November Revolution'). Verbal parallels of this sort are highly suggestive, but whether or not Heym had the workings of his own country in mind, the general point is that there are similarities in the attitude to the past adopted by such societies, and in the way in which they need to interpret it. The 'ruler' is, among other things, historian-in-chief, and his view of the past is unchallengeable. Different views cannot coexist alongside his highly selective vision, a vision which allows him to appropriate those aspects of his heritage which suit his needs best.

One of Heym's main concerns in this novel is the nature of historical truth, and he shows a major interest in the problems that face the independent historian in a repressive society. Historical evidence, suggests the author, must always bow to religious constraints, and political intervention will be the inevitable consequence of failure to respect these. The very word 'truth' is in fact a frequent one in this novel, just as it has figured frequently in a number of others and in Heym's polemical writings. It is a concept which allows of different interpretations, and Heym brings this out bluntly in the following example from 'Die Langeweile von Minsk': 'Nun gibt es Leute, die argumentieren: Schön – aber was ist die Wahrheit? Gibt es nicht tausend Varianten der Wahrheit, je nach Standpunkt und Weltanschauung des Betrachters?'[16] ('Now there are people who will argue: fine – but what is the truth? Aren't there a thousand variations of truth, each one dependant on the actual viewpoint of the observer and his philosophy of life?') – *The King David Report* puts the same point in more poetic terms: 'Blessed be the name of the Lord our God, whose truth is like a field arrayed with flowers of many colours, for each man to pick the one striking his fancy' (p. 39) The truth which Ethan seeks takes the form of evidence which can help determine the succession of events, the motivation of every critical action, and the consequences which each of these was to have. But for King Solomon and his advisers there is a different form of truth: that which they claim to be based on the word of God as interpreted by the prophets and priests. For them, truth is a relative concept, and all facts must be seen in relation to an overriding idea. If facts seem at variance with their religious doctrines, then the facts must be wrong! Facts can only serve to illustrate and strengthen dogma, they must never make it questionable or weaken it in any way. It is therefore not surprising to find great stress being laid on the importance of *guiding* the people in their understanding of the 'truth' – the masses must not be allowed to think for themselves and, paradoxically, elaborate deceit can be readily condoned whenever 'truth' needs to be disseminated. There is consequently little doubt about the attitude which must be adopted in the recording of history, and it is indicated by one of the chief ideologues of Solomon's state, Nathan the prophet. First Nathan puts forward the basic idea, then he emphasises how it must not be tainted: 'Once we are agreed that David is the chosen of the Lord, then everything he does is for the good of Israel. But as knowledge of the facts may lead a person to dangerous thoughts, the facts must be presented so as to direct the mind into the proper channels' (p. 82). By this stage of the novel the relationship between religion and modern political ideology is emerging quite clearly. The reader will consequently be tempted to substitute 'the party' for 'the Lord', producing the well-known argument of how the party is always right. True, the biblical framework may conceal that argument from some readers, but as Nathan develops his point, his words become less specifically religious. His advice for the political historian may contain delightful euphemisms ('dangerous thoughts', 'proper channels'), yet it is firmly prescriptive. Nathan is, of course, here dealing indirectly with a central problem of both *The King David Report*, of 'Stalin verläßt den Raum', and of socialist historiography in general: the treatment of taboo. Just as the rule of Stalin produced a number of topics on which investigation was officially prohibited, so too did the rule of David encompass a number of episodes which brought into question the nature of that King's relationship with Jahweh. Nathan recognises it would be diffi-cult to omit such 'dangerous' facts from the historical record. By its very nature, the taboo exerts a fascination. Further, too many people know what actually took place. There may have been a successful purge of every descendant of Saul; but even if those descendants cannot now speak, those who eliminated them can. Similarly, if the record is falsified, *someone* must be responsible for its falsification. This Achilles' heel of totali-tarian historiography is implied at several points throughout the novel, mainly through the discussions of the working policy that the commission will have to adopt. Ethan the Ezrahite, whose view is sought directly by King Solomon, quickly formulates a compromise to satisfy all parties. He attempts to flatter his hearers into acceptance, and his syco-phancy is humorous on two counts: first, as linguistic parody of the language of the Authorised Version; and second, because we know what he, as a would-be independent his-torian, really thinks:

I began by saying that I was most grateful to the mighty lords on the Commission, because they had put the problem so neatly and spoken on it so sagaciously. On the basis of their debate, I said, I had listed the various possibilities of dealing with undesirable matter: (a) tell it all, (b) tell it with discretion, (c) don't tell it. To tell it all (possibility a) was obviously unwise; people were quick to draw the wrong conclusions from facts and to form wrong opinions of persons whom we wished to be highly regarded. Not to tell it (possibility c) was equally unwise; things had a way of being noised about and people always picked up what they were not supposed to know. This left us with possibility (b): tell it with discretion. Discretion, I said, was not the same as lying; surely the Wisest of Kings, Solomon, would never condone lying in a history of his father King David. Discretion was truth controlled by wisdom. (p. 84)

Ethan here emphasises the importance of seeing in context. 'Wisdom' effectively represents present concerns and stan-dards, while 'truth' represents the past. The result is that the interpretation of the past is always dependent on the consider-ations of the present. Taken out of context, these words provide a plausible justification for actually rewriting the past, the

logical outcome of which is the *reductio ad absurdum* we find in
Winston Smith's rewriting of *The Times* in *Nineteen Eighty-Four*.
But Ethan's elegant defence of the half-truth is undercut by
what he really thinks and what this policy degenerates into.
The irony of speeches such as this makes us realise that the
history of King David, as desirable in the eyes of King
Solomon, will rest upon gross distortion of the 'truth' and that
it will be controlled by a selfish political expediency rather
than by wisdom.

Such cynical observations are virtually all reinforced by
Heym's consistently light-hearted use of language. The novel is
certainly his wittiest. As in *The Queen*, he adapts his style
ingeniously to that of a former age, and much of our enjoyment
derives from the euphemisms, understatement, and periphra-
sis, from the regular tension between statement and implication. Unlike that of the earlier work, though, this writing is
parodic rather than spoof. Occasionally modern vocabulary
and modern concepts stand out from the otherwise meticulously chosen biblical phraseology and the divine attitudes, and
Heym takes regular pleasure in destroying the illusion of biblical dignity. When, for example, we are being told the story of
David and Goliath, we hear what King Saul has promised to
any man who can kill the giant: riches, his own daughter, and,
at the top of the list, a tax-free house! Money, in fact, motivates
so many of the Israelites. Ethan is much concerned about his
pay and conditions when he takes on the role as editor of the
'report'. He hints to Solomon that he would like his sons to be
educated free of charge, in addition to his being paid the wage
of a minor prophet, and he later curses himself for not having
asked for travelling expenses. Heym revels in pseudo-biblical
euphemisms, such as his invention 'May God do unto me such
and such, if it isn't . . .', and its intensive form: 'May God do
unto my such and such and more also, if it isn't . . .'. And he
exploits, for its openly cruder value, the (biblical) concept of
those who 'pisseth against the wall'. One of his neatest formulations is the repeated devaluation of the great report's title.
Even the grandest in Solomon's entourage are prepared to
refer to it as 'The Report on the Amazing Rise and so forth'.

This truncated form suggests the speakers' dismissive views of its fundamental purpose.

It is obvious that the concept of 'truth' which is put forward by Solomon's priests and prophets – and in particular their way of justifying its uses – bears a close similarity to that which has been promulgated by a number of political movements, and in particular by twentieth-century Communism. It is equally obvious that the problems of the Old Testament historian are, by analogy, also those of an historian in contemporary Communist society. What may be less obvious is that the problems of that historian are those of the intellectual *in general* in a totalitarian state. In such a society an alternative point of view is denied all those active in the humanities and political sciences, and Ethan the Ezrahite is sufficiently clearly an intellectual for him to have representative function. His position contrasts markedly with that of orthodox intellectuals, for their activities are considerably easier. For them, adherence to the word of Lord Jahweh/the doctrines of modern Communism does not carry with it any dangers, and it is likely to carry rich rewards. Those who can reconcile dogma with history have always prospered. Thus Ethan himself can envisage grand opportunities on his first visit to Solomon's court, opportunities still available to those in the totalitarian state: 'I ... saw that I might end, as some writers did, with my head cut off and my body nailed to the city wall, but that, on the other hand, I might wax fat and prosperous if I guarded my tongue and used my stylus wisely' (p. 11). (Ethan designates himself by his other profession here ('writer'), thus widening the relevance of his observations at an early stage of the novel.) However, his 'weakness for truth', his strong intellectual curiosity, and, just as significant, the desire of the participants to ensure he really does learn what took place, prevent him from conforming to the wishes of his masters. He cannot hope to convey his findings directly, and so he has to resort to subterfuge in order to alert his readers to a different way of viewing the evidence. He hopes for a 'word here and a line there by which later generations would perceive what really came to pass' (p. 11), 'a dim signal to generations to come' (p. 239). Heym is suggesting that it is precisely this intention which is the source of certain failings of the Old Testament. Some inconsistencies are actually deliberate: a provocation to read between the lines.

Given the firm paralleling of political backgrounds (ancient Israel/modern totalitarianism) as well as that of the two writers (Ethan/Heym), we would expect the twentieth-century figure to see in the fate of his forbear an adumbration of his own. In this respect Heym seemingly inverts the optimistic situation he had portrayed in *The Queen* ... When Ethan's subversive aims are discovered, he is hauled before King Solomon. The penalty for crimes such as these is usually death, but the execution of such a well-known figure might lead to embarrassing speculation among the masses. Solomon therefore adopts a novel solution and sentences him to be 'silenced to death'. Nothing he says or writes is to be made available to the people. Ethan has thus achieved his modest aim at considerable cost and his sentence has a parallel with the fates of dissident historians in the modern world. In the case of the Soviet Union under Stalin, for example, only minimal deviation was tolerated, and historians and writers remained unpublished, were imprisoned and sometimes even executed for failure to observe certain requirements. Even in the eighties, scope for dissent was highly restricted in certain areas, though the accession of Gorbachev marked the beginning of a proper end to ideological pressure. True, at the time *The King David Report* was being written, writers were no longer being executed for failure to accept the tenets of Marxism–Leninim; but they were certainly being harassed and denied publishing outlets for refusing to do so. This is where the fate of Ethan, anachronism that it clearly is, fits so neatly into the allegorical framework. It also reflects the situation of Heym himself at the point of writing. As far as he could tell, he could at any moment be silenced to death far more effectively than simply denying him the opportunity to publish in his own land. This is what makes the composition of *The King David Report* such an important act of literary bravery.

I have, of course, just been dealing with the pessimistic

conclusions of the novel, but I think it is important to emphasise that they find their counterbalance elsewhere. First, in the image of the final sentence, which may be seen to relativise much that has gone before. As the historian leaves the town which has brought him sorrow and disgrace, he turns to condemn it:

When we had crossed the brook Kidron and climbed the crest beyond, I stopped for a last look at the city of David. And I saw it lying there upon its hills, and I wanted to curse it; but I could not do it, for a great splendour of the Lord lay over Jerusholayim in the light of the morning.

It is surely significant that the succession of humiliations which the writer has been forced to undergo, and the perversions of the truth which he has been forced to witness, are nevertheless firmly challenged by the symbolic brightness with which the author chooses to conclude. By this strategic emphasis on Ethan's recognition of the glory of his God, Heym offers a symbol of hope for the Communist cause also. Whatever perversions of his message Jahweh's representatives on earth have brought about, Jahweh himself remains a glorious ideal. The true spirit of Marx likewise lives on, despite the failings of his successors.

Equally important a consideration is the fact this novel was published at all. At the time of writing, Heym was effectively condemned to 'silence' in his own country, and it was only by adopting a method similar to Ethan's that he might hope to be able to reach print if there were to be another political 'thaw'. To Heym's delight, the easing of restrictions came shortly after completion of the novel, and by 1973 a small edition of *Der König-David-Bericht* had indeed been published in East Berlin. Heym's oblique method of criticism had thus borne fruit, and the novel was even featured briefly in the official East German *Geschichte der deutschen Literatur*. It was designated 'ein Gleichnis raffinierter Herrschaftsmethoden' ('an allegory of cunning exercise of power'), and the entry tactfully concluded: 'Durch die starke Verallgemeinerung bleibt das Gleichnis sehr abstrakt' ('Through the strong generalising method the allegory remains very abstract') (vol. 11, p. 607).

A final positive implication of this book is that the historian –

and the writer in general – wields a power which is feared even by despots. The socialist countries in general long regarded literature as an important ideological weapon, and the mixture of respect and unease shown towards Ethan (and Defoe) is an acknowledgment of his power to shape the views of posterity. As he did in *The Queen*, Heym is reminding the reader of the heavy burden carried by the writer, and he was doubtless encouraging himself further to use his own power wisely.

Heym had not written a bestseller for many years, but the publication of *King David* proved a turning point; every succeeding novel was to generate considerable sales. The impetus here came from a good marketing campaign by his new publisher, Kindler, and from the warmth of the first reviews. In the UK, for example, *The Times*, *The Sunday Times*, and *The Guardian* were all rich in their praise,[17] and the novel was in due course reprinted several times. In West Germany, Marcel Reich-Ranicki was, by his standards, warm: Günter Zehm was ecstatic; but the most influential review was probably that of Heinrich Böll in *Der Spiegel*.[18] Böll provided a particularly rich comment which the publishers were to exploit fully: 'Man möchte aus diesem Buch pausenlos zitieren. Stefan Heym ist durch die Nähte geschlüpft, die der offizielle David-Text hat; mit Phantasie, Witz und Frechheit ...' ('The reader is tempted to quote from this book without a break. Stefan Heym has slipped through the seams of the official story of King David; with imagination, wit and impudence ...'). From this point onwards *Der Spiegel* devoted far more attention to Heym, his difficult political position, and his writing. And it also provided him with an outlet for some of his most urgent pleas at particularly difficult points of GDR history.

The early seventies brought another source of strength: in 1971 Heym had remarried. The career of his new wife matched that of his first: Inge had been engaged in the film industry (in this case the state company DEFA). Beautiful, sensitive, and quietly efficient, she provided an external stimulus to Heym's way of thinking and provided companionship and firm support at times of stress. Heym was therefore well prepared for the troubles which the new decade was to bring.

CHAPTER 8

Centre of controversy again: Honecker's first period

A change of leadership in the socialist countries rarely used to signify a sudden change in political direction. In order to be even considered a suitable candidate for the highest party office, it was necessary to have been a conforming member of the ruling elite for some considerable time and to have won promotion within it through clear devotion to the cause.[1] Erich Honecker's rise to the position of First Secretary of the Central Committee was achieved through precisely this sort of career. He had been a 'Young Pioneer' in the Communist Party when he was ten, Secretary of the Communist Youth for the Saar as early as 1931, had spent ten years in jail under the Nazis (1935–45), and had been a full member of the Politbüro since 1958. Throughout his life he had been a firm supporter of Moscow. As the man entrusted with state security in 1961, he had carried responsibility for the building of the Berlin Wall. His most noteworthy act in cultural politics had been his condemnation of Heym and other writers at the Eleventh Session of the Central Committee in 1965.

The general sense of satisfaction among the GDR populace at the appointment of Honecker was more a sense of relief at the demise of the inflexible and aging Ulbricht, who had held control in the Soviet Zone/GDR for more than twenty-five years. The latter had incurred public Soviet displeasure over his unease at closer relations with West Germany, but failing health made his 'request' to be relieved of his post quite credible. By comparison with many other eastern bloc rulers, and especially his successors in the GDR, his departure was honourable. Honecker was fortunate to take over at an

163

auspicious period of GDR history. He came to power just before the eighth *Parteitag* of the SED in June 1971, as East–West détente between the superpowers was already well advanced. There was a Four-Power Berlin agreement in September of that year, which allowed, among other things, West Berliners to visit the GDR (a considerable number of them had relatives there). The spirit of this agreement was mutual co-operation between the two Germanies, and it led, a year later, to the rescinding of a crucial law on visits to the GDR by former citizens. (Hitherto anyone who had left the GDR illegally faced prosecution on their return.) Very many more in the East were thus able to benefit from western visits and all the tangible benefits which they brought. Most important, however, was the Basic Treaty between the Democratic and Federal Republics of 21 December 1972, which not only provided for co-operation between the two states on various commercial, scientific and cultural matters, but also for them to respect each other's independence in both internal and external affairs. The GDR, in other words, had at last gained its long-sought goal of political recognition by its western neighbour, and the Federal Republic took the inevitable further step of rescinding the so-called 'Hallstein-Doctrine', that infamous ruling by Foreign Secretary Hallstein in the fifties, that the FRG would break off relations with any state which *did* recognise the GDR. To the delight of East German citizens, a flood of political recognitions now took place. Britain and France waited two months until February 1973, but the bulk of Europe had preceded them.

The removal of 'second-class' status was greeted with great satisfaction in the GDR, and there were other striking events in this period from which Honecker and his populace could derive special satisfaction: growing economic capacity, for example, which had ensured the GDR's achieving a position in COMECON second only to the USSR. In a completely different area, a law to legalise abortion was approved by Parliament in 1972, providing a desperately needed sense of security for many anxious women. And as a final example, in another totally unrelated area, one could cite the enormous sense of national pride which followed the Munich Olympics (1972). Sport, and especially athletics, had always been taken seriously in the country, and vast sums were spent not so much on the general public as on the selection and training of a sports elite. International competition became an area in which the GDR considered it could gain the recognition which was being denied in the political arena, and in this respect it was phenomenally successful. In the Mexico Olympics in 1968 more Gold Medals had been won by the GDR than by the Federal Republic, but the great triumph came in Munich – that is, in a state which at that point did not officially recognise them. Here the GDR did not simply win more Gold, Silver, and Bronze medals than their hosts, but they actually won more Bronze medals than did the Soviet Union. This provided enormous pleasure for a populace which had deeply resented the role of the USSR in their affairs, and which still felt deep unease over Soviet military intervention in Czechoslovakia four years previously.

An excursus on the political background would seem slightly out of place in a study of most literary figures in the west; and one on the importance of national sport even more so. But the GDR success in these areas created a far more positive mood in the country, and one which influenced the leadership's attitude towards what might be tolerated – especially in the sphere of culture.

As suggested earlier, the socialist countries as a whole have a particularly high estimation of the role culture can play in the development of a society, and it was not long after his accession to power that Honecker made a surprisingly conciliatory statement on the arts. Although he employed standard clichés to confirm their importance to socialist development, stressed the value of socialist realism, and warned of the dangers surrounding imperialist culture, the tone he adopted was unexpected, His denunciation of the 'enemy' was less extreme than usual, and he revealed a sense of understanding for the difficulties in the arts. His most important remark was that artists needed new forms of expression for their depiction of the present age, and that the party recognised their difficulties in the search for these. His comment seemed tantamount to encouragement of experiment: 'Gerade weil wir um die Mühen, um die Kompliziertheit der künstlerischen Schaffensprozesse wissen, bringen wir der schöpferischen Suche nach neuen Formen volles Verständnis entgegen'[2] ('Precisely because we are aware of the difficulties, the complexity of the processes of artistic creation, we are fully sympathetic towards the creative artists' search for new forms'). Some six months later, in December 1971, came the statement which had since been quoted in practically every survey of GDR literature in the seventies:

Wenn man von der festen Position des Sozialismus ausgeht, kann es meines Erachtens auf dem Gebiet von Kunst und Literatur keine Tabus geben. Das betrifft sowohl die Fragen der inhaltlichen Gestaltung als auch des Stils – kurz gesagt: die Fragen dessen, was man die künstlerische Meisterschaft nennt.[3]

Providing one sets out from the firm position of socialism, then in my opinion there can be no taboos in the field of art and literature. That applies both to questions of presentation of content and to style – in short: the questions of what are referred to as 'artistic mastery'.

Honecker claimed that this was a view which had emerged naturally after the Eighth Conference, yet the choice of the concept 'taboos' was entirely his own. In selecting so unambiguous a word, and one which Heym himself had often used, he was conceding that certain subjects had indeed been regarded as untouchable. And in the second part of his statement, which is often overlooked, he was suggesting that there need no longer be any means of composition which was inappropriate for an East German writer – provided, of course, the writer's basic viewpoint was that of socialism. Honecker could not have forseen the consequences of these words, which were born of a new optimism in the country and which in certain respects gave official endorsement to what figures like Heym and Christa Wolf had already achieved in the late sixties. The 'thaw' which was to follow was at its greatest for the following two years. Thereafter some of the former problems began to return, and an abrupt, but foreseeable end to liberalism was signalled by the exile of Wolf Biermann in November 1976.

A principal beneficiary of the new mood was Stefan Heym. His East German publishers, who must likewise have feared an early end to the Honecker honeymoon, co-operated to the full (they had not been allowed to publish anything since the two fairy tales of 1966). In 1972, then, *Lenz* was reprinted (in a slightly revised translation by the author); in that year too 'Die richtige Einstellung' appeared in the journal *Sinn und Form* (it had appeared in the West in 1967, and in the East only in English translation);[4] in 1973 *Der König-David-Bericht* appeared; and early in 1974 *Lassalle* and *Die Schmähschrift*. True, print runs were short, and the few reviews were not entirely complimentary. The metaphorical implications for the GDR of *Die Schmähschrift* and *König David* were ignored, and the latter was viewed as an attack on feudal and capitalist societies only. But the books *were* published, and among the GDR's avid reading populace each copy would find far more than a single reader. The same held true for the other major works of fiction of these years, such as Günter de Bruyn's *Preisverleihung* (1972), Ulrich Plenzdorf's *Die neuen Leiden des jungen W.* (1973), Irmtraud Morgner's *Leben und Abenteuer des Trobadora Beatriz* (1974), and Volker Braun's *Unvollendete Geschichte* (1975). Honecker's first years were certainly among the richest in GDR literature.

The manuscript of *King David* was being completed as this hopeful climate was breaking, and so Heym could now return, with greater expectations, to *A Day Marked X*. The revision, deletions, additions, and stylistic improvements were undertaken with the usual scrupulous care, and in 1973 Heym set about finding a publisher for the new version, *Five Days in June*. In the East the Verlag Neues Leben was pleased to sign a contract, although it was one to which they would fail to adhere. In the West, Heym's obvious choice was the Kindler Verlag, with whom he had hitherto been well satisfied. Their decision to reject the manuscript was presumably made on political grounds, despite their denial, but it cost them dearly in missed royalties and the loss of all Heym's later bestsellers. The Bertelsmann Verlag, by contrast, warmly welcomed the manuscript, invested in a fine marketing campaign, and reaped handsome profits. The author retained their services for every succeeding book.

The contents of *Five Days* have been discussed above in connection with *Der Tag X* (see pp. 93–102). What needs to be noted at this point is that the novel enjoyed immense success in the West, was reviewed very widely, and generated as much reflection on political issues as it did on literary values.[5] Several aspects of such a reception were embarrassing to the GDR cultural functionaries. First, that the party's mistakes were being highlighted not by an embittered exile or a hostile western critic, but by someone who wished socialism proper to succeed; second, that the novel became an instant bestseller and received such extensive coverage in the press of all political inclinations (in the GDR publicity and print run would have been minimal); and third, a book which had been denied publication since the late fifties could still not appear in its own country. There were limits to openness in the East, and they were reached with *Five Days*. Although it would appear that the novel did come close to reaching print in the GDR, it was not finally published until after Honecker himself had lost power and signs of unification were emerging.

The eastern rejection of *5 Tage* probably marks a turning point in GDR literature more aptly than does the exile of Wolf Biermann in November 1976. The novel was published in October 1974, by which point the hopes of the earliest Honecker period were diminishing. Economic problems were growing, exacerbated by spiralling world energy costs which were completely outside the GDR's control. And the Politbüro must also have been distinctly uneasy about certain literary works which had appeared. Although their authors may have claimed to be socialists, the works themselves did not always appear to be written 'from the firm position of socialism'. Honecker had noted this in a speech of May 1973, although his unease did not yet have any noticeable effects on publishing policy.[6] By July 1974, though, Reiner Kunze was being offered the alternative of a comfortable existence if he conformed, or imprisonment in harsh conditions if he persisted in his individualism.[7]

The worst period for the government, though, was the autumn of 1976, and the first embarrassment arose in a very different area of society – the reluctantly tolerated church. In August, Pastor Brüsewitz committed suicide by publicly setting fire to himself in protest at GDR treatment of religion. The event drew wide international publicity, despite the GDR attempts to pass off the victim as mentally disturbed. In September Reiner Kunze published (in the West) his series of sketches, *Die wunderbaren Jahre*, a succession of sharp attacks on the GDR and its disturbing methods of implementing socialism. It produced a strong reaction in the West, and it led to Kunze's being deprived of his membership of the Writers' Union on 3 November. And then, on 16 November, Wolf Biermann was stripped of his GDR citizenship while on a short tour of the West. This was the first time he had been allowed to leave the country for very many years, and, indeed, the first time he had been allowed to perform at all (since the ban on public performance introduced by Honecker at the Eleventh Session in 1965); and although the grounds given to justify his expulsion were that he had made offensive remarks about his country while singing in Cologne, it would appear virtually certain that he was allowed out of the GDR simply in order to refuse him re-admission. The age of show trials had clearly passed, but what better way to remind all other writers of the party's powers and direct public attention to those who were failing the country by ridiculing it? In theory the plan must have seemed perfect; in practice it proved one of the most serious miscalculations ever made.

The public, and especially writers and artists, protested forcefully. The most serious attack came from a small group of the most prominent writers, who gathered at Stephan Hermlin's to discuss the best course of action. They quickly decided on a public statement which would be delivered to their own press offices in the first instance; but in order to put pressure on what they knew to be a totally government-controlled organisation, copies were also taken to the French press agency and to Reuters (by Stefan Heym) for release several hours later. The text was brief and balanced. It acknowledged Biermann's failings, but noted his talent, and it urged that the measures taken be reconsidered. To give it an ideological trust, it alluded to Marx's '18th Brumaire' and the importance of constant self-criticism. There was no response from the GDR leadership, despite the fact they must have learnt of it immediately. Western publications therefore went ahead, with international coverage. Eastern citizens learnt of the statement only through western television news.

Those first (twelve) signatories of the open letter had no idea of the vehemence of the attack on them which would follow from their government, nor did they have any idea of how many other writers, artists, and actors would rush to become co-signatories in the following days. Heym was independent and the strongest of all to resist pressure – which is possibly why he escaped unharmed. Gerhard Wolf (Christa Wolf's husband), by contrast, was excluded from the party immediately. His wife, together with several others, was removed from the executive of the Berlin Writers' Union. Jurek Becker protested forcefully at the treatment of Gerhard Wolf, and he himself then lost party membership. In the meanwhile, the poet Jürgen Fuchs was arrested and so too were two young critical song writers, Christian Kunert and Gerulf Pannach. Robert Havemann was put under house arrest.

The aim of pressures of this sort was initially to encourage all signatories of the letter to withdraw their support. Volker Braun did in fact, do so, but then he courageously decided to withdraw his withdrawal! That was a promising sign for GDR dissenters, and in spite of the undisguised anger of the GDR leadership – and the distinct likelihood of reprisals – over a hundred other figures added their names to the statement over the following weeks.[8] Many of these were to leave the Republic in the course of the next few years, together with numerous other prominent figures. Among writers, the following period saw the departure of Günter Kunert, Sarah Kirsch, Reiner Kunze, Jurek Becker, Thomas Brasch, Erich Loest, Karl-Heinz Jakobs, Bernd Jentzsch, Rolf Schneider; actors and actresses like Katharina Thalbach, Manfred Krug, Angelica Domröse. Composers like Tilo Medek. Biermann's expulsion, and the permission granted to so many others to follow him to the West, proved that the leadership preferred to see troublesome figures on the other side of the border, whatever the loss in cultural terms.

Heym decided to cancel all trips outside the Republic in the immediate aftermath of the Biermann affair for fear he too might be denied a return. Inside the Republic itself he spoke in his normal frank manner. On 31 March 1977, at the meeting of the Berlin Section of the Writers' Union which formally discussed Biermann's exile, he sharply criticised the Party's main representative, Konrad Naumann (a member of the Politbüro). He neatly rejected Naumann's angrily expressed view that only the party was fit to judge its own actions, and he warned that the policy of exiling writers represented a shelving rather than a solving of the problems which the Republic faced. He concluded, amid a noisy mixture of opposition and support, that the only way forward was open and honest exchange of opinions (*Wege und Umwege*, pp. 428–32). For all the fervour of his speech, Heym cannot have had high expectations of any real change in party policy. On the contrary, he, like others, feared the reintroduction of much harsher censorship. In this respect they were pleasantly surprised. Writers had been composing in a more adventurous spirit over the last few years, and a number of manuscripts were reaching the point of completion. If the worst fate was now only exile, then risks were worth taking. And equally surprisingly, publishers were prepared to comply. Although attempts were still made to encourage writers to change, adapt, modify, if those writers were prepared to fight and to negotiate compromises on what needed change, the resultant volumes were able to maintain the liberal trend established since 1972. The prime example here is probably Erich Loest's *Es geht seinen Gang*, for which a contract had been signed with the Mitteldeutscher Verlag in 1974, that is, when the thaw was still apparently in full flood. By the time the novel was completed, however, circumstances had changed and the publishers demanded numerous, and major, alterations in the work. Even more were demanded after the Biermann affair. But Loest persevered, and after a succession of battles with the publishers (and, of course, with those in the Ministry of Culture who stood behind them but who remained unseen) the book finally appeared. The first printing was sold out immediately, and although a second was promised, Loest was then informed this had been prohibited. It was a clear sign of the changed times that Loest decided to fight against this and that he finally won the concession that a second, small, printing would appear with another publisher (an obscure one). Like Heym with *Der Tag X*, Loest was actually paid by the Mitteldeutscher Verlag for an edition which they did not bring out! Heym had shown that fighting could produce results, and Loest may well have been influenced by his example. His experiences here he turned into a book about the novel, *Der vierte Zensor*, which he published in the West after he left the GDR in 1981. But not all writers had the courage or the perseverance of Loest and Heym. Only those who were prepared to take such risks were rewarded. This rarely included the young.

There were two important reasons why Heym chose to remain in the GDR, apart from the obvious one that he preferred a full sense of challenge. The first was that this was the country in which he felt a duty to his readership, as well as a sense of communion with them; the second was that he still hoped a proper form of socialism might develop there. His hopes here are well reflected in two articles he wrote for the *New York Times* before the Biermann affair. Both 'The tender little buds of East Germany' (1973) and 'Letter from East Germany' (1975) acknowledge failings in the country, but find sufficient evidence of progress to look forward far more positively than he had ever done before. In one sense, though, Heym's assessment of the political and cultural situations was irrelevant to what he decided to write: he wrote what he wished, refused to be intimidated by the authorities, continued to ridicule their ludicrous media language,[9] and actually made some aspect of their behaviour a subject in every major work of this period. The next grand undertaking was no exception, and it was one which once again was to lead to public vilification, stripping of rights, prosecution, and even the introduction of a new law to the penal code.

The seventies revealed an increasing number of authors choosing to depict writers and their problems.[10] Heym had begun with *King David*, and the germ of *Collin* is to be found in 'Der Gleichgültige', a short story which contains a suggestion on its opening page that the date of composition was 1973 – shortly before work on the novel itself must have begun. The plot of the shorter work bears certain superficial similarities to that of the longer, but it is in their themes that the two reveal their closest point of contact: both are concerned with the attempts of a successful socialist writer to suppress disturbing aspects of the past.

In 'Der Gleichgültige', a famous novelist has been publishing his memoirs, chapter by chapter, and has just dealt with an awkward 'show trial' of 1949. This was an occasion for which he was actually asked by the leader of the country himself to provide an eye-witness account, but the writer's principal memory is of others' reports only: he fell ill just before the trial began, and was thus able to stay in the comfort and security of his bed. In retrospect he is even more grateful for the sudden illness, for in the de-Stalinsation year of 1956 it transpired that the trial had been staged, the accusations prefabricated.

This cosy view of the writer's lack of involvement in the affair is given a nasty jolt shortly after this chapter of his memoirs appears: the editor of a former second-rate journal is able to confound him by producing an old manuscript which proves the author did indeed attend the trial and actually wrote a report on it. This had been turned down by the major organ of the day, as also by the second-rate journal (which feared to publish what the leading party journal had avoided). The reason for the non-publication is clear only now, at such a distance from the events. The author had concluded his article with a sense of disbelief at the defendant's 'indifference' – his gross acts of treachery had not, it seemed, been conducted out of a sense of hatred of Communism (which might have made them understandable). This insight by the novelist – albeit an unwitting one – clearly touched on the sham of the whole trial and made his article unacceptable.

There are a number of key points made in this short, but carefully constructed and thematically barbed story. First, the fact that the novelist was absolutely convinced that he had not attended the trial at all. The strength of his mind to blot out the past was total. Second, unexpected aspects of the records had been preserved. As was pointed out in connection with *The King David Report*, the Achilles' heel of totalitarian states is that records are kept and that if they are falsified, someone will know about the falsification. Finally, and perhaps most troublingly, the chapter of the novelists' memoirs which deals with the trial (which Heym playfully gives the title 'Chapter 13') will not be corrected, even though it is inaccurate. It has now appeared as the official version, and the publisher is not willing to see it altered.

This uneasy, false relationship with the past is responsible for the condition which precipitates the events of Heym's next novel. The writer Hans Collin has had a distinguished career in the GDR, but his fame extends back as far as his first novel about the Spanish Civil War. During his period in the International Brigade, his company commander, a certain Georg Havelka, had had him sent back from the front line precisely because he was a writer and should therefore be preserved in order to record for posterity what he had witnessed. Collin does survive, is an exile in Mexico, and returns to the GDR after the war. He is a conformist, and eventually becomes a classic of socialist literature in his own lifetime. But, in his sixties, he feels dissatisfied with what he has done, and on the prompting of his friend the critic Theodor Pollock, he decides to write his memoirs. The attempt to do so has unfortunate consequences: circulatory problems lead to hospitalisation, and it is uncertain whether his condition is actually physical or psychosomatic. The director of the exclusive clinic to which he has been taken is convinced that Collin 'needs' his illness, that it is an excuse for not facing his past. Probing the depths of this writer's unconscious would be dangerous, he feels, for full recognition of his situation might be worse then a simple physical illness.

The physician therefore advises his junior doctor to 'let sleeping dogs lie', advice which is ignored. The young and idealistic Dr Christine Roth encourages Collin to face up to the ghosts in his past. She succeeds in getting him to recognise a major part of his creative block lies in his failure to intercede on behalf of his former commander in Spain, an act which could possibly have helped the innocent man avoid a six-year prison sentence. Collin is transformed by this insight into past failure, but it leads only to exaggerated hopes. He discharges himself from hospital, claims he will now write without any taboos, and begins to work further on his memoirs. Before long, however, he has died of circulatory problems.

Collin's condition is initially shrouded in a certain mystery. Is it 'genuine'? Is it the product of his imagination (but physically threatening nonetheless)? Is it, consequently, in some way symbolic, given that Collin himself symbolises a certain type of socialist writer? The uncertain nature of the illness raises doubts about the appropriate treatment. If it is indeed psychological in origin, might the cure be worse than the condition? In other words, might the necessity to face the past be even more enervating than enduring the disease? Indeed, could it lead to premature death? There is a final issue surrounding the psychological factor, and this lies in an unexpected area – throughout the novel there are references to voodoo and the methods used by primitive tribes to exorcise illness. At one stage it does in fact seem that voodoo practices reflect certain aspects of Collin's problems. We are led to expect, therefore, that the final resolution may well relate to ancient remedies, and we are encouraged to speculate on what that resolution might be. These three strands – the exact nature of the illness, whether disease is preferable to cure, and the implications of primeval customs – are neatly interwoven in the novel, with now one, now the other being brought to our attention.

Collin is instinctively attracted by voodoo ideas, which are first raised in a formal medical context: Christine Roth reflects silently on the aura which surrounds her chief, Gerlinger, and recalls that thousands of years ago the shamans had performed

with almost equally good results (pp. 10/11). Faith in the
healer is what counts in the case of an illness which is primarily
psychological, and Christine secretly wishes to see herself as
successful in this domain. Her unease with her son's troubled
imagination leads us to wonder, however, whether she can be
wholly successful with the far more complex Collin.

For Urack, chief of the secret police and a fellow inmate in
the hospital, there is a different attraction in the beliefs of these
tribes: the idea that you can rid yourself of an illness by passing
it on to another (a 'scapegoat'). This takes firm hold in his
otherwise logical and calculating mind, culminating in the
view that his survival is dependent on the death of Collin (an
idea with which he can easily infect the highly suggestible
writer).

Collin himself is gripped by two different aspects of primitive
thinking. First, he is frightened by the notion that an illness
could be passed on to him; yet when he leaves hospital he is
confident that he has in fact transmitted it to Urack (whose
sudden deterioration has been marked). Second, Collin is also
aware of death following a different type of voodoo: the driving
out from the tribe of someone who has broken its laws. Once
outside the tribe, the victim cannot survive. Now when Collin
leaves hospital, this is precisely the course on which he is set: he
is intent on writing all he knows, exposing the past failings and
crimes of the tribe, and thus, as he inwardly recognises, banish-
ing himself from it. There is a further disturbing aspect to
publishing memoirs, and this surfaces only once in Collin's
mind. On his journey home, Collin briefly reflects that it might
not be his usual public in the East, but certain sensationalist
publishers in the West who would be waiting for his manuscript, a realisation which produces a sudden and clearly
symbolic pain in his heart. This is the first of several adumbra-
tive touches in the final chapter.

That chapter is generally impressive for its understatement.
In the guise of simple narrative and conversation, Heym draws
together all the main issues which have previously been raised.
He relies, of course, on the reader's having grasped the essence
of Collin's dilemma earlier in the novel, despite the fact it is a

dilemma which is formulated fully on one occasion – in the middle of the work. Only at this point does Collin state boldly the two alternatives with which he is faced: either to exclude himself 'from the ranks of those with whom I've been sticking together my whole life and who, all things considered, have been taking care of me quite nicely', or to continue with 'the self-imposed curbs, the sterility, the hollow glory' (p. 131). The critic Pollock puts the conflict in more pithy terms: 'the conflict between his fear of the voodoo death on the one hand and his struggle against being coerced into a permanent castration of his intellectual self, on the other' (p. 133). The dichotomy does not reappear in such sharp form. Although the voodoo references continue, Collin never again gives expression to his self-doubt, that of the impotent party hack. But this single remark suffices to make us aware of another dimension to his initial illness, and, more importantly, of the irresolvable nature of his mental and physical predicament.

Despite the gloomy prognosis for Collin, Heym plays with our expectations by showing us Urack's sudden deterioration. Following the voodoo symbolism, we expect Collin to thrive, and this he gleefully does. The corollary, however, is that Collin will suffer if Urack recovers, and news of the latter's vigorous progress has the expected detrimental effect. Shortly afterwards, as the symbolism leads us to predict, Collin falls victim to an attack similar to his first one.

Collin was only the second of Heym's published novels to be set in the GDR. It develops the theme of 'Der Gleichgültige' with regard to memory, repression, and health, and it provides a fuller study of the 'show trial'. Here it is not only the point of view of the victim which is portrayed – in one of the most dramatic sections of the novel – but also the viewpoint of the writer who had to witness it, and, intriguingly, the secret police chief who organised it. This sensitive, and sometimes painful, study of the predicament of the socialist writer covers several periods of GDR history which are generally avoided and which raise fundamental questions about the morality under which the socialist state operated. It is Heym's most open statement on the secret agencies which try to ensure political conformity,

but it is quite unlike so many exposés of the Communist secret
police in that it actually allows them to provide a partial
defence of their aims. For although there is a revolting depiction of the degrading and inhumane torture to which certain
characters are subjected, the figure who is largely responsible
for such activities is given a prominent, and sometimes sympathetic role in the novel. Urack, head of the secret police,
unswerving and indefatigable socialist, finds himself in the
same hospital as Collin. The latter's illness, although psychological in origin, has developed physical symptoms. Urack's,
by contrast, is physical in origin, but he develops psychological
problems. Some of these may actually relate to his recognition
of injustice in earlier stages of the Republic's history, and
although he has no difficulty in justifying these in argument,
his mental disturbances suggest that they may nevertheless
weigh on his conscience.

Urack is not presented as an evil man, even though some of
the activities which he has sanctioned are depicted as evil. His
defence is the classical one: that everything was done for the
sake of a great ideal, the progress towards socialist utopia. In
this respect he rejects as naive Collin's view of life: 'What does a
fellow like Collin know of the causes, and how one thing grows
out of another, and who did what with whom and for what
purpose' (p. 44). This phraseology is important for Urack, who
repeats it in arguing with his wife over what he considers that
equally naive views of his grandson: 'an injustice is an injustice
not in every case, because everything depends on who does
what and for which purpose' (p. 99). Urack's philosophy has a
perfect pedigree, as Peter Graves has pointed out in his careful
study of the individual's relation to the state in this novel.[11]
Urack is not advancing anything which is not to be found in
Marx, Engels, and Lenin, and yet he is in a grey area of
government morality, that in which the methods employed
might be seen to run counter to the ideal which is being sought.
Graves selects an East German edition of a Soviet work on
Marxist–Leninist ethics in order to make this point: 'Das Ziel
rechtfertigt nicht einfach ein beliebiges Mittel ... wählt man
Mittel, die dem Ziel nicht entsprechen, führt das zu einem

unerwünschten Resultat und entstellt dadurch die Natur des Zieles'[12] ('The end does not justify the introduction of any possible means whatsoever . . . If means are adopted which are not commensurate with the end, an undesirable result is achieved and the nature of that end is consequently corrupted'). This is essentially a post-Stalinist view, and its basic humanitarian stance is not one with which Urack can at any point be associated. He reveals no regrets over the past; he accepts that injustices will occur; and he gladly tolerates them. Yet Urack's confidence is undercut by the fact that his methods have completely failed to change the world in the way initially expected, by the methods his organisation needs to adopt, and by his own grandson's defection to the West. He is seen as a partial anachronism in a state which has developed far beyond the high Stalinist era of the fifties. The notion that it mattered little if one eliminated one or two more than was necessary – if by that means one was ensuring the progress of socialism – has long been discredited. Power has been abused too often for us to trust those who wield it.

This novel, then, represents yet another encounter with Stalinism – as we have already seen in *Defoe*, *King David* and 'Der Gleichgültige', works which all feature trials where the defendant has been judged guilty even before he is brought before a judge. In *Collin* we see the two sides of Stalinist justice: the secret tribunal from which the public are excluded, and the show trial, which the public is encouraged to attend. Indeed, some of the public are virtually compelled to attend, largely so that they can recognise the danger which they would be in if they were to oppose the regime in any way. The condemnation in *Collin* is not only historical, however, for one of the arguments Heym was advancing is that Stalinism was not dead in the GDR. His attack had contemporary relevance.

The principal means of establishing parallels between past and present was not by any allegorical method, but by depicting well-known and readily recognisable individuals. More than any other novel by Heym, this one is a *roman à clef*. True, the central figure himself is not to be equated with any one particular writer – whatever identifiable mannerisms, personal

history and literary interests Heym has invested him with –
but there are numerous other figures in the novel whose brief
characterisation allows them to be seen as modelled on one
figure in real life only. Thus, for example, the references to
'Curd' as being a minister with thick glasses, as having an
adventurous past behind him, and being a poet who lectured
in a tone of ponderous pathos, point inescapably to Johannes
Becher. 'Weinreb', the urbane and distinguished poet, makes
reference to his days in the French resistance, clinching the
parallel with Stephan Hermlin. 'Pamela Piddelkoe', bony and
domineering mistress of the Republic's most strife-ridden
theatre company, can only be the Director of the Berliner
Ensemble, Brecht's widow, Helene Weigel. And the distinguished Hungarian philosopher and critic 'Keres', who briefly
becomes a minister, can only be Georg Lukács. The pathetic
Stalinist scapegoats, 'Faber' and 'Havelka' are also barely
disguised. The former has clear similarities with Paul Merker,
sometime Secretary of State in the Ministry of Land Economy,
who, like Faber, was actually made manager of a restaurant
before he was taken away and tried, partly as a 'Zionist
agent', in 1952. And the fate of Havelka is that of several
members of the so-called 'Harich-Gruppe' (principally Wolfgang Harich, Walter Janka, Manfred Hertwig, and Bernhard
Steinberger), who were prosecuted in grand show trials in
1957.[13] Various intellectuals were invited to be present at
these trials, including, interestingly, one of the doyens of
socialist realism, Anna Seghers. The latter did not speak out
on this occasion; she, and others, were obviously afraid to do
so for fear a comparable fate might befall them. As a result,
the state confirmed its control of intellectuals. Memory of the
unjustice to Harich, Janka, and the others, was to live on for a
considerable period.

In these figures, then, the novel operates mainly as a *roman à
clef*, and the central figure of this historical constellation is not
Collin (who is symbolic rather than individual), but Urack,
Minister of State Security.[14] Comparatively little detective
work is necessary here, where Heym seems to take pleasure in
actually stressing rather than simply hinting at the parallels.
Urack's career openly reflects that of Erich Mielke, with not

only underground activities, the Spanish International Brigade, internment in France, and exile in the Soviet Union, but also work throughout his period in the GDR with the secret police. What is most striking about these careers, however, is that the secret police is being controlled in the 1970s by the same man who controlled it at the height of Stalinism in the fifties. The fear that continuity is assured after Urack's ultimate retirement is evident in the way Urack's probable successor, Bergmann, does not differ substantially from his superior, yet the most troubling indictment of the ministry as a whole comes largely through an aside. When Urack, not quite mentally stable following the defection of his grandson, escapes from the hospital and returns to his ministry in order to attend the weekly staff meeting, he tirades against the pusillanimous attitude which his department has taken in the past and demands more radical measures. As it is reported to Theodor Pollock by Bergmann:

the mistake had not been that a number of people had been wrongly arrested, wrongly accused, and wrongly sentenced; how could anything have been wrong that was done in the interest of the dictatorship of the proletariat? Our mistake consisted in our constant back tracking, our constant concessions – to the intellectuals, to the church, to the youth, to the masses hungry for consumption, to the West. Wherever you turned in this country you were confronted with a sullen, barely hidden discontent. Despite our vast collection of questionnaires and reports, despite our system of files that encompassed everybody and that were evaluated and ready to be fed into the nearest computer, we had failed to put the necessary fear into people and often enough had allowed them to make damned fools of us. (p. 234)

Urack's words could be dismissed as the ravings of a temporarily disturbed mind, but they echo earlier comments on the need for firm control. And the really troubling aspect to his savage exposé is the report of Bergmann that 'they surely fell on sympathetic ears' (p. 234). The desire to rule by terror is, then, still firmly part of the system.

Heym does not spare us the horrors of Stalinist imprisonment, torture, interrogation, and show trial. In the persecuted figures of Faber and Havelka – both innocent of the charges of which they are accused – we see the lengths to which the secret police will go in order to extract confessions of the most ludicrous kind. Their need for such confessions is simple: mistakes and failures in party policy must never be blamed on the party itself – a scapegoat must be found. It is simply the misfortune of Faber and Havelka that they happened to be the obvious sacrificial objects at the time. Urack actually expresses anger that Faber in particular refused to recognise the necessity for his prosecution. Faber, after all, knew the system and the importance of submitting to it.

Urack's discussion of Faber's predicament raises another vexed question of Communist societies. Urack claims that if he had been in Faber's position, then he would probably have acted in much the same way. Yet his fundamental point is that he would never have found himself in Faber's position: his character was totally different, and to Urack's mind, one's character determines one's destiny. Heym's underlying question here is one raised in *Lassalle*. Is it the Communist system which creates characters like Urack, with his rigid view that 'immoral' actions are justified by the higher morality of the state (suggestively expressed as a 'relativisation' of Kant's categorical imperative, that what is good for the party is good)? Or is it rather that characters like Urack create such a system?

Whatever the answer, the effect is seen to be disastrous for individuals and for society as a whole. Collin makes his own accusation as he learns that Urack's grandson has defected to the West: 'Why all the trouble you took over Faber, and over the many others, if the sons turn their backs on us?' (pp. 219/20). In 1989, when Hungary threw open its border to the West and allowed a mass exodus of East Germans, Heym was making precisely the same point on West German television.

The critical reactions to *Collin* were mixed. Jürgen Serke hailed the volume as 'politisch abgewogen und ästhetisch gelungen' ('politically balanced and aesthetically successful'),[15] whereas Wolf Biermann expressed concern over the language, which he considered neither 'East' nor 'West' German, and lacking in character.[16] Certainly, some of the dialogues lack a natural flow, and there is perhaps too much interior monologue designed to guide us in our interpretation. This could be seen as emphasis on the communication of ideas at the expense of realism, but such a weakness is off-set by the constant variation in point of view, by Heym's ability to create suspense, and by sections of truly dramatic narrative. It is perhaps significant that all events recalled from the past are written with vigour.

The plot itself is well and tautly structured, with the author drawing together characters with a common history in their pre-war years, but whose development in the GDR has been highly dissimilar. All these old campaigners are meticulously drawn, with particular care to physical gesture and personal idiosyncrasy. The only blemish here is in the means Heym uses to establish the present relationship between these figures, which relies to a certain extent on coincidental contacts, largely through the figure of Christine Roth. Christine is the only one of the characters to lack full credibility, possibly as a result of her having to play too many roles: as physician to two of the central characters, but also as confidante of the one and lover of the other's grandson; as confidante of the third central character of the novel (Pollock), as well as object of his repressed affections; as amateur psychiatrist; as mother; as wife. Christine is usually dominated by those whom she is in contact. She thus rarely emerges as an independent figure.

Some critics were unfavourable in their response to the novel. Heym's view of his own work was that it represented 'Unterhaltungsliteratur' and that a fundamental part of his purpose as a writer was actually to *entertain* his readers. For a number of years, however, various hostile critics had employed more derogatory concepts, such as 'Trivialliteratur' or even 'Kolportage' (suggesting that the excitement and suspense was an end in itself rather than a means of retaining the reader's interest for a high purpose). There were also accusations that he was exploiting his position as a GDR dissident for the purpose of sales in the West, and that his works were easily manipulable by the market.

The suggestion that Heym was exploiting his persecution fails to acknowledge political realities. It is, in addition, an accusation which could be levelled against any eastern writer who chose to publish in the West when there was no possibility of doing so in the East. On the other hand, there can be little doubt that some of Heym's novels were indeed manipulated by shrewd marketing agents – *5 Tage* and *Collin* itself are the principal examples. The question, then, is whether Heym intended such works to be manipulable and composed them according to a market formula. To judge from the evidence within the texts themselves, the answer is negative. With the sole exception of *Hostages*, these works actually *attack* numerous aspects of the society for which they were published. One should also note that 'manipulation' is usually only possible in a restricted market – the large number of translations which were commissioned suggests there are qualities here which transcend national concerns. (*Hostages* was translated into fifteen other languages; *The Crusaders* into more than twenty). Although the judgment of the reading public may not be a reliable guide to literary qualities, Heym's international success does indicate that he achieved his aim of entertainment. And with it, of course, the exposure of Stalinist methods and widespread dissemination of humane views.

If there were divided views on aspects of composition, all reviewers were unanimous on one point: Heym's 'bravery' in publishing the novel. None were specific about what this actually amounted to, apparently taking it for granted that readers would recognise its dimensions. I suspect, however, that few at the time did in fact appreciate these; the passage of time now allows us to evaluate his actions more clearly.

To write a book which contains harsh words on one's own secret police is obviously courageous in itself, but to model the head of the fictional service on the head of the real-life organisation runs an even greater risk. The timing of publication should also be borne in mind. The first draft had been completed just after the Biermann affair of late 1976, and Heym, who regularly travelled to the West, was likely to fall between two stools: possible exile in the West (should he temporarily travel), or possible imprisonment in the GDR (should he decide to stay). Towards the later stages of revision there were several well-publicised trials of writers in the Soviet Union, and, in the GDR itself, Rudolf Bahro was arrested and prose-cuted for supposedly supplying information to the West (when his 'crime' was essentially publishing in the West certain per-sonal views that were in part critical of the East – exactly what Heym had done.) In mid-1978 Bahro was sentenced to eight years imprisonment, and the beginning of 1979, when *Collin* appeared in Munich, was one of the most threatening periods for intellectuals in the history of the Republic. If they were prosecuted, the chances of a fair trial were virtually nil.[17] It has been noted that if Christa Wolf had published her Novelle *Was bleibt* in 1979, that would have been an act of 'heroic resist-ance'. She did not, but waited until 1990.[18] Heym, by contrast, was indeed heroic in his resistance, and in April 1979 he published a denunciation of the Büro für Urheberrechte, that institution responsible for vetting manuscripts before they could be published abroad. Heym ridiculed the office's futile attempts to prevent authors publishing in the West (writers could buy themselves freedom, he claimed, for a fine of 300 Marks), he exposed the office's new concern with supposed 'Currency imports' as a more insidious way of suppressing free speech (the fine could now rise to 10,000 Marks and there could be imprisonment of up to five years), and he compared these methods to those of the USA in the early fifties. In addition, he published the article in the *Frankfurter Allgemeine*. In the following year he allowed it to be reprinted in *Der Spiegel*.

Heym was also running risks in another area. The fictional hero, Hans Collin, may have had slight personal touches of the author himself, but as *writers* the two were totally different. In the figure of Collin it was a certain type of writer who was being attacked: those whose private criticism of the Party was never given expression in their books. This included, of course, a fair percentage of the Writers' Union, and certain aspects in the characterisation of Collin make it clear he is to be regarded as typical of that organisation. Heym ran the risk of ostracism from here too, then, and in due course he was indeed expelled from the Union. He was also fined 9,000 Marks in the law courts for not submitting his manuscript to the Büro für Urheberrechte and supposedly evading currency exchange controls on foreign royalties. To his relief, he was not imprisoned. Heym refused to be bowed by the drawn-out proceedings. After keeping silent during the pre-trial interrogations, he spoke his mind in an interview which was broadcast, amid some fanfare, by West German television.[19] This created a minor international scandal as the interviewer concerned was banned from the Republic, and Heym's fearless attack on the GDR authorities undoubtedly clinched the verdict of 'guilty' when the trial actually took place shortly afterwards. The whole affair also led to the hasty introduction of a new East German law, the notorious 'Paragraph 219' of the Criminal Code. Under this section, which aroused considerable alarm among West German journalists, severe restrictions were imposed on GDR citizens in their dealings with foreigners. Imprisonment of up to five years could be imposed on anyone who communicated information which could be seen to 'damage' the GDR, a vague, blanket description which could obviously be made to fit almost any form of communication. The same penalty applied to any author who failed to submit a manuscript to the Büro für Urheberrechte. This 'Lex Heym' (as it quickly came to be known) came into force on 1 August 1979, and on the day before Heym allowed a hard-hitting interview to be broadcast on West German television.[20] In what was claimed to be 'das erregendste Interview des Jahres' ('the most exciting interview of the year') (*Die Welt*), he prophesied a 'großes Schweigen' ('a grand silence') which would have far-reaching consequences, and this formulation achieved enormous circulation in the West.

But Heym's courage and outspokenness bore fruit. Not simply in the vastly increased sales of *Collin* in the West (and later the filming of the novel), but above all in the moral lead given to other writers in the GDR. Not only did several well-known authors oppose the GDR press vilification and Heym's expulsion from the Writers' Union from the very start (an act of bravery which was to cost them their own membership, with all its associated and considerable privileges), but at the actual meeting to discuss expulsion, Heym's words swayed a sizeable number.[21] As he recalls in his memoirs, given the prevailing political climate the support of twenty per cent was 'bemerkenswert' (p. 836). That is a major understatement. In a country where support for any decision from a party body was usually one hundred per cent, that was a substantial victory. It undoubtedly influenced the union's future policy, and with it, that of the Politbüro. By the end of 1980 Heym had again begun to publish in the West – without seeking approval. He was never to be prosecuted for it.

CHAPTER 9

An easier struggle: the eighties

The 1980s were to prove once again what the history of the Republic as a whole had revealed: the further the totalitarian straitjacket was loosened, the more difficult it became to tighten it again. So although periodic attempts would indeed be made to reassert party control in the course of this decade, they were to prove largely ineffectual in anything other than the short term. Ironically, though, party intervention was in one respect less necessary. Quite simply, there were fewer writers and artists to whom pressure needed to be applied. The heavy exodus following the Biermann affair had begun an irreversible trend which the authorities appeared to welcome. Their view was clearly that an exile could well make unwelcome statements 'abroad', but that the damage done by these would be restricted. The real danger lay in those who chose to remain in the Republic: in particular those outspoken figures who commanded wide support and who could rely on their international standing for some form of protection. The principals here were obviously Christa Wolf and Stefan Heym.

Heym's activities in the eighties are marked by fewer journalistic functions on the one hand, and more public lectures and TV appearances on the other. More than any other East German figure, he relished TV performance – at which he was particularly good and for which he was in constant demand. He had long been aware of the power of the screen, recognising that its impact was more forceful than that of the printed page and that it was also a means of reaching the East German audience which was denied his public appearance and his writing.[1] He had appeared regularly since the inter-German journalism agreement of November 1972, and his excellent relationship with key individuals in the western media had been of considerable value in the period around his trial for 'currency violation'. As the new decade developed, however, he was to use the media less for personal issues and more for topics with broader human relevance: first, the future of Germany as a divided country; and second, world peace and the removal of atomic weapons. These two issues were also to feature in his novels of the eighties: *Ahasver*, with its warning of apocalypse; and *Schwarzenberg*, with its reminder of an honest attempt at socialism in a part of Germany which had remained unoccupied in 1945. This was also the period of carefully gathering previously published materials: *Wege und Umwege* (1980, expanded edition 1985), which consisted of essays, speeches and lectures from five decades; *Reden an den Feind* (1986), broadcasts from the war; *Nachruf* (1988), the memoirs; and finally *Einmischung* (1990), interviews, speeches and lectures from the eighties. This steady stream of publications testified to Heym's continuing industry and versatility, and although the publication of *Schwarzenberg* was considered by certain critics to mark a decline relative to his earlier fiction, there is no evidence of deterioration in the essays, speeches, or the repartee in interviews. The average length of Heym's essays and speeches also grows at this stage. Solid financial security (arising from excellent sales in the West) presumably removed completely the need to publish quickly in order to maintain his own and his wife's standard of living.

With maturity, Heym's novels have tended to differ from one another far more than did those of the early years. The first three, for example, showed relatively few differences in attitude, authorial perspective, or techniques of narration. The historical novels of the middle period are likewise characterised by a comparable stance: they are in the main traditional, realistic works resting on careful research and execution. But there is a turning point in Heym's whole approach, and this seems to follow the death of his first wife, Gertrude. From *The Queen* onward there is broader range in subject-matter, greater variety in narrative perspective, wider perspective on life in general, and greater inventiveness in the use of language.

Was Heym in some ways inhibited by Gertrude's influence, or was this development bound to have taken place anyway? Gertrude was a willing and obviously highly beneficial critic, but were her expectations of something cinematic, a script easily adaptable to the screen, in fact a subconscious determiner of her husband's methods? Or can the changes be in part attributed to an even firmer determination to oppose censorship and perpetual calls for a sterile realism? For whatever reason, the novels of the seventies and eighties reveal much bolder pursuits and a far richer sense of humour, qualities which are both evident in the next major work to reach print.

The Wandering Jew probably ranks as Heym's second most successful novel from a literary critical point of view. Its complex structure, sophisticated use of language, subtle working out of theme, have impressed critics of both German and English versions. But there is one feature of the novel which has received barely any attention, and it is one which contributes substantially to the work's appeal: its humour. The irony, the wit, the satire, the parody. It is these elements, therefore, to which I should like to give comparatively more weight in my analysis, but in relation, of course, to the principal themes they support: bigotry, hypocrisy, the danger of following dogma blindly, man's inhumanity to man, the likely destruction of the earth.

Our initial impression is of three separate strands of plot and time, although as Rodney Fisher has pointed out, closer scrutiny reveals there are actually four.[2] These operate at very different stages of world history and points of space. The novel has an extra-terrestrial dimension, and its axes lie in the earthly and the eternal, the modern and the primeval, the rational and the miraculous. The conception is fantastic, yet many parts of the work are realistic and thoroughly researched. The result is a critical and unsettling entertainment, which brings biblical history, medieval German history, and contemporary events into a close relationship and which suggests the unchangeability and imperfectibility of Man.

The first strand is set in a limbo, where the participants move regularly in space and time and in which various spirits dispute their opinions of Man and of how his future should be shaped. These spirits include God, Lucifer, Christ after his Crucifixion, and also the figure of Ahasver, who is depicted as an angel who fell from God's favour when he refused to bow down before Adam. Ahasver is thus seen from the beginning as a rebel, and the word 'revolutionary' is actually used to describe him on the first page of the novel. The choice of such a word is typical: throughout the text unexpected appellations give a modern edge to the historical/spiritual subject-matter, reminding the East German reader in particular of parallel situations in his own country or in the socialist countries in general.

The second strand bears on moments in the life of Christ – in the wildernness, at the Last Supper, and on the way to Calvary. At all of these Ahasver is present, but in constantly changing form: as a satanic tempter, in the guise of a beloved disciple (John), and finally as a figure denying Christ a moment's rest on his final earthly journey. For the latter act Ahasver is condemned to eternal 'wandering' until the Second Coming. After the Crucifixion Christ becomes a spirit, and his encounters with Ahasver now take place in another realm.

The third strand is centred on sixteenth-century Germany, and there are historically accurate passages – as well as spoof sections – on Luther, Melanchthon, and an ambitious (and equally historical) young cleric who rises to be Superintendent of Schleswig, Paul von Eitzen. There is a firm and detailed plot to this strand, which occupies more space than any other, and it includes a mysterious figure called 'Leuchtentrager' ('Lucifer' in human form), as well as various manifestations of Ahasver (who now features as the traditional 'Wandering Jew'). It initially appears as if Paul von Eitzen is to be the hero of the novel, for we are tempted to identify with this young, if slightly foolish, young scholar and to sympathise with him as he is so obviously led astray by Leuchtentrager/Lucifer, his guardian demon. Our identification is short-lived, however, for Eitzen quickly reveals himself as a self-seeking, lascivious, and hypocritical opportunist. His constant hounding of Ahasver is carried out for revenge, and the loss of his soul to the devil is seen as the inevitable consequence of his unchristian activities. His primary source of inspiration, Martin Luther, is also seen as a dangerous influence, bigoted and uncharitable in his fervent attacks on the Jews.

The final strand takes the action to the actual time of Heym's composition, 1980, and it comprises a correspondence between an East German Professor of 'Scientific Atheism', Siegfried Beifuß, and a Professor at the Hebrew University of Jerusalem, Jochanaan Leuchtentrager. The latter claims to know Ahasver personally, produces a variety of different items of information to 'prove' his eternal wandering, and finally arrives in East Berlin in order to attest his companion's existence. Beifuß initially reacts dismissively to the claims of his correspondent, but he becomes increasingly animated, despite the fact that his Marxist beliefs exclude the occurrence of miracles. Occasional letters from the East German 'Ministry of Higher Education' and the secret police enliven this strand, which concludes in Beifuß's being seized by his visitors and dragged in magical flight over the Berlin Wall.

Each chapter of the novel switches to a different strand, but it is the figure of Ahasver which unites all four. Heym gleefully and ingeniously expands his legend, which appeared in Europe around the thirteenth century and gained widespread popularity in Germany in the seventeenth.[3] He uses aspects of it to interpret features of modern and medieval society, religious history, the creation of the world, and also of its end. Although this interpretation is playful and frequently extravagant, it is clothed in a fully researched historical setting, and precise, highly evocative, depiction of background detail. Further, Heym uses more central motifs and incidental details of the legend than any of the many other writers who have exploited it.

The villain of the legend is Ahasver. Having denied Christ a resting place he is condemned to eternal wandering, and the same is seen to hold true for his people, the Jews. But in Heym's novel the only figure who is *not* a villain would seem to be

Ahasver. He alone is capable of loving his neighbour, and it is precisely his love for humanity which leads him to reject Christ. He is annoyed that Jesus, who could have transformed the world had he wished, nevertheless meekly submitted himself to his father's will. Ahasver would much prefer Jesus to assist humanity in a direct, revolutionary way, but the latter prefers to suffer for the redemption of mankind in the world to come. Jesus, then, is regarded by Ahasver as a failure, and the same applies to God, who will tolerate hunger, plague, and countless injustices. Great church figures like Luther and Melanchthon are no better. Luther in particular is portrayed as an ugly glutton and a vicious anti-Semite whose failure to continue his support for the exploited peasants was an act of self-seeking. The central figure of the major strand, Paul von Eitzen, is comparably distasteful. His rise to a position of supreme authority in the church is sustained not by love of his fellow men but by a desire for power; and his goal is achieved through sycophancy, ruthless adherence to dogma, and occasional terror. Eitzen's unwitting selling of his soul to the devil is one of the numerous compromises he will make with his conscience for the sake of personal success. He thus becomes the central anti-hero of a book full of religious villains.

Eitzen, Luther, and also in some degree Siegfried Beifuß, are seen as inadequate representatives of their representative creeds, and a quotation from Ezekiel (which actually occurs twice in the text), underlines this theme of the unworthy leader: 'Thus says the Lord God, Behold I am against the shepherds; and I will require my flock at their hand, and cause them to cease from feeding their flock; neither shall the shepherds feed themselves anymore; for I will deliver my flock from their mouth, that they may not be meat for them' (p. 29 and, with changes in the punctuation, p. 287). Heym refuses to identify this quotation other than to refer to it as a passage from Ezekiel, and so most readers are driven to scouring the whole Book of that prophet in order to discover its context. The chapter from which this verse is taken (34:10) does in fact bear unambiguously on the novel: Ezekiel warns of shepherds who betray their flock and seek to satisfy their own physical needs at the expense of those they should be nurturing. The principal butt of such a critique is obviously Paul von Eitzen, but the historical paralleling of the novel encourages our identification of others.

The subject-matter of the book, its pessimistic theme, and its cynical view of man, would not at first sight obviously lend themselves to a humorous treatment. Yet the novel contains an abundance of comic elements, and it is, of course, conceived as a travesty of the legend. The careful research which underlies it is itself regularly exploited for the purpose of satire on academe.

Perhaps the first element of humour to strike us is the parody of biblical and medieval language. Heym patterns his style on archaic devices in his sources (e.g. Luther's translation of the Bible; the Ahasver 'Volksbuch'), but deliberate colloquialism, modernisms, and euphemisms reveal that his adoption of archaic tone, rhythm, and language is artificial, and that the contents carry modern relevance.

We can study an example of this in the very first lines of the novel: the summary which precedes the opening chapter.

> Wherein it is related how God, to the great joy of
> the angels, created man, and two revolu-
> tionaries happen to differ on a basic
> question

The first half of this sentence parodies the construction of biblical formulations. The archaic 'wherein', for example; the impersonal form employed in order to give maximum prominence to the word 'God'; the delaying of the second verb and its object; and the overstatement in the '*great* joy of the angels'. The symmetrical layout of this summary creates the impression of dignity and control, as well as enhancing the medieval aura. However, this dignity is undercut by the contrastingly simple structure and almost conversational tone of the second part, the unexpected presence of 'revolutionaries' (after the emphasis on the spiritual), and the legal dryness of 'a basic question'. The second part of the sentence is shorter than the first, too, and this contributes to the sense of anti-climax: the conclusion falls (deliberately) flat after the grandiloquence of the opening.

Heym's command over language is evident in the quite different sort of parody we find in the correspondence of Professors Leuchtentrager and Beifuß. The following example is taken from the middle of the novel, as Beifuß yet again tries to prove that immortality is impossible:

Dear Colleague,

I wrote to you only a week ago; if after so brief an interval I do so again it is because I am worried that I may not have given sufficient emphasis to a thought I deem closely related to the entire Ahasverus matter. Let me add that my views on this point are fully shared by the collective of my Institute which has pledged to assemble by the First of May, the worldwide festival of the working class, the material for an essay on the reactionary character of the myth of the transmigration of the soul. (p. 140)

As Beifuß indicates, this is his second letter within a week, a fact which acquires its significance only within the context of the full correspondence. We later discover that this letter and the preceding one both arrive in Israel on the same day; and before writing his first letter, Beifuß had received advice/warning from the 'Ministry of Higher Education' that he should devote himself in the correspondence more fully to the question of religion and 'imperialist expansionism, particularly in relation to Israel' (p. 94). Beifuß fails to do this in the first, more individualistic letter; in the second (we are led to deduce) he is driven by pressure from within his collective as well as from the Ministry. He therefore writes in a more official tone and actually rounds off his final argument with one of the best-known quotations from Marx. The fact he is being pressurised to adhere to Party doctrine is clear not only from the tone and contents of the letter, but also from the fact that it arrives in Israel on the same day as the preceding one. The latter has clearly been held up by the censorship office to see whether a firmer tone was being adopted in the supplementary letter, and the two are obviously released, all too clumsily, at the same point in time!

Beifuß's introductory paragraph makes it clear that the contents of this letter are not entirely his own. Although the opening tone is urgent and has the hint of a personal touch (lacking, interestingly, in the original German, which is officialese throughout), it quickly lapses into bureaucratic jargon and long-windedness. In the second section the personal yields to the impersonal and the abstract, and there is an artificial air of political enthusiasm. The jargon ('collective', 'worldwide festival of the working class', 'reactionary character'), together with the heavy phraseology ('pledged to assemble', 'reactionary character of the myth of the transmigration of the soul') makes this a typical example of East German officialese, with its preference for nouns, abstractions, clichés, and undue length. In every letter which is written in the GDR, Heym satirises not only the language, but also the narrow-mindedness and political caution of the correspondent.

Heym's parody of language extends to all parts of the novel, even to those sections devoted to the spiritual realms. Here the tone is essentially that of the Bible: not just the New, but also the Old Testament. A certain lyricism enters at points, when the highest realms of the spiritual world are reached, and here the source of inspiration seems specifically the Revelation of St John. But as in the Eitzen and Beifuß strands, the tone is essentially parodistic; this is reinforced by the contents, which regularly stand in total contrast to those of the originals.

Heym's liking for irony is evident in most of his fiction, as well as in his journalism. In *The Wandering Jew* the possibilities are considerable, for key aims are to expose inadequacy, hypocrisy, and dogmatism, and to suggest other levels at which the text should be understood. In this respect some of the pointers are quite forthright, for example, the unexpected word 'revolutionaries' in the first chapter heading, or such generalised statements as Ahasver's to Jesus: 'Rabbi, I said, the imperfection of man has been the excuse of every revolution that failed to achieve what it set out to do' (p. 198). The ostensible subject of discussion here is Christ's sacrifice for the world (which Ahasver claims to have been fruitless), but the issue is broadened by an inappropriate terminology. Comparably striking is the use of the anachronistic 'dissidents' (p. 72) with reference to the work of fallen angels in medieval society: 'telling how the bad angels were also busy among the authorities, creating mischief and disturbing the peace and harmony of the state by abetting dissidents or appearing as witnesses for them' (pp. 71/2). The irony runs at a further level here, since the author himself is a prime example of such attempts to question the authority of the state.

Two equally prominent examples of linguistic playfulness are to be found in the words 'existing' and 'real', taken from that popular formulation 'der real existierende Sozialismus [in der DDR]' (in contrast to that which was claimed to exist or which it was hoped might in due course come to exist);[4] and in the description of Eitzen's equivalent of the secret police: 'and therefore the talk of the people is being listened to in the inns and marketplaces of Eiderstedt county, and even inside their own homes people are not safe from watchers who are trying to find out whether they are having suspicious thoughts or own one or other of those little books written by...' (p. 234). Regular reminders of present-day oppressive methods encourage reflection on more general aspects of contact between the periods of time depicted in the novel.

There is humour of a wittier and more frivolous sort too, often of a blasphemous and sexual nature. Eitzen's entire love-life is seen to be doomed, whether he fall impotent before his ugly (but wealthy) wife, or before the ravishing beauty of the Countess Ehrentreu (a glaringly inappropriate name), who initially praises the erotic nimbleness of Eitzen's fingers and ascribes their dexterity to frequent leafing through the Holy Scriptures. Generally deflating and cynical comments also abound, such as the fact that the cock which crowed thrice to Simon Peter has long since been turned into a fricassée (p. 135); that Judas, treasurer of the disciples' common purse, is troubled by inflation and embarrassed by the need to buy extra wine for the Passover (p. 75); or when Luther, seemingly about to embrace Eitzen, thinks better of it and leaves the young cleric instead with only the vapour of beer and onions (p. 88).

More than any other of Heym's works, *Ahasver* exploits sexual comedy, and that to underline an unusual theme: the sacrifice of sexual satisfaction to clerical advancement. This has broad implications when viewed in the general guise of careerism at the expense of integrity, for a comparable issue is to be found in the Beifuß sub-plot. Beifuß's enslavement to dogma is comparable to Eitzen's, with both figures having gained promotion by strict adherence to their respective party line. Both bear the hallmark of the stereotype party function-ary, devoid of personal opinion, limited in intellect and imagination, and dependent on the writings of others for their inspiration and authority. Eitzen, in fact, is virtually a Stalinist *avant la lettre*. He will enforce respect of his religion through brutality, and hypocritically refuses to recognise that his sup-posed ideals are in any way compromised by such behaviour. The resulting gruesome episodes stand in almost grotesque contrast to the sexual comedy which frequently surrounds them.

Moments of sexual frustration recur throughout the novel, but they are at their most intense whenever Eitzen makes a decision in favour of dogma or preferment. The first instance occurs when he prepares himself for his degree examination: the wager with his personal devil is that he will have his heart's desire (the chambermaid Margriet – an echo of Goethe's 'Gretchen') if he is *not* questioned on the subject predicted by Leuchtentrager. Eitzen 'loses' the wager. Assisted by Leuch-tentrager, he passes the exam with flying colours, and thus has no claim to Margriet. Instead he is obliged to take the unat-tractive Barbara Steder, to whom he is betrothed on account of her father's position and her expected inheritance. The first sexual union of the plain Barbara and the equally unattractive Eitzen is again controlled by Leuchtentrager, who arouses the passion of both with flattering comments (an echo of the 'Garden' scene in *Faust* I) and magic wine (an echo of the witch's magic potion in 'Witch's Kitchen'). The literary paral-lels reveal a gulf between the grandeur of the truly Faustian vision and the pettiness of Eitzen's. His mind is never on his wife, but on reincarnations of the sensual Margriet. As they unite sexually, Eitzen and Barbara are each thinking of someone else (a grotesque echo, perhaps, of *Die Wahlverwandt-schaften*, for the deformed child of this union resembles

Leuchtentrager). When they awake, they find themselves lying not among the grandeur which the wine had led them to imagine, but in a stinking low pub from which their money and fine clothes have disappeared. Eitzen's marriage to Barbara is repeatedly portrayed in terms of such anticlimax and failure, and his other sexual adventures in similar, almost slapstick manner. The narrator recounts these events in mock-excited, and mockingly erotic terms, consistently relating sexual disappointment to questionable triumph in church affairs.

In the course of this novel Heym attacks targets both ancient and modern, and it is not only the Beifuß sub-plot which relates the themes of the work to the GDR. In addition to political and humanitarian questions, Heym is also concerned with such fundamental issues as world peace/world destruction. This has long been a major personal concern of his, and the writing of the novel coincided with notable advances in the East German peace movement. We see a partial reflection of these in two of the four strands.

Heym had been an early supporter of this (unofficial) peace movement, together with his long-standing acquaintance Stephan Hermlin (who became the leading literary figure). Its membership had grown slowly since the early seventies, but a significant moment came at an international conference in East Berlin on the 13/14 December 1981, at which no fewer than ninety-five writers, artists, and scientists gathered to discuss disarmament and peace in Europe ('Berliner Begegnung zur Friedensförderung').[5] Because of the impossibility of finding accommodation to stage their discussions or talks, and also because there was much support from the church, the movement relied almost exclusively on church premises for its gatherings. Atheists and Christians thus came together, questioning eastern as well as western arms strategy. The symbol of the movement was adopted in 1979 and was based on the Old Testament prophecy of Micah (4:3), that in the final days of the earth swords would be beaten into ploughshares. Badges with the insignia (based, rather shrewdly, on the *Soviet* sculpture which stands outside the United Nations building in New York) became increasingly popular in the GDR. Like all forms of opposition – which is alien to the thinking of a Communist state – they caused alarm to the government, which banned the wearing of them in the spring of 1982.

It is against this background that certain parts of *The Wandering Jew* need to be seen; in particular the actual allusion to Micah (p. 193) and the vision of nuclear Armageddon (pp. 262/3). At both these points Heym is directing attention to a GDR problem and to a wider world issue. The GDR dilemma lay in the fact that the government had originally supported the peace movement in the West, in particular the 'Krefelder Appell' (which was aimed more at western governments than at eastern ones), but had then reacted repressively to a movement within its own borders criticising Soviet, as well as western nuclear power, and calling for general disarmament. Heym repeats this call in chapter 25 of the novel by allowing Jesus, in his second coming, to portray the extent of nuclear capacity. Armageddon is seen by him not as something likely to be initiated by the heavenly hosts, but by man himself. It is the horror of this realisation which leads Jesus to reconsider his earthly existence and to acknowledge its pointlessness. Humanity must be changed by more drastic means than meekness and self-sacrifice.

Just as the peace movement had criticised both East and West, so too does Heym. But his attack is broader, for the condemnation is not only of politicians and ideologies, but also of organised religion.

Another prominent area of Heym's attack is anti-semitism. In his keynote address at the opening of the Annual Convention of the International Council of Christians and Jews in 1982, Heym spoke regretfully of the tribulations of the Jews since the time of Christ. The whole lecture is clearly related to the themes of *The Wandering Jew*, and the author devotes a complete paragraph, in fact, to Luther's fervent and hostile attitudes. He recalls that the booklet against the Jews, written by Luther, was still being used by the Nazis in their propaganda efforts. In the novel, Heym intimates that the GDR authorities are anxious to underplay the negative aspects of Luther in order to ensure a successful international 'Luther

Year' (1983) in their country (which is also Luther's homeland): an opportunity for prestige and foreign income. *Ashasver*, published in 1981, suggests that unquestioning glorification of Luther would not simply be hypocritical, but contemptible.

The great 'reformer' is portrayed advocating the burning of Jewish synagogues and schools, confiscation of their scriptures, and forcing them to manual labour. His words inspire others. Eitzen follows the lead of his mentor, preaching vigorously against the Jews and trying to blackmail or harass them into conversion to Christianity. This depiction, like that of Luther, is based on thorough research. But modern anti-semitism is also featured. There is a short section devoted to the Warsaw ghetto, allusions to the gas chambers, and even a hint of East German hostility to the state of Israel (p. 227). In his Convention address Heym had openly lamented the persecution of the Jews in the socialist countries, which he regarded as a particular breach of socialist humanitarianism. In the novel, this theme is concealed behind a more general plea for tolerance. As in his other works, Heym has recognised the need for literature to exercise a maieutic as well as a didactic function.

The note of hope – however slight – on which Heym prefers to conclude his novels, is probably at its weakest in *Ahasver*. Although the author himself rejected the charge of pessimism,[6] critics have rarely been prepared to view the novel's conclusion positively. Malcolm Pender, for example, regards the work as further evidence of an increasingly gloomy view of the historical process, and he considers that all three of its layers describe the 'unchanging nature of human behaviour and the regression of all revolutionary movement to reaction'.[7]

Pender's claim cannot be disregarded, and it is part of his well-illustrated thesis that there are contradictions in Heym's writing and that a sense of fatalism is actually evident as early as the forties. Such a view can easily be sustained by giving only slightly more weight to particular sections of the novels than to others: the balance is certainly fine in some of the later works, and in the absence of unambiguous authorial guidance the reader's response will only reflect individual personality. I would suggest this is not the case in the fifties, when Heym's optimism is strong and his guidance firm (for example, in the programmatically entitled 'Die Veränderung im Menschen', one of the short stories in *Die Kannibalen*), but the capacity for, and the pace of, change, does seem much reduced by the time of *Ahasver*. In this text hope survives principally in the unbowed figure of the revolutionary Ahasver himself. It is not to be detected in the plot.

Whatever our reaction to Heym's fiction, the author's belief in the changeability of man is raised constantly in his public statements. From the early fifties through to the late eighties, his articles, essays, interviews and speeches all bear witness to a belief in human progress. The statements are, if anything, more optimistic in the later period. As Heym put it in an interview after the publication of *Ahasver*, his view of literature was that of 'erziehen' ('to educate') in the sense of 'Veränderung in jemandem hervorrufen'[8] ('bring about change in someone'). Such an end is achieved in this novel not by showing the triumph of the revolutionaries, but by proving the need for further revolution – especially in the search for international peace.

The reception of *Ahasver* was more favourable than that of any novel since *King David*. Although Peter Pawlik's review in *Die Zeit* was only lukewarm, this was quickly compensated for by the exceptionally positive response of Jurek Becker in *Der Spiegel*, and then the first scholarly review by Jörg Bilke in *Neue Deutsche Hefte*. The English translation, which first appeared in New York, was hailed by D. J. Enright as a 'brilliant theological fantasy'.[9]

For all its complexity and theological allusions, the novel sold extremely well. Further, the GDR authorities decided to take no steps to prosecute Heym for failing to submit the manuscript to the copyright office before allowing it to be considered abroad. This represented yet another victory against authority and the censor, and further encouragement to others to publish without restraint in the Federal Republic.

Shortly after the publication of *Ahasver* Heym predicted that the novel would not appear in the GDR for some time. What would be offensive was its anti-authoritarian attitude, 'wir unterwerfen uns nicht' ('we will not submit') (*Wege*, p. 474). He was correct, and seven years were to elapse between the appearance of the novel in the West (1981) and the East (1988). In some respects this is slightly surprising. By comparison with earlier years, these ones were stable enough in the GDR: it was in other socialist countries that difficulties and crises were more obvious. The decade had begun, for example, with strikes in Poland and the rise of the free trade union 'Solidarity'. Its amazing support from the Polish workforce and its pressure for reform led to various repressive measures and eventually to the introduction of martial law in December 1981. The actions of 'Solidarity' were much discussed in the GDR, but no comparable East German force emerged; it was in Hungary that brief strikes were inspired by the Polish example. In these years too, Moscow itself was experiencing problems. The poorly-disguised ill-health of Brezhnev, and the deteriorating Soviet economy, gave cause for concern. Unease was not allayed by the appointment of the elderly Andropov (after Brezhnev's death in 1982), swiftly followed by the equally frail Chernenko (1984). Not until the appointment of Gorbachev in 1985 was any sense of strength and vitality evident in the leadership of the Soviet Union. Such a succession of Soviet changes was somewhat unsettling for Honecker's government, which still felt a strong need to follow Moscow's wishes; further, the security of the GDR was to a large extent dependent on the presence of Soviet forces.

Within the GDR itself, confrontation between citizens and the police was relatively limited and peaceful, although open, popular demonstrations were becoming more common – sometimes to be brought to an end with force. The principal challenge came from the church, which did not only represent religious views but which provided a growing semi-public platform and focus for dissident forces, particularly those from the peace movement.[10] But the peace and anti-nuclear banners camouflaged much broader unease with GDR conditions and the growing desire of many to emigrate. Dramatic escapes across the border were no longer common, or indeed, necessary.

The first sensational-but-peaceful exit route was that of six who managed to enter the US embassy in East Berlin and request asylum. Although later asylum-seekers were unsuccessful here, others soon managed to gain an exit by penetrating the West German Permanent Mission in East Berlin; and then, in April 1984, there was the well-publicised case of thirty-five who escaped by penetrating the West German embassy in Prague. International scandal, and any open sign of dissatisfaction or opposition, was most unwelcome to the GDR authorities. They became far more responsive to official applications to leave, not just those by dissident writers; nevertheless, there was amazement in the country when in November 1984 the Federal Republic announced that no fewer than 36,123 had been allowed to move permanently to the West in the first nine months of that year.[11] Although the number fell to 18,000 in 1985 and 20,000 in 1986, an equally significant statistic is the number of legal visitors to the Federal Republic. In 1986 this stood at 573,000 *excluding* those of pensionable age and for whom travel was freely allowed.[12] This figure rose even higher in 1987. Such 'appeasement' of the populace may have been stabilising in the short term, but there were still large numbers who wished to leave or who wished to visit and who were not granted permission to do so. In addition, the direct experiences – by so many – of the material situation in the West can only have fuelled dissatisfaction with the GDR's sluggish economic performance and have led to that decisive vote, in March 1990, for swift unification.

As usual, Heym commented on numerous aspects of the national and international scene in the course of this period: the situation in Poland after martial law, for example ('Zu Polen', broadcast on the Sender Freies Berlin); the dangers of nuclear armament ('Über den Frieden', a speech to trade unionists in Dortmund); demonstrations and the church in the GDR ('Plötzlich hebt sich der Boden', interview with *Der Spiegel*); the responsibility of the individual ('Überlegungen 1983', speech at a writer's conference in West Berlin); and repeated remarks, in lectures and interviews, on the peace movement in the GDR and elsewhere. There is also much comment on both German states and on their future, the highlight of this being the 1983 Munich speech 'Über Deutschland'. This lively lecture is one of the longest Heym has ever written, and it ranges over history, literature, language, and politics. In it, as in all these pieces of the eighties, Heym is constantly alert for parallels – historical, contemporary and international – and he delights, as ever, in contradictions and in novel combinations of well-known views. At times throughout this speech he both praises and condemns each part of the nation, seemingly caring little whether he upsets any part of his audience and, indeed, seemingly intent on disturbing practically every segment of that audience at *some* point. In this respect he was operating in sharp contrast to the politicians: he was not at excessive pains to proclaim the 'achievements' of his own country or to denounce the 'failures' of the other, but to present an apparently balanced, critical assessment of the nation and its future. By appearing objective, his words carried weight.

As can be seen from the places of delivery or publication of these contributions to international dialogue, none of them found their way into print in the East. Despite the fact that during this period the GDR authorities allowed the publication of such critical novels as Helga Schutz's *Julia oder Erziehung zum Chorgesang* (1980), Christoph Hein's *Der fremde Freund* (1982) and Eberhard Hilsche's *Die Weltzeituhr* (1983), Heym nevertheless remained forbidden. There was clearly a difference between publishing (in small print runs) the criticism of the less well known and that of the internationally famous. Such a policy was poor for the GDR's image both at home and abroad, and it was also futile. The many visitors to the West (as indicated above) had ample opportunity to acquire Heym's works, increasingly available in cheap paperback form.

The decision to ban Heym was one of many counter-productive government policies which found their conclusion in the final collapse of the Republic. If the leadership had been prepared to give more rein to open discussion – which was still resisted long after Gorbachev's calls for *glasnost* – much frustration could have been released and it might have been possible to progress more gradually and in a far more balanced way to the concessions eventually granted in desperation by a government determined to retain power. Heym could have contributed enormously to such a dialogue, just as he had done in the fifties with 'Offen gesagt'. He maintained again in the eighties that his suggestions were far from dangerous for the country, and could only be beneficial to it (*Wege*, p. 490). This was undoubtedly true, but the government failed to recognise the positive value of Heym's consistent defence of socialism as a superior ideology to capitalism, and of the GDR as a superior state to the Federal Republic. The eulogies of the party faithful, and the self-congratulatory speeches in the official press or at party congresses, were (if actually read) dismissed with laughter by the outside world and even by a good number of the inhabitants of the GDR. The support of the querulous Heym was by contrast taken seriously. It may not be an exaggeration to suggest that he did far more for the image of the GDR in the Federal Republic than did any other figure in the East, politician or otherwise. At home, however, his criticism was deemed to outweigh his support. To the end, he could never be sure whether the following day would bring his arrest for treason.

While lecturing on the future of Germany, Heym was also delving into its past. The result was *Schwarzenberg* (1984), the only one of his novels which has not yet appeared in English translation. Although few of the first readers of this work believed its author had created anything other than an exciting tale of how a socialist democracy *might* have developed on German soil after 1945, Heym, as in all his historical fiction, had actually composed a novel which was based on research. In contrast to earlier works, however, his sources were in this case highly restricted. He knew from an old friend that an independent state, Schwarzenberg, had been created in a small area of the south which the American and Soviet forces had – for whatever reason – failed to enter, but he was unable to establish much more. Most of the records had been removed for an obvious reason: the notion that a socialist democracy could be established on German soil, without the assistance of the USSR, was not at all welcome to a party which adulated Moscow. Heym therefore had to content himself with a minimum of records, a one-sided dissertation written in the fifties, and tape recordings made by his old friend, a leading member of the 'action committee' which took power and ran a state of what may have been as many as 350,000 people.

The plot unfolds through three different sources. First, the memories of Kadletz, a Communist during the Third Reich who is thrust into a position of power in the action committee set up immediately after the war ends. Second, a sequence of 'military interludes', which focus on the activities of the American and Soviet forces, and also on a marauding troop of Nazi soldiers who wish to avoid the prisoner-of-war camp. And finally, untitled chapters focussing largely on the figure of Max Wolfram, a Jewish intellectual of left-wing tendencies and utopian ideals, who has survived the Nazi death-cell. A post-script, undated, depicts Wolfram as a popular, but disillu-sioned professor at Leipzig University.

The 'Republic' of Schwarzenberg lasted seven weeks. Heym traces its practical problems as well as its ideological ones: the difficulty of ousting petty Nazis from their positions of power, for example, and the delicate negotiations with the conquerors in both East and West. We see the beginnings of a postal service (the Republic printed its own stamps) and of trade with the Occupation Zones; the arrest of the Nazi Gauleiter of Saxony, and the continuing dangers from marauding Nazi troops. Against this background of day-to-day practical difficulties, there is also concern for the state's legitimacy and the problem. of drawing up a constitution.

Just as stability seems assured, the Soviet army moves in to occupy territory up to the line agreed at Yalta. Even without that agreement, Heym suggests, occupation would have been inevitable. The Soviets knew what the Americans did not: Schwarzenberg contained deposits of uranium. The future of the Soviet atomic bomb lay in this curious workers' republic, and there was therefore a pressing need to possess the land. Only the Soviet fifth columnist in the action committee,

Reinsiepe, is aware of this, and Heym's depiction of this figure, and his mysterious activities, provides one of the principal enigmas of the work.

What would attract Heym to such material? Clearly, it provided him with one of his standard subjects and themes: a form of revolution, and the consequent paradoxes surrounding freedom in an emergent socialist utopia. This utopia itself, however, lay within a particular context and was partly controlled by it: by the Red Army in the East and by the Americans in the West. The major points of comparison are thus those of Communism and capitalism, and the novel derives its intellectual force from the questioning of utopianism against the background of these contrasting ideologies.

The 'revolution' in question was minor and it was only possible because the National Socialist armies had been defeated by the Allies; but it nevertheless represented a seizure of power in a country with a history of unsuccessful revolutions. Its uniqueness is emphasised in Kadletz's reflections on the situation after the Nazis have been ousted:

Aber vergessen wir doch nicht, daß es in Deutschland noch nie gelungen war, eine Revolution aus eigener Kraft zum Siege zu führen; alle Bemühungen in der Richtung waren stets in Blut erstickt worden; so daß unsere erfolgreiche schwarzenbergische, so klein und schäbig sie auch erscheinen mag, immerhin ein Präzedenzfall ist und als ein bescheidenes Beispiel für künftige Versuche dienen könnte. (p. 61.)

But let us also remember that at no time in their history have the German people ever succeeded in staging a victorious revolution; all their efforts in that vein miscarried and were drowned in blood; so that the success of our pint-sized Schwarzenbergian one at least sets a precedent that may serve as a modest example for future attempts. (Rendering by Stefan Heym)

Kadletz's comments gain their significance from the fact he is making these observations not from the point of view of the forties, but from the seventies. The perspective is further complicated by our knowledge that Kadletz was a Communist at the time of the 'revolution'. There is no indication in the text, however, of whether his views have changed since then or whether the present government has failed to meet his expectations. At all events, his words contain a barely veiled incentive to further, and much grander, peaceful revolution.

The sub-title of this particular chapter carries echoes of a more ominous transfer of power: 'Machtübernahme' ('Taking power') offers a parallel to the Nazi 'Machtergreifung' ('seizure of power') of 1933. What parallels does Schwarzenberg have with the Third Reich, or in what ways can its republic be seen as a model? Does this sub-title actually carry a warning, despite the positive viewpoint from which what follows is related?

The dangers of even the most enlightened form of government are alluded to in the novel, principally by means of Max Wolfram's reflections on a constitution. Wolfram has touches of Ernst Bloch about him: his study of utopias, his subsequent professorship at Leipzig University, and the fact that in the seminar we see him conducting, one of the students refers to Schwarzenberg as 'eine große Hoffnung' ('a great hope') (an echo of Bloch's major work, *Das Prinzip Hoffnung* (*The Principle of Hope*)). But by the end Wolfram has rejected the notion that hope existed for Schwarzenberg, describing it instead as 'eine große Illusion' ('a great illusion'). We cannot tell whether this remark reflects the caution of a man who feels himself under constant scrutiny, whether it is the product of Soviet 're-education', or whether it does reflect the wisdom of experience. Wolfram's earlier views have led to suffering and imprisonment at the hands of the Nazis, and we know of a long-term enforced period in the Soviet Union. But even in his Schwarzenberg period, Wolfram's hopes were ill-founded, and his untested political idealism is revealed as potentially dangerous. His aim is a socialist utopia, and he is given the task of drafting its constitution. While others labour hard at practical and physical problems, he dabbles in an intellectual exercise. Wolfram has regular self-doubts, and his laborious drafting is recognised as futile by the reader. Historical knowledge, quite apart from narrative hints, suggest his utopianism is impractical. Like many other intellectuals depicted by Heym, his grasp of politics is inadequate. His hope that freedom and necessity

could be harmonised are undercut by his recognition that even
the ideal state will need forms of protection in terms of army
and police, and although he believes that his method of using a
variety of figures, with responsibility for separate aspects of
government, should mean that no charismatic figure will be
able to seize power, we cannot but recall one of the findings of
his doctoral dissertation: according to his intellectual Nazi
persecutor, all the previous utopias studied by Wolfram did
constitute dictatorships.

Wolfram is an idealised character, and at least two critics
have considered him lacking in credibility.[13] Despite his appal-
ling experiences, he remains politically naive. He is not practical either, and he is repeatedly trapped in compromising
situations. His final position – as a frustrated socialist liberal –
places him alongside Heym's numerous other defeated
idealists, but principally alongside Thomas Benda, who was
equally unable to reconcile the demands of freedom and
government. Heym's thinking on this issue thus reveals surprising consistency over a period in excess of thirty years.

Wolfram is not the only idealist in the novel, although he is
the most extreme. Kadletz has also suffered for his (Communist) beliefs, and so too has Reinsiepe, who spent the whole of the
Third Reich in Soviet exile. There are, however, clear differences between these figures. For all his pride in calling himself
a Communist, Kadletz reveals uncertainty. He is too quick to
acknowledge the value of the social democratic way of thinking, and not sufficiently single-minded in his dedication to the
Communist cause. Reinsiepe, by contrast, is wholly and inde-
fatigably committed to that ideal, and the strength of his
long-term views is presented as a source of admiration on the
one hand, and of concern on the other. The humanitarian sides
to his character are seen to have suffered in his dedication to a
long-term, and probably questionable, goal.

In contrast to the inflexible and long-term goals of Communism stand the immediate, practical and humane aspects of
Social Democracy, and the fundamental difference in attitude
between these two political viewpoints is brought out by
Kadletz in his recollection of his colleague, the Social Demo-

crat Viebig. The latter took great pains to provide straw for the wagons to be used in repatriating the Soviet slave labourers, and this was something, Kadletz admits, he himself would never have contemplated. Viebig's action leads Kadletz to programmatic reflection on different aims and methods:

Ich habe mich manchmal gefragt, warum gerade ehemalige Sozial-demokraten zur Verwaltungsarbeit tendieren, und hier wiederum zum Wirtschafts- und Sozialwesen, und ich nehme an, das kommt daher, daß in ihnen noch etwas nachwirkt von dem in den Anfängen der Arbeiterbewegung so prävalenten Drang, dem leidenden Pro-letariat direkt und praktisch zu helfen; die weiter links stehenden Gruppen, besonders wir Kommunisten, haben eher Fernziele im Auge, weitreichende Projekte weltverändernder Natur, und unser Ziel ist es, den Menschen revolutionäre, um nicht zu sagen utopische Gedanken einzuimpfen, die, wenn überhaupt, erst in der langen Perspektive zu verwirklichen sind und daher im Alltag, wo es um Bier und Wurst geht, weniger ins Gewicht fallen. (p. 168)

I have asked myself more than once why it is that former social democrats have this penchant for administrative work and, within its context, above all for the social services. I presume it is because they still are motivated by some residue of aspirations prevalent in the beginnings of the organised working class movement, the urge to give direct and practical aid to the suffering proletariat; the groups farther to the left, especially we Communists, tend to think of more distant aims, of far-reaching projects to change the whole world, and we strive to fill people's minds with revolutionary, if not to say utopian thought which requires a long perspective for its realisation and which therefore has less weight when it's a question of beer and sausages. (Rendering by Stefan Heym)

These lines are typical of Kadletz's leisurely thought-processes, his constant explanations and often anecdotal examples. Here his contrasting of two ideologies concludes on a somewhat bathetic note: the sudden, concrete illustration of 'Bier und Wurst' ('beer and sausages') is curiously at odds with the grand abstractions which have been previously employed. There is a slight sense of disdain in initially praising the humanity of the Social Democrats, but then associating them with trivial, culinary pursuits, while the glorious ideals of the Communists are referred to only in radical terms. There is the potentially comic risk of overstatement, in fact, with the succession of grandiose concepts: 'Fernziele', 'weitreichend', 'weltverändernd', 'Revolutionäre', 'utopisch' ('more distant aims', 'far-reaching', 'to change the whole world', 'revolutionary', 'utopian'). And yet Kadletz's language and analogy are more a reflection on his own manner of thinking than an evaluation of the Social Democrats. Indeed, the choice of such language may be seen as one of his means of protecting himself from the fear that there are failings in the ideology to which he subscribes. Such failings may be here dismissed by allusions to beer and sausages, but the true nature of Communist transgressions becomes clearer in the gradual revelations concerning the fate of those who are here being repatriated, and then, of course, in Reinsiepe's final political justification – a declaration that everything he did had to be subservient to his political mission. He was conforming, of course, to the Leninist principle of subordinating all individual feelings to an abstract ideal – the Communist utopia. Kadletz, by contrast, is repeatedly troubled by the excesses of the party in which he has placed his trust. In this respect his feelings compare with various characters in Heym's earlier fiction, in particular Wollin (in *The Architects*) and Collin. The anti-Stalinist stance of the early novels is firmly maintained.

If the arrival of the Soviet forces, with their questionable political principles, is seen as unfortunate by the citizens of Schwarzenberg, the alternative (extreme) is not viewed in any more favourable a light. Earlier in the novel the American forces are caricatured as selfish capitalist entrepreneurs, with far more of an interest in the economic future of Schwarzenberg than in its political independence and idealism. They, too, would have made poor masters.

The conclusion to Heym's most recent novel is not defeatist, for the principal aim of the 'postscript' seems clearly to restore a note of optimism. In these final pages, set in the seventies or even early eighties, Wolfram is seen concluding his university lectures on 'Soziale Strukturen in utopischen Gesellschaften' ('Social structures in utopian societies') with a brief question-and-answer session. Wolfram's replies to his questioners reveal that his own utopianism has been eradicated: his responses are very much party-line, a rejection of past utopian thinkers in favour of 'scientific' socialism. His youthful audience, however, reveals much greater hope for change than he does, and one member is even prepared to assert open dissatisfaction with the actual state of socialism in the GDR. He is the son of one of the Schwarzenberg action committee, and it is clear that he has inherited his father's belief in a truly socialist society. As in numerous other novels, Heym pins his hopes on youth.

Between (western) publication of *Schwarzenberg* and the end of the Republic, the gulf between writers and state became even greater – as did that between the state and its ordinary citizens. True, there were fewer pronouncements by functionaries on the role of literature in a socialist society (the Writers' Union itself took over much of this function), but when suggestions or criticism were actually made by the functionaries, their remarks seemed wholly out of touch with actual literary developments. Not surprisingly, such statements were ignored by all figures of any stature, and one can only assume that the functionaries were directing their encouragement at publishers and others involved in the editorial process rather than at writers themselves. One typically incongruous statement came shortly after the appearance of *Schwarzenberg* and just before the thirty-fifth anniversary of the Republic. The intelligent, and in many respects sensitive Klaus Höpcke (Deputy Minister of Culture, and with responsibility for literature) called for 'sozial aktivierende Werke und in ihnen Helden, die Taten für den Fortschritt vollbringen'[14] ('works which have an activating impact on society and which feature heroes who perform deeds for progress'). This was an undisguised reference to the 'positive hero', and the article later made reference to another basic aspect of socialist realism, 'das Typische' ('the typical'). Small wonder that Manfred Jäger sub-titled his article on this piece 'Höpckes Griff in die Mottenkiste der 50er Jahre'[15] ('Höpcke rummages among the mothballs of the fifties')! Höpcke was not alone, and his views were soon echoed by Erich Honecker. In September of that year the latter

demanded works 'in deren Mittelpunkt der aktiv geschichts-
gestaltende Held, die Arbeiterklasse und ihre Repräsentanten
stehen'[16] ('at the centre of which stand the hero who is actively
shaping history, the working class and its representatives'). A
year later the official position remained the same. Kurt Hager,
the leading cultural functionary, quoted and firmly endorsed
Honecker's words when addressing the Writers' Union.[17] In
his (twenty-two-page) speech, Hager again dredged ancient
concepts from a much earlier period of GDR literature and
stressed their contemporary relevance. 'Wir orientieren uns auf
eine lebensnahe und lebenswahre Kunst, eine parteiliche und
volksverbundene Kunst des sozialistischen Realismus in der
ganzen　Weite　und　Vielfalt　seiner　künstlerischen
Ausdrucksmöglichkeiten und Gestaltungsweisen' ('We aim at
art which is close to life and true to life, art which adopts the
party-line and which is close to the people, socialist realism in
the complete breadth and variety of its artistic modes of expression and means of creation'). Such words could barely apply to
the list of prominent figures whom Hager had earlier quoted,
'die die DDR-Literatur national und international repräsen-
tieren' ('who represent GDR literature nationally and internationally') (Heym's name, the widest seller in international
terms, was omitted.) Hager's divorce from the GDR public too
was clear in his dimissive response to Gorbachev's reformist
policies. In an interview with the West German popular
weekly *stern*, he suggested that when a neighbour changed his
wallpaper, one did not have to follow suit.[18] The image soon
became popular currency and was repeatedly mocked by
Heym. In June 1988 Honecker was still feebly making the same
unconvincing point: that changes in the Soviet Union were
inspired by purely Soviet circumstances.

Whatever the public utterances of such powerful figures, the
politicians failed to exercise full control over literary publications in this period. True, the need for formal approval of
literary texts remained – and was still to drive out certain
frustrated figures like Gabriele Eckart, who was subjected to
what she claimed was a form of 'psychoterror'[19] – but J. H.
Reid has shown quite clearly how works actually published in

this period made a mockery of certain earlier clampdowns. A large number of novels and plays which had been banned in their time were now printed or staged without too much difficulty.[20] Once again, though, one obvious exception proved to be Stefan Heym. To understand why this should be so, we need to consider the role of the publishers and the attitude which the leadership held towards Heym.

As we have seen, the Politbüro's views on literature were unequivocal and were probably aimed more at the editorial figures who had to collaborate with authors rather than at the creative figures themselves. The question then arises, why did the editors not reflect the firm ideological stance of their superiors? Principally, perhaps, because these editors wanted good books by the most eminent figures of the Republic. They can have had little satisfaction in publishing works by the party hacks. Second, they knew that if they antagonised their best authors and demanded too many changes before publication, then there was the risk that such authors might leave the Republic. A large number of the most talented had already done so, and their works were now forever lost. A third reason was that frustrated authors, rather than leave the country, might simply send their manuscripts abroad. Heym had shown this could be done with impunity, and there was the consequent risk that many others might follow. This could well explain the relaxation towards those others; and also the vindictive refusal to accept any manuscript by Heym, whose example had deprived East German publishers of works they would have relished. Only after his seventy-fifth birthday (1988) was Heym again to be published in the GDR – and even then in initially restricted form.

Although it was possible to ban Heym's writing, the man himself managed to remain the best-known 'non-person' of the Republic by appearing more often than ever on western TV and by writing regularly for western publications. His face was as well known as that of the leading politicians, and on the streets he was immediately recognised by everyone, from all walks of life. The future of Germany remained one of his prime concerns (the texts included in *Einmischung* give ample testimony to his concern for this issue), and his writing and appearances before the opening of the Wall became frequent and passionate. On this issue he was far more committed than any other writer in either East or West.

Heym was in a firm position to comment on the contemporary situation, because he had just been involved in an extensive review of GDR history. In the course of 1984-7 he had tried to relive the past by exploring his substantial records of previous events in his private archive. The aim was neither academic nor nostalgic, but a means of preparing himself for his most signficant task of the eighties: the composition of his autobiography. *Nachruf*, which appeared in 1988, covered the whole of Heym's life up to the point of composition. To the disappointment of some, however, it devoted well over half of its 844 pages to his experiences before entering the Republic. The pace of these memoirs is leisurely, and they contain possibly too much detail of relatively minor episodes in his career.[21] But the writing at numerous points is captivating – particularly at moments of confrontation – and Heym's life story does engage fully with the major points of GDR history and cultural politics. As we have seen, he remained firmly at the centre of controversy and became involved in some way with every major event. Given his long-standing interest in the forces of history, it is not surprising that these memoirs are concerned far more with factual detail and historical accuracy than with questions of his own personality and identity. His personal, erotic, and literary success takes far less space than his involvement with social or political developments – or, in the war years, than the fight against National Socialism.

Autobiographies by modern German writers – in contrast to those by politicians and the like – have tended towards the techniques of fiction. We find discontinuous narrative, multiple levels of narration, even hints of an 'unreliable narrator'. Heym's approach is strictly traditional. He is determined to present a continuous and unambiguous narrative, and he makes only one concession to modern trends: varying his narrative viewpoint between first and third persons, a technique which only occasionally lends the writing an impression of fiction but which certainly enhances the impression of a *critical* autobiography. Yet Heym is only moderately critical of himself, and he is also indulgent towards most others. He is prepared to see positive qualities even in figures like Ulbricht and Honecker, although these are balanced, of course, by evidence of their shortcomings. For all his tribulations, Heym is never self-pitying or sentimental. And he also avoids the obvious, and justifiable temptation towards self-glorification.

Serialisation of some of the best chapters (in *Der Spiegel*) produced the expected good sales, but even the publishers' expectations were surpassed – the volume soon went into a second printing. Despite size and cost (DM 48.00), over 50,000 copies were sold before the end of the year (1988). As usual, the book was not made available in the GDR.

Heym faced considerable physical problems in these years – torn leg ligaments which did not heal well, difficulties with his hip joint, a failed cataract operation which led to the loss of an eye – but in spite of these he faced the demands of 1989 with energy and resourcefulness. He had observed the development of *glasnost* and *perestroika* in the Soviet Union with rising expectations, initially doubtful of whether Gorbachev could achieve anything against the strong vested interests of those anxious to see no change, but then realising the hope which nevertheless existed, not least for the GDR. He was dismayed by the GDR leadership's resistance to change, which seemed as firm as that of Bulgaria. While all its immediate neighbours were introducing liberalising policies, the GDR remained unrepentingly regressive in its attitude. To the amazement of most, it was not following the line dictated by Moscow. The only major occasion on which this had previously occurred had been when Ulbricht opposed a closer relationship with West Germany – a key factor in his downfall.

Why should the East German leadership have opposed Gorbachev's reforms, and which of them did they find particularly troubling? Perhaps the new frankness towards the past was the most embarrassing, for it brought an obligation to confront the earlier years of their own country in a comparably open manner, something for which Heym had been calling since the

sixties. Soviet intellectuals had given expression to many frustrations – the mistakes, indeed, the crimes of the past; the
suppression of these; the ruthlessness of Stalinism; and the
corruption which had obtained only a few years previously
under Brezhnev. The GDR leadership had good cause to fear
comparable self-scrutiny, for so many of its members had been
in post at the very foundation of the Republic and had implemented Stalinist policies for most of their lives. In the space of
nearly forty years, the Republic had known only two leaders
and their personally selected associates. The responsibility for
mistakes was therefore very tightly held. Another Soviet
concern had been the destruction of the environment, and this
too was a matter on which the GDR seemingly had much to
fear. The reception of Hanns Cibulka's *Swantow* (1981/2) had
already given clear evidence of that: uncensored part-
publication in *Neue Deutsche Literatur* had aroused firm government disapproval, with the result that the book version,
published with difficulty well over a year later, showed evidence of major deletions and revisions.[22]

Whatever the feelings of the leadership, GDR culture certainly appeared to benefit from *glasnost*. Works which had
previously been banned found their way into print, and
volumes from outside the GDR which had hitherto not been
permitted were also allowed. The Writers' Union itself began
to move with this tide, and at their Tenth Congress (November
1987) they went so far as to grant access to western journalists
and TV cameras. The presence of outsiders was of great value
to the progressives. At an early stage of the congress Horst
Matthies called for a change in the proceedings in order to
allow more time for free discussion – as it was being encouraged
in the Soviet Union. The proposal was defeated, but this did
not stop Günter de Bruyn from making a speech in which he
called for the abolition of 'was ich sonst Zensur nenne, hier
aber, ... Druckgenehmigungspraxis nennen will'[23] ('what I
otherwise call censorship, but I will here ... refer to as the
means of obtaining permission to publish'). He also read a
letter from Christa Wolf which urged open discussion and
coming to terms with such past events as the exile of Wolf

Biermann and the exclusion of various colleagues from the Writers' Union. In one of the discussion groups, Christoph Hein spoke fervently against censorship, which he described as 'paradox, menschenfeindlich, überlebt, nutzlos, volksfeindlich ... Die Zensur ist strafbar, denn sie schädigt im hohen Grad das Ansehen der DDR und kommt einer "öffentlichen Herabwürdigung" gleich'[24] ('paradoxical, anti-social, outdated, useless, hostile to the people ... Censorship is something punishable, for it damages to a considerable degree the reputation of the GDR and is tantamount to "public degradation"'). That nothing was achieved by this speech, or by the words of de Bruyn or Matthies, is unsurprising. The remarkable point is that such views were voiced at all. What they reveal is a changed climate in which writers felt the raising of such previously taboo issues was permissible. The implications were auspicious, and for Heym they turned out to be official recognition of his seventy-fifth birthday. In the April 1988 issue of *Neue Deutsche Literatur*, official organ of the Union which had excluded him almost ten years before, three chapters of *Ahasver* appeared.[25] In the September issue, his whimsical 'Das Wachsmuth-Syndrom' was featured, some fifteen years after it had been published in the West. And in the course of the year the complete novel *Ahasver* was also to appear with an eastern imprint.

Such events were not isolated. They reflected a different, and uncertain mood in the literary field. They need, however, to be seen against the more general background of repression in social and political life, and the leadership's firm rejection of *glasnost* as a policy appropriate for the GDR.

Although 1987 had in some respects seemed a promising year for civil liberties, certain concessions may be attributed to Honecker's wish for a semblance of liberalism in view of his impending visit to the Federal Republic. Thus, for example, the year saw the abolition of the death penalty and an amnesty for a very large number of prisoners (both criminal and political). These gestures coincided with the extensive 750th anniversary celebrations for Berlin, where major building programmes were restoring much of the city's former architectural splendour. Yet in the same year there had been very obvious problems: the visit by Reagan to West Berlin in June, for example, when he had called on Gorbachev to 'tear down' the Wall – something the East German leadership may well have feared as a possibility in view of the liberalising tendencies in Moscow. Shortly before this there had been clashes between East German police and several thousand rebellious youths who had gathered near the Wall to hear a rock concert given on the western side. Summers are easier for demonstrations (and the siting of the concert may have been a partial provocation by the West), but the following winter produced a protest which struck firmly at socialist ideology. On 17 January 1988, the anniversary of the death of Rosa Luxemburg and Karl Liebknecht, the official eastern rally was faced with a counter-demonstration. Press reports suggested well over 100 were detained – a figure not reached since 1953, and disturbing for a country in which demonstrations were permitted to be organised only by official bodies and were invariably pro-government – and a small number were given prison sentences ranging between six and twelve months. Thousands of East Germans began holding almost daily protests at further rallies in response to these convictions, and as a result of this pressure (and western protests) all those who had been imprisoned were released by early February. In March, however, there were another eighty arrests during simultaneous human rights demonstrations in East Berlin, Leipzig, Dresden, and Wismar. And in October some eighty persons were arrested (with the use of considerable force) for demonstrating against censorship of church publications. Throughout 1988, in fact, there was constant civil tension with a succession of smaller and larger public protests over the suppression of political discussion, the continuing limitation of exit visas, the lack of non-military alternatives to the compulsory military service, and the need for more action on ecology and peace. The church espoused all these causes, and became increasingly outspoken in its support of these groups.

Once established, the anti-government demonstrations could not be stopped, and in 1989 the pattern was repeated,

beginning again with the anniversary celebrations for Luxemburg and Liebknecht. On this occasion, though, it was in
Leipzig that eighty arrests were made, showing the firm spread
of protest to cities other than Berlin. Relations between the
Soviet Union and the East German leadership were by this
point under considerable strain, as Honecker's government
continued to assert its opposition to liberalising tendencies; one
way of doing so was by increasing the pressures on opposition
groups (especially religious, disarmament, and groups representing the estimated 300,000 who had been refused permission
to emigrate), but such pressure had limited and possibly
counter-productive effect. Much surprise was also caused by
the banning, late in 1988, of the Soviet news digest *Sputnik*. The
eastern authorities claimed that history was being distorted by
this (official) Soviet publication, and the same objection was
levelled against five Soviet films which were banned from the
GDR. The real reason for this action was perfectly plain. Such
developments in the Soviet Union demanded comparable
efforts should be made in the GDR, but the leadership still
feared facing the ghosts which would be raised by considering
their own past. The implications of *Collin* were as fresh as ever,
and the pressures from without could not be concealed from
the populace. As Heym pointed out in an interview for the
Swiss paper *Die Weltwoche*, the East Germans knew of the
attempts by the editor of *Pravda* to stir up his colleagues, and
they also knew that Gorbachev's speeches were being censored
before being reported in the GDR.[26] Such a policy could not
be maintained for long and was soon abandoned. There was
little point in falsification if the full texts were being broadcast
from the other side of the Wall.

Open disagreement with Moscow was unprecedented, and
gave cause for concern to a very different group of GDR
citizens: the party faithful. The leadership had lost confidence
on a broad scale.

The developments in the latter part of 1989 are well known:
the rise of unofficial opposition groups with widespread
support (for example, Neues Forum); a dramatic increase in
the use of the churches as meeting grounds for dissidents; the

beginnings of large-scale escapes to the Federal Republic via third countries; unprecedented mass demonstrations in cities outside the capital, especially Leipzig; and then mass escapes through the newly opened Hungarian border, the latter being generously encouraged by a well-organised Federal Republic. There followed the resignation of the ailing and obviously incompetent Honecker, the desperate attempts by his successor Krenz to safeguard his own position by keeping abreast of popular demands for rapid and radical reform; and then the panic decision to allow free travel to the West. Once that move had been conceded, the collapse of the old guard was assured. They had no experience in dealing with a populace which now recognised its own power and which could also emigrate at will. The following decision to sacrifice the hated secret police meant that the government no longer had any means of enforcing unpopular policies or inhibiting free speech. Free elections were the natural consequence.

Heym expressed his views on most aspects of these developments, the keynote of this period being cautious foresight rather than critical warning. For example, he spoke to a Jugoslavian conference of writers on the implications of Chernobyl and the super-power meeting in Rekyavik, commented in numerous interviews on the implications of *glasnost* and its non-appearance in the GDR, reflected repeatedly on the future of Germany, and also regularly reminded his listeners or readers of the mistakes or crimes committed by the Germans in the past – their treatment of the Jews, in particular. It is true that this latter theme had not been strong in his writing for many years, and was probably revived through the writing of his memoirs. The need to recall and reflect on the past also led to the introduction of more anecdotes from earlier years, as Heym noted various aspects of history repeating itself. There is also one remarkably far-sighted piece which was published anonymously in *Der Spiegel*: an imaginary scene set at some point in the future at which tourists are given a historical introduction to a small remaining section of the Berlin Wall. Yet for all Heym's mockery of the Wall itself, he was still defending the GDR as a state and a wholly acceptable alternative to the Federal Republic. An interesting late example of this is his long and astute review of Peter Merseburger's *Grenz-gänger* (1988), in which Heym uses the review (in *Der Spiegel*) as a platform to commend the economic achievements of his country.

All these later pieces are typical of Heym's breadth of vision, as well as his irony and the capacity to think in opposites. They are wholly in his tradition of composition as it had been established over five decades. There is a change, however, with the pieces from 1989 – particularly with those which appeared as the feelings in the GDR were beginning to rise decisively in late summer. The writing now has a more urgent ring to it – there is more intense self-questioning, sharper use of historical flashbacks and comparisons, blunter condemnation of the illiberal and short-sighted policies of the leadership, and a swifter succession of arguments. There is also more variation in the cadences, with a sense of breathlessness sometimes being employed to increase the sense of drama. The tone is occa-sionally fearful, and it is clear Heym is troubled by develop-ments in which he should in fact take a certain pleasure: for instance, the apparent demise of an inadequate leadership. Far more than the writing of others at this point, Heym's pieces reveal awareness of the dangerous implications of such a collapse. While welcoming certain changes, he can recognise the difficulties which others will bring. His principal fear, I would suggest, is that socialism may be undermined and dis-credited to such an extent that the majority will be reluctant to embrace it again. The view that materialist concerns could sweep aside long-held socialist principles comes out in his essay 'Aschermittwoch' and in his speech to a large demonstration in December – that is, after the opening of the Wall.[27] For such views Heym was later to be attacked – most notably by Monika Maron, who accused him of double standards and who ridi-culed eastern writers in general in their call for a rejection of West German capitalism.[28]

In the period before the collapse Heym was arguing inten-sively for a restructured form of socialism; the speed with which the eastern populace swung away from this and effectively voted for capitalism suggests he was at this stage out of touch with popular opinion. The demand for a higher standard of living and for consumer goods without queues was greater than that for a reformed ideology. At this point, of course, the notion of much higher prices and large-scale unemployment – as a concomitant of financial 'progress' – had not been widely recognised.

Heym did foresee the dangers of hasty progress, and his essays in *Die Zeit* and *Der Spiegel* are among the best in his career. Passionate, but balanced, they plead for the saving of socialism under a different leadership. Heym's hopes here were ill-founded, however. Unlike Moscow, East Berlin had not produced a Gorbachev: someone from within the ranks of the party who nevertheless recognised the need for radical change and who possessed the necessary confidence and vigour to pursue it. None of the younger members of the Politbüro revealed sufficient charisma or diplomatic skills to lead the Republic to a new type of government, nor were there any figures on the fringes of the party with sufficient experience or competence to step into a position of authority. The best (figures like Rudolf Bahro) had either managed to leave the country voluntarily, or had been forced out after imprisonment. Heym's pleas were therefore in vain – not least because he had once again been denied a platform in his own country. The change came with 'Aschermittwoch', published in both *Der Spiegel* and *Junge Welt* (December 1989), a *cri de coeur* for an independent, socialist Republic. But underlying its passionate argument there is the feeling that the GDR has been lost.

The GDR was indeed lost, and many of the ideals for which it had stood were quickly forgotten – even by some of its previously ardent supporters. In the belief that only within a united Germany was a truly prosperous future to be ensured, there was widespread rejection of the calls for an independent socialist state (most notably, of the document 'Für unser Land', an appeal signed by a number of prominent writers, including Heym), and the determination to ensure an abundance of consumer goods then led to humiliating defeat for the reformed socialist parties in the free elections of March 1990. Heym was soon vindicated in his fear that a restoration of capitalism would eradicate all East German social achievements. The forces behind conservative restoration had, after all, been a theme in various novels (especially *The Crusaders, Lenz*), and their reappearance in the GDR provided him with a theme which runs through every one of the short stories in his final volume to date: *Auf Sand gebaut* (October 1990).

Most of these seven short pieces employ a semi-guileless, first-person narrator who suddenly finds himself outflanked by the rapid developments following the revolution – or 'Wende', to use the popular eastern euphemism. The new victors are those who have hitherto proved shrewd, adaptable, and successful in the old GDR, and who can readily modify their behaviour to what is actually an equivalent style of political manoeuvering, collaboration, or simple opportunism in the limbo between 'Wende' and unification. These cynical stories remind one of Heym's *Cannibals* – the image of the predator fits perfectly – but the tone is lighter and the humour less bitter. They present an image of a Republic which has lost all idealism, of careerists who have cynically adapted to change, and of an aggressive West Germany which, with American advice, has subtly influenced the East Germans' thinking on a united Germany. Heym sees nothing positive in the unified Germany which is to come, and the symbolism of the title piece reinforces the idea that the new Germany will be as unstable as the old.

Heym, then, has become a dissenter once more – in the third German state in which he has existed.

CHAPTER 10

The achievement

Durch die Darstellung von Gefühlen und Schicksalen habe ich mich bemüht, den Menschen etwas zu geben, ihnen vielleicht auch ein wenig vorwärtszuhelfen und so zur Veränderung unserer Welt beizutragen.

(*Wege*, p. 21)

By writing about the feelings and fortunes of individuals, I have tried to give something to humanity, perhaps also to help people on, and by this means to contribute in a small way to changing our world.

Heym has devoted his whole adult life to the causes in which he believed. Apart from a small number of fairy tales, lyric poems and similar short pieces, his novels, essays and speeches all address political issues which were in some way connected with the development of democratic socialism. His entire intellectual and emotional energy was invested in portraying the problems surrounding certain ideals of truth, freedom, and democracy, on exposing the evils of fascism and Stalinism, and in pleading for a better world. To this end he constantly took serious risks, and he often espoused causes which he knew to be out of favour. True, his attacks on bureaucracy, injustice, and Stalinism found many grateful listeners in more than one country, but he did not shrink from voicing opinions which he knew could damage his popularity and his income. For many years after the war, for example, he was severe in his assessment of the Germans and the German mentality, and even in the late 1980s he was still criticising sections of West German society for their silence during the Third Reich. In the East it was not only officialdom he attacked. He deplored the sudden surge of materialism in East Germany after the Wall was removed, and this at a point when the East German public would for the first time have unrestricted access to all his works. As he himself commented in another speech at this time, he knew that his remarks would not be welcomed by many – but plain speaking had always been his hallmark.

The suppression of heterodox views has occurred regularly throughout the history of civilisation, and Heym stands in a long tradition of persecuted writers – particularly German authors. Like many of his predecessors, his successes have been both political and literary. In politics we have seen how his stand against authority began in Germany and continued in the USA. It was in the GDR, however, that he took most risks, and it was here that his achievements were greatest. He repeatedly endangered his own freedom, but in so doing he exposed injustice, encouraged questioning, and provided that all-important example for others. Without his lead, opposition in the GDR would have been far weaker. In the literary sphere it might have crumbled completely. To his fellow artists he not only illustrated the possibilities of writing 'between the lines', but he also showed the opportunities for undisguised dissent, often by means of foreign outlets.

In literature Heym quickly established an international reputation on which he was able to rely for much of his career. The issues on which he focussed tended to be general and timeless. His novels were translated into over twenty languages, and the sales of certain works exceeded a million copies. With later novels political factors may well have played a role in this success: a certain proportion of his audience was anxious to read what it considered the 'scandalous truth' about the GDR, and the author's image as a persecuted dissident doubtless gave him further appeal. Yet Heym did not choose to exploit this position in writing fiction. He could easily have expanded his readership by being sensationalist in his revelations, but his method represented a defence of the socialist ideal as much as a critique of what was commonly referred to as 'der real existierende Sozialismus' ('the form of socialism which actually exists'). This may be one of the reasons why his greatest admirers lay in that country whose leaders regularly refused him permission to publish. Another reason may be found in his consistent position as an unproblematic storyteller with an unselfconscious narrative: he remained an unashamed realist throughout his career, exploiting non-realistic methods on only a handful of occasions and insisting that the duty of the true artist is to entertain and to appeal to his reading public as a whole. By following these precepts Heym demonstrated the possibilities of socially committed writing, while assuring for himself a large and loyal readership on both sides of the Berlin Wall.

2 THE EARLY YEARS: REVOLT AND EXILE

1 There is an absence of detailed information on Heym's early career. The present outline owes much to Heym's memories, *Nachruf*, and to a series of conversations with the author conducted over a number of years.

2 In the final stages of completing this study Heym advised me that he had discovered an even earlier poem. This had appeared in 'Jugendstimme', a section of the *Chemnitzer Volksstimme*, as early as February 1930. Heym was at this point only sixteen years old. The sentiments are again anti-military:

Nie Wieder Krieg!
Es reitet der Tod auf einem Gerippe
und mäht und mäht mit grausamer Hand.
  Kanonen donnern,
  Raketen blitzen,
  Granaten heulen,
  Tanks rollen heran.
Gasschwaden senken
sich tief auf die Erde,
und keine Rettung
gibt's vor dem Tod.
Es liegen Leichen
in jedem Trichter,
Fleischfetzen kleben
an jeder Wand.
Ein großes Morden
von Graben zu Graben.
Der Himmel speit Flammen,
die Hölle ist hier!

Du hätlst reiche Ernte, Gevatter Tod!
Dein härer Gewand ist von Blute rot!

Wofür?

Frauen, wollt ihr wieder eure Kinder opfern?
Männer, wollt ihr wieder hingeschlachtet werden?
Söhne, wollt ihr wieder eure Zukunft geben für ein Nichts?
Nein, wir wollen leben, uns nicht töten lassen!
Niemals wieder wollen wir die Waffen heben gegen Brüder!
Nie wieder Krieg!

Never again war!
Death comes riding on a skeleton
and mows down and mows down with a cruel hand.
Guns thunder,
Rockets flash,
Shells whine,
Tanks roll up.
Clouds of gas sink
deep onto the earth,
and there is no way of saving
oneself from death.
Corpses are lying
in every crater,
Pieces of flesh
stick to every wall.
A grand scale of murder
from trench to trench.
The sky spits forth flames
and hell is now here.

Old Friend Death, a rich harvest you reaped!
Your hair shirt in red blood is steeped!

And for what?

Women, do you again want to sacrifice your children?
Men, do you again want to be slaughtered?
Sons, do you again want to sacrifice your future days for nothing?
No, we want to live, not let ourselves be killed.
Never again do we want to raise weapons against our brothers.

Never again war!

3 The poem is reproduced in the second edition of *Wege und Umwege*, a collection of Heym's most important shorter pieces to

appear between 1931 and 1985, pp. 23–4. This edition is one of the fourteen volumes in the Goldmann *Werkausgabe*, to which all references will be made unless otherwise stated. Reference to works in English will in all cases be to the first edition. For full details of Heym's publications, see the first part of the Bibliography.

4 Facsimiles of the detailed newspaper report in the *Chemnitzer Tageblatt* of 1 October 1931 are included in the first pages of the (unpaginated) *Beiträge zu einer Biographie*.

5 Heym recalls this objection, typical of cultural policy in the early fifties, in 'Das Volk will echten Realismus. Beobachtungen zum literarischen Leben in der DDR', p. 3.

6 Ibid.

7 For example, the UK: M. Dorman, 'The state versus the writer: recent developments in Stefan Heym's struggle against the GDR's Kulturpolitik'; the USA: entry in *International Biographical Dictionary of Central European Emigrés*, vol. 2, edited by Herbert A. Strauss and Werner Roder; West Germany: Hans-Albert Walter, *Deutsche Exilliteratur 1933–50*, vol. 4, 'Exilpresse'; the GDR: the entry in Gerhard Seidel's bibliography of *Das Wort*, *Das Wort, Moskau 1936–1939, Bibliographie einer Zeitschrift*.

8 For a brief assessment of the achievement of the *DVE*, see Robert Cazden, *German Exile Literature in America, 1933–50*, pp. 42–4. A more detailed survey is provided by R. Zachau in 'Stefan Heym als Herausgeber des kommunistischen *Deutschen Volksecho* (New York, 1937–1939)'; other relevant material is contained in Zachau's doctoral dissertation, 'Stefan Heym in Amerika'. Another doctoral dissertation also devotes some space to this period of Heym's career: Inge D. Dube, 'Das Amerika-Bild Stefan Heyms'.

3 FIRST NOVELS

1 For Heym's careful explanation of his aims, see 'Wie *Der Fall Glasenapp* entstand'.

2 Orville Prescott, 'Books of the times', *New York Times*, 16 October 1942.

3 'Stefan Heyms Auseinandersetzung mit Faschismus, Militarismus und Kapitalismus', p. 118.

4 See Hans Habe, 'Abschied von Stefan Heym', p. 10.

5 The interview with Habe is recalled in *Nachruf*, pp. 390–1. Heym is generous in his assessment of Habe's motivation here. Habe, by contrast, expressed violent anti-Communist feelings in his vicious 'Abschied von Stefan Heym'.

6 *American Novels of the Second World War*, p. 56.
7 'I arrive at socialism by train', p. 229.
8 *New York Daily Worker*, 16 September 1948, p. 3.
9 Review by Richard Plant, 12 September 1948, p. 37.
10 *New Republic*, 27 September 1948, pp. 33–4.

4 WRITING FOR CAUSES

1 For further details of Tolstoy's firm views on history and historiography, see R. F. Christian, *Tolstoy. A Critical Introduction*, especially pp. 154–8.
2 These stories were first written in English and then translated into German by Heym and Ellen Zunk. They appeared as *Die Kannibalen und andere Erzählungen* in 1953. The original English-language pieces were not published as a collection until 1957 in the Paul List (Leipzig) series of 'Panther Books'.
3 For further details of Heym's translation skills, see my article 'Using the "Self-translator" as a model: the translations of Stefan Heym'; also the dissertation by Marina Höller, 'Stefan Heym als zweisprachiger Schriftsteller', especially pp. 102–6. Ms Höller rightly detects less confidence in Heym's later translations from German into English, as his daily experience of the English language becomes more distant. This coincides with the point, of course, at which Heym begins to use German as his first language of composition.

5 RETURN TO GERMANY: THE STRUGGLES OF THE FIFTIES

1 For an introduction to the changing view of the writer in the GDR, with particular reference to the politico-cultural background, see the most helpful article by Ian Wallace, 'Teacher or partner? The role of the writer in the GDR'.
2 For a brief survey of writers' earnings and some of their privileges, see, for example, *Hansers Sozialgeschichte der deutschen Literatur*, vol. 11, ed. Hans-Jürgen Schmitt, pp. 57–66.
3 Reprinted in Elimar Schubbe, *Dokumente zur Kunst-, Literatur- und Kulturpolitik der SED*, p. 108. The three volumes in this series of documents from the GDR will henceforth be referred to as 'Schubbe, *Dokumente*', 'Rüß, *Dokumente*'; and 'Lübbe, *Dokumente*'.
4 Comparable difficulties were faced by Ludwig Renn, Hanns Eisler, and even Bertolt Brecht. Hans-Dietrich Sander lists the numerous casualties of what he terms the 'erste Kulturkampf der

SED' on pp. 104–7 of *Geschichte der Schönen Literatur in der DDR*. This includes a lengthy quotation from Kantorowicz's diary, which describes the Kafka-like feeling of oppression which certain writers were experiencing.

5 For details of the frustrations to which writers were subjected, see, for example, Janet Swaffar's interview with Gabriele Eckart, especially pp. 318–27.

6 The most detailed study is that by Arnulf Baring, *Uprising in East Germany: 17 June 1953*, a slightly revised version of the German edition which was published several years earlier. This volume should be read in conjunction with the detailed comments by the French reviewer, Félix Lusset. Also of value is the collection of essays edited by Ilse Spittmann and Karl Wilhelm Fricke, *17. Juni 1953. Arbeiteraufstand in der DDR*. The latter includes a number of accounts by leading East German figures of the time, including Heym's 'Memorandum' which was published in the *Tägliche Rundschau* on 21 June.

For the standard East German view, see the relevant chapter in *Geschichte der deutschen Arbeiterbewegung in acht Bänden* edited by the Institut für Marxismus-Leninismus beim Zentralkomitee der SED, vol. 7. The East German view has, however, been revised over the years, and Heinrich Mohr has contrasted two short histories of the GDR in order to illustrate a shift in attitude between the Ulbricht years and those of Honecker. Taking Stefan Dornberg's widely read *Kurze Geschichte der DDR* (1964) as representative of the former, he shows how by 1974 the depiction is less emotional, more factual, and that there is an attempt to see the events in a greater international perspective (his second example is *DDR. Werden und Wachsen: Zur Geschichte der Deutschen Demokratischen Republik*, written by Rolf Badstübner et al.). For full details, see Mohr's article 'Der 17. Juni als Thema der Literatur in der DDR', in *Die deutsche Teilung im Spiegel der Literatur*, pp. 43–84.

7 See his article 'Beobachtungen zum Pressewesen in der DDR' (July 1953), reprinted in *Wege*, pp. 209–17.

8 It is not, however, possible to speak of any clear influence from Brecht on Heym's method as a whole, and the technique of inverted expectations is repeatedly evident in the *Volksecho* articles. There are, nonetheless, occasional Brechtian echoes. Stephan Bock, in his warm survey of Heym's journalism in the early fifties, quotes a passage from Heym's 'Offener Brief an Herbert Warnke' which bases itself on Brecht's 'Fragen eines lesenden Arbeiters' (Bock, *Literatur Gesellschaft Nation*, p. 193). Heym anticipates any criticism of plagiarism by himself referring

to Brecht. Another possible influence here is, of course, Karl Kraus.

9 These two key sentences are also quoted by Sander in his brief discussion of the 'Nacherstedter Brief', which he regards as something orchestrated by powers higher than the workers themselves (*Geschichte der Schönen Literatur*, pp. 148–9). A more positive view is expressed by Stephan Bock in *Literatur Gesellschaft Nation*, pp. 140–5.

10 See his review of the collection, 'Licht und Schatten', p. 124.

11 For the clear division of interpretation between East and West, see my 'History and political literature'. Valuable points are also made by Heinrich Mohr in 'Der 17. Juni als Thema der Literatur in der DDR', by Johannes Pernkopf in his volume *Der 17. Juni 1953 in der Literatur der beiden deutschen Staaten*, and by Rudolf Wichard in 'Der 17. Juni 1953 im Spiegel der DDR-Literatur'. A full bibliography of East German literature on this subject has been compiled by Stephan Bock, *Der 17. Juni in der Literatur der DDR. Eine Bibliographie (1953–1979)*.

12 For details of Heym's personal, dramatic experiences, see *Nachruf*, pp. 563–9. A key revelation here is that Heym managed to prevent the Writers' Union from issuing a totally inappropriate statement on the events. Some information on the range of his researches for the novel is provided on pp. 582–6.

13 See Heym's interview with Adalbert Reif, 'Auf beiden Seiten ist der 17. Juni umgelogen worden', p. 6. This was a point, however, that Heym was already making in June 1953. As he put it in one of his major newspaper articles: 'Es ist klar daß der unmittelbare Anlaß zum 17. Juni auf die Agentenarbeit der Westmächte zurückzuführen ist. Sonst wäre ja nicht zu gleicher Zeit an so vielen Stellen in dieser organisierten Form losgeschlagen worden. Die Ursache aber ist nicht der Anlaß – und die Ursache zu den Ereignissen liegt in der DDR' ('It is clear that the immediate cause of 17 June can be traced to the work of western agents. How can one otherwise explain that attacks in this organised form broke out at the same time in so many different places? But there is a difference between the immediate cause and the origins: and the origins of these events lie in the GDR'). The whole article is a powerful denunciation of the party for its inadequate relations with the people. See *Wege und Umwege*, pp. 261–8 (267). The only other literary figure who was prepared to commit himself openly at this point was Erich Loest. See in particular his article 'Elfenbeinturm und rote Fahne'.

14 'Heilige Kühe aus Ost und West', interview with Karl Corino.

15 'Gruppenbild mit Genosse', p. 179.
16 For example, Michael Ratcliffe in his review 'Straight between the eyes'; Günter Zehm, 'Der schwarze Tag des Stefan Heym'.
17 For example, Fritz Raddatz in the above-mentioned review. Raddatz's shrewd observation here holds good for Heym's fiction as a whole: 'Er kann Menschen großartig *gegeneinander* setzen, das Miteinander gerät ihm oft banal' (p. 176) ('He is splendid at setting people *against* one another, but at actually *bringing* them together he can be quite banal.') It is the coincidences surrounding the figure of Goodie Cass to which most exception has been taken.
18 *Zitat und Montage*, p. 144.

6 THE USES OF HISTORY

1 See Heym's account in *Nachruf*, pp. 656 and 660–1. More favourable reactions by party members are quoted on page 657.
2 'Birth of a spectre', p. 269.
3 Wolfgang Joho, 'Tragikomische Ouvertüre'.
4 The most helpful introduction to the movement, which also attempts to see it in a wider framework, remains that by Bernhard Greiner, *Von der Allegorie zur Idylle: Die Literatur der Arbeitswelt in der DDR*, especially pp. 99–190.
5 The full text of Khrushchev's speech, together with a commentary, is provided in Bertram D. Wolfe, *Khrushchev and Stalin's Ghost: Text, Background and Meaning of Khrushchev's Secret Report to the Twentieth Congress on the Night of February 24–25, 1956*.
6 See the opening paragraphs of his essay 'Zu einigen Fragen der Literatur und Kunst', which was given prominence in *Neues Deutschland* (27 July 1956); it is reprinted in Schubbe, *Dokumente*, pp. 440–5.
7 See his speech at the 'Sitzung der Präsidialrates des Kulturbundes zur demokratischen Erneuerung Deutschlands', delivered on 22 February 1957. Relevant extracts reprinted in Schubbe, *Dokumente*, pp. 455–60; see especially p. 456.
8 See Hager's long speech of 25 March 1963, 'Parteilichkeit und Volksverbundenheit unserer Literatur und Kunst', reprinted in Schubbe, *Dokumente*, pp. 859–79; see especially p. 877.
9 *German Writers in Soviet Exile, 1933–45*.
10 In his study, Pike quotes from two letters by Herzfelde. These express concern over the situation of 'innocent' colleagues (p. 215). Pike might have considered the sentiments expressed here more cautiously. The sincerity of views expressed in all

hearsay evidence, as well as in letters, must remain in doubt. Self-preservation, and subsequent preservation of self-image, obviously play a significant part in all statements.

11 Ulbricht divorced his first wife, who had never left Germany, in 1951; immediately afterwards he married Lotte Wendt.

12 The speech was delivered at some point during the colloquium, 1–5 December 1964. It appeared in *Die Zeit* on 5 February 1965.

13 According to Heym's later self-defence after the '11. Plenum des ZK der SED', this was Dr Pollatschek of the *Berliner Zeitung*. Heym ascribed the letter of attack on him by two 'workers', as published in the *BZ* for 10 December 1965, to the paper's anger at his exposure of their actions. See *Wege*, p. 369.

14 *Nachruf*, pp. 729–30. This sense of affinity is also admitted in conversation with David Binder, who reviewed the book for the *International Herald Tribune*: 'Asked whether *Lassalle* was a labor of love, Mr Heym retorted: "He was a bastard. But damn it, I got to like him. Maybe there is an affinity. He was a Jew and a revolutionary. I am a Jew and a Socialist. He was a fantastic character, not just one person but many combined, and he is all but forgotten. Marx and Engels were sanctified. But nobody ever mentions Lassalle. I came to feel he was a fallen angel."'

15 'Der Sinn für das Wesentliche. Stefan Heym, *Lassalle*'. Neubert was reviewing the first East German edition, of course, which appeared only in 1974, some five years after first publication in the West. His hostility was not shared by other GDR reviewers, who used this early part of the Honecker era to express themselves more openly. After predictable comments on Heym's treatment of Marx and Engels, the *Neues Deutschland* reviewer (Harald Wessell) called the novel 'ein reizvolles Buch' ('a charming book'). Christoph Funke (*Der Morgen*) found his reading 'unterhaltsam und abenteuerlich' ('an entertaining adventure'). And Günter Ebert (*Freie Erde*), despite some reservations about depicting Lassalle from the point of view of the bourgeoisie, could praise the novel as 'eine erzählerische Glanzleistung' ('a superb narrative achievement').

7 THE USES OF LITERATURE

1 For a brief outline of the careers of Havemann and Biermann within the larger context of oppositional activity, see K. Fricke, *Opposition und Widerstand in der DDR*, especially pp. 158–9 and 176–8; or, for the later period, R. Woods, *Opposition in the GDR under Honecker, 1971–85*, pp. 24–31

2 W. V. Blomster in *Books Abroad*. Despite this fundamental error, the review is otherwise sensitive, and Blomster is generous in his praise. The work is likewise extolled by Werner Brettschneider, who regards it as 'in ihrer Kürze und Geschlossenheit das literarisch vollendetste Werk Stefan Heyms' ('in its brevity and taut construction it is, in literary terms, Heym's most accomplished work') (*Zwischen literarischer Autonomie und Staatsdienst*, p. 91); R. K. Zachau, often hostile in his assessment, considers this work 'ein Meisterwerk der modernen politischen Satire' ('a masterpiece of modern political satire') (*Stefan Heym*, p. 72).

3 For details of this debate, see Manfred Jäger, *Kultur und Politik in der DDR*, pp. 125–31, and *Hansers Sozialgeschichte der deutschen Literatur*, vol. 11, pp. 279–83.

4 'People must feel free' [interview with Timothy Nater], p. 60.

5 The first review was that by Hermann Kähler, 'Christa Wolfs Elegie', which appeared in *Sinn und Form* early in 1969. Ironically, this lukewarm assessment was one of the best Christa Wolf was to receive. Very few other reviews actually appeared, in line with East German policy of not drawing attention to what was undesirable. Although the novel bears the publication date '1968', copies were not in fact released until 1969. There is considerable doubt about the size of the original print run (see Heinrich Mohr, 'Produktive Sehnsucht. Struktur, Thematik und politische Relevanz von Christa Wolfs *Nachdenken über Christa T.*', pp. 216–17), and the volume itself was not reprinted until 1973.

6 *VI. Deutscher Schriftstellerkongress vom 28. bis 30. Mai 1969: Protokoll*, especially pp. 55–6.

7 This was revealed by Kant many years later, when he expressed bitterness over the delay. His account is contained in a conversation he allowed to be printed by the West German left-wing publication *Kürbiskern* some ten years later (1980). The novel had been serialised in advance (thus avoiding the rigorous censorship procedures imposed on books), so when the novel as a whole did not appear, it was obvious to readers that there was official disapproval. See 'Von Helden, Autoren und Präsidentensorgen', especially pp. 121–2.

8 *The King David Report*, London, 1973; *Der König-David-Bericht*, Munich, 1972.

9 Interview with Robert Moskin, reprinted in *The Queen against Defoe*, p. 120.

10 For details of other treatments, see my article 'Problems of socialist historiography: the example of Stefan Heym's *The King David*

Report', pp. 131–8. This article treats certain aspects of the novel in slightly more depth than does the present chapter.

11 *What is History?*, p. 17.

12 The issue is, for example, treated in two of the other most important novels to be written in the GDR: Hermann Kant's *Die Aula*, pp. 258–66; and Christa Wolf's *Kindheitsmuster*, p. 360.

13 The parallel between David and Stalin is accepted unquestioningly by Marcel Reich-Ranicki ('König David alias Stalin') and by Heinrich Böll ('Der Lorbeer ist immer noch bitter', pp. 158–9). David Roberts, on the other hand, has taken the main parallel as David–Lenin, with a consequent paralleling of Solomon–Stalin (see his stimulating 'Stefan Heym: *Der König-David-Bericht'*, p. 204). Reinhard Zachau, however, suggests that the only parallels to be found are with Stalin and Beria (*Stefan Heym*, p. 75).

14 In his infamous 'Secret Report to the Twentieth Congress on the Night February 24–25 1956', Khruschev actually called for a new history of the recent past – to be edited, moreover, in accordance with party principles. (The full text of this speech is contained in Bertram D. Wolfe, *Khruschev and Stalin's Ghost. Text, Background and Meaning of Khruschev's Secret Report to the Twentieth Congress on the Night of February 24–25, 1956.*) There are striking parallels between Khruschev's list of crimes perpetrated by Stalin and those which are perpetrated by Heym's David. Although Heym's title might suggest he was influenced by Khruschev's 'Report', Heym himself has admitted in conversation the inspiration came rather from that of Dr A. C. Kinsey! That the parallels between the specific crimes of Stalin and David are thus coincidental, underlines the continuity of method to be seen in the totalitarian system.

15 'Die Verbesserung der Forschung und Lehre in der Geschichtswissenschaft der Deutschen Demokratischen Republik', quoted by W. Conze in 'Die deutsche Geschichtswissenschaft seit 1945', p. 8. The Central Committee's paper is replete with similar grandiose intentions, and in particular with the notion of 'unsere Aufgabe' ('our task'). This phrase, so common in GDR political jargon, is regularly exploited in the German version of the novel. An example from the fifth chapter stands in a clearly ironic relationship to the Central Committee's formulation: 'Unsre Aufgabe ist es, die Größe unsres Zeitalters zu widerspiegeln, indem wir einen glücklichen Mittelweg wählen zwischen dem, was ist, und dem was die Menschen glauben sollen' (p. 48). It is perhaps worth noting that the phrase, which obviously lacks a sense of irony for the English-language reader, would seem to

have been inserted deliberately in the German translation. It is lacking in the English original: 'We are to strike a happy medium between what is and what we want people to believe' (p. 42).

16 *Wege und Umwege*, p. 354.

17 Michael Ratcliffe in *The Times*; Clancy Sigal in *The Sunday Times*; Robert Nye in *The Guardian*.

18 Marcel Reich-Ranicki in *Die Zeit*; Günter Zehm in *Die Welt*; Heinrich Böll in *Der Spiegel*.

8 CENTRE OF CONTROVERSY AGAIN: HONECKER'S FIRST PERIOD

1 For information on typical career patterns of the GDR political elite around the time of Honecker's accession, see P. C. Ludz, *The German Democratic Republic from the Sixties to the Seventies*, pp. 41–5. Ludz provides an exhaustive analysis of trends in the composition of the SED leadership bodies in chapter 3 of his earlier study, *Parteielite im Wandel*.

2 See his 'Bericht des ZK an den VIII. Parteitag' of 15 June 1971, part of which was given prominence in the *Neue Deutsche Literatur* issue for August of that year ('Inhaltliche Tiefe und meisterhafte Gestaltung'). The quotation is reprinted in Rüß, *Dokumente*, p. 181.

3 Part of his final speech to the '4. Tagung des ZK der SED', printed in *Neues Deutschland* on 18 December 1971. Reprinted in Rüß, *Dokumente*, p. 287.

4 This peculiar circumstance is explained by the fact that the translation, 'The proper approach', was included in an anthology edited ('on behalf of the Presidium of the PEN-Centre, German Democratic Republic') by Wieland Herzfelde and Günther Cwojdrak. The GDR was thus able to give the impression abroad that such pieces were being published in the country itself.

5 See, for example: Anon., 'Der Ostberliner Aufstand – aus der Sicht eines DDR-Autors' (*Neue Zürcher Zeitung*); Jörg B. Bilke, 'Stefan Heym und der 17. Juni 1953' (*Frankfurter Hefte*); A. Mytze, 'Stefan Heyms Report des 17. Juni 1953' (*Die Presse*); Fritz J. Raddatz, 'Gruppenbild mit Genosse' (*Der Spiegel*); Wilfried F. Schoeller, 'Fünf umstrittene Tage im Juli (*Frankfurter Rundschau*); Wolfgang Werth, 'Nachdenken über Martin W.' (*Süddeutsche Zeitung*); Günter Zehm, 'Der schwarze Tag des Stefan Heym' (*Die Welt*).

6 See his 'Bericht des Politbüros an die 9. Tagung des Zentralkomitees', printed in *Neues Deutschland* on 29 May 1973. Reprinted in Rüß, *Dokumente*, pp. 776–8. See especially p. 777.

7 Kunze's own version of the alternatives he was offered were not revealed until 1981 (in an interview for *stern*). For the wording, and for a useful survey of the politico-cultural situation at this point, see Derek Fogg, 'Exodus from a promised land. The Biermann affair', pp. 139–40.

8 A full list of the signatories and co-signatories is to be found in Lübbe, *Dokumente*, p. 111.

9 For example, his witty survey of the GDR news programme 'Aktuelle Kamera', which carried the sarcastic title 'Je voller der Mund, desto leerer die Sprüche'. This appeared in West Germany (*stern*) and the UK (*New Statesman*), but not in the GDR.

10 For a study of this particular feature of GDR literature, see Wolfgang Müller, *Dichter-Helden in der DDR-Literatur der siebziger Jahre*. Müller considers *Collin* on pp. 93–9.

11 'Authority, the state and the individual: Stefan Heym's *Collin*'.

12 Ibid., p. 345. Graves is here quoting from A. I. Titarenko and others, *Marxistische-Leninistische Ethik*, p. 154.

13 Janka's own testimony is now available: *Schwierigkeiten mit der Wahrheit*. It appeared in the West after the fall of Honecker.

14 In *Nachruf*, Heym suggests that if there is a model for the figure of Urack, then it is not Mielke but Richard Stahlmann: the latter had a long and distinguished secret service career for the Communist Party, and highlights of it are mentioned by Heym on p. 815. Stahlmann served under Mielke and became almost paranoic under his pressure. His name was not, however, widely known in East Germany, and the eastern public, like the western critics, would probably have overlooked this aspect of the *clef*.

15 'Die Austreibung des Bösen', p. 82.

16 'Tapferfeige Intellektuelle', p. 41.

17 For details of the GDR's abuse of the International Convention on Civil and Political Rights in this particular period, see, for example, David Childs, *The GDR. Moscow's German Ally*, pp. 225–6.

18 See Julian Roberts's analysis of the debate which Christa Wolf's actions aroused, 'Crucifying Christa' (*The Guardian*, 23 August 1990). Roberts summarises the main view against her as follows: 'although publication in 1979 would have been an act of heroic resistance, in 1990 it is a cheap attempt to represent herself as the victim of a system of which she was the beneficiary'.

19 For the text of this interview, see *Wege und Umwege*, pp. 440–1. For Heym's own details of the trial, see *Nachruf*, pp. 832–3.

20 Reprinted in *Wege und Umwege*, pp. 440–52.

21 For the text of Heym's self-defence, see *Wege und Umwege*, pp. 442–8. Heym's knowledge of the (indirect) pressures on members of the union is brought out in the conclusion of this speech, where he concedes the difficulties some will have in deciding to vote as they might wish. He is quite frank: 'Wir alle wissen, was für den einzelnen von seinem Votum abhängen mag: Westreisen und Stipendien, Auflagen und Aufführungen, Verfilmungen und Preise aller Art' (p. 447) ('We all know what depends on the way each individual votes: trips to the West and grants, editions and performances, film versions of your works and all sorts of prizes'). The speech concludes with Heym reminding his colleagues that the ultimate judge of their conduct will be the public and posterity.

Heym gave copies of this manuscript to *Neues Deutschland* and other East German media, but it was not accepted by them. It first appeared in the *Frankfurter Allgemeine Zeitung* of 22 June 1979, p. 25. The decision to seek publication in the West may be seen as another example of Heym's tactical bravery.

9 AN EASIER STRUGGLE: THE EIGHTIES

1 In the course of the eighties, East German viewing of West German TV programmes was extensive. In 1986, Roger Woods suggested that '80 to 90 per cent of potential viewers watch them' (*Opposition in the GDR under Honecker*, p. 9). Although East German sports programmes probably remained unrivalled, the livelier (and, of course, more sensational) methods of presentation in western programmes ensured far larger audiences. Heym himself commented on his popularity in the western media as early as 1975 (*Wege*, p. 395). Ten years later he could still lament 'Wie es jetzt ist, kann ich mich mit den Bürgen der DDR nur über das Westfernsehen verständigen' ('As things now stand, I can communicate with GDR citizens only by means of West German television') (*Einmischung*, p. 96).

2 'Stefan Heym's *Ahasver*: structure and principles', 232–4. Nancy Lauckner suggests a more precise division, claiming there are four 'time levels' (the time of Creation, Jesus' time, the sixteenth century, and the twentieth century) and a 'level that transcends time'. ('Stefan Heym's revolutionary Wandering Jew. A warning and a hope for the future', p. 67.)

3 A very full treatment of the legend is provided by George K. Anderson in *The Legend of the Wandering Jew*. Its relevance to Heym is well surveyed by H.-P. Ecker, *Poetisierung als Kritik*, pp. 15–37.

4 The importance of the pun for Heym can be seen by the fact that he preserves it in English translation, but at a different point in the novel. In the German version it is introduced at the conclusion, with reference to the 'real existierende Loch' ('actually existing hole') in the wall from which Beifuß is taken by the devil (p. 246). In the English version it is used by Eitzen to refer to Ahasver when he attends the death of the former's father (p. 133). On both occasions the words refer to something which, in the eyes of the speaker, should not properly exist.

5 For details, see for example Fricke, *Opposition und Widerstand*, p. 196, or Woods, *Opposition in the GDR*, pp. 36–41; 185–213.

6 The issue of pessimism is taken up in the interviews by both Hartmut Panskus ('Gelitten und nicht mehr') and Hans Wolf- schütz ('Diskussion mit dem Teufel. "Der ewige Konflikt – das ist ja das Hoffnungsvolle"').

7 See 'Stefan Heym', p. 45.

8 See Hans Wolfschültz, 'Gespräch mit Stefan Heym', p. 14.

9 See Peter Pawlik, 'Pallawatsch. Stefan Heyms Roman *Ahasver*'; Jurek Becker, '*Ahasver*. Der ewige Jude gibt keine Ruhe'; Jörg B. Bilke, 'Stefan Heym: *Ahasver*'; D. J. Enright, 'Beer, onions, and damnation'.

10 For a most helpful survey of the 'dynamics of the triangular relationship between State, Church, and autonomous peace movement in the GDR', see John Sandford, 'The Church, the State, and the peace movement in the GDR'.

11 See Hermann Weber, *Die DDR 1945–1986*, p. 240.

12 Ibid., p. 100.

13 Jay Rosselini, 'Der Weg zum "dritten Weg"', p. 60; Klaus Bölling, 'Kleine Schritte statt großer Sprünge', p. 34. Theo Honnef considers all the characters lacking in human terms: 'Es macht eine Schwäche des Romans aus, daß Heym seine Personen in erster Linie als Träger von Ideen sieht' ('A failing of the novel lies in the fact that Heym sees his characters in the first instance as vehicles for ideas') ('"Wir haben schon wieder . . ."', p. 149).

14 'Tatkräftiges Handeln für den Sozialismus bewirken', p. 4.

15 Jäger's mocking review suggests that the principal reason for the emergence of such outmoded views was a need for the 'Verschär- fung des ideologischen Kampfes zwischen Sozialismus und Imperialismus' ('intensification of the ideological struggle between socialism and imperialism') (p. 794).

16 Honecker's call was reported in *Neues Deutschland* on 21 Septem- ber 1984. For a brief discussion of this within the context of Hermann Kant's position in the Writers' Union, see Harald

Kleinschmid, 'Tapferkeit und Vorsicht. Unklarheiten in der Kulturpolitik der DDR', especially p. 118.

17 'Probleme der Kulturpolitik vor dem XI. Parteitag der SED. Rede im Vorstand des Schriftstellerverbandes der DDR, 26 September 1985', p. 9. Hager quotes Honecker's earlier remarks in full on p. 17.

18 For details, see 'Kurt Hager beantwortete Fragen der Illustrierten *stern*'.

19 See her conversation with Janet Swaffar, in which she also gives an illuminating account of the complex procedures needed to be taken, even in the eighties, before a book could be accepted for publication. One particular comment is worth quoting in this respect: 'But cultural politics in the GDR are totally unpredictable.' See Janet Swaffar, '"Schließlich schreibt man immer in erster Linie für sich selbst": Ein Gespräch mit Gabriele Eckart', pp. 318–19. The same point is made by Dennis Tate in his fine survey of cultural politics in the seventies: 'We are faced ... with an occasionally bewildering, and often unpredictable, cultural landscape.' See 'Beyond "Kulturpolitik": the GDR's established authors and the challenge of the 1980s", p. 25.

20 See J. H. Reid, *Writing without Taboos*, pp. 50–9.

21 For a contrary view, see the exceptionally warm review by Klara Droge, who concluded by referring to 'diese große Autobiographie, die trotz ihrer Länge von fast 850 Seiten kleinbedruckten Seiten keine Zeile Langweile zuläßt' ('this great autobiography does not contain a single dull line, despite a length of almost 850 pages of small print') (p. 130).

22 For full details of the storm aroused by this work, see Anita Mallinckrodt, 'Environmental dialogue in the GDR. The literary challenge to the sanctity of "progress"', especially pp. 14–20. This article is of much value to a general understanding of cultural politics in the GDR.

23 De Bruyn's speech is given in full in the March issue of *NDL* for 1988. For Christa Wolf's letter, see pp. 88–9; for de Bruyn's soon famous reference to 'Druckgenehmigungspraxis', see p. 85.

24 This speech was reported in *Die Zeit* on 4 December 1987 and by Harald Kleinschmid in his review of the congress ('Probelauf für Glasnost – Zum X. Schriftstellerkongreß der DDR', p. 56). It was not featured, however, in the above-mentioned issue of *NDL*, which gave only a brief summary of the discussion groups' deliberations.

25 *NDL* 36, no. 4 (April 1988), 20–45. The extract concluded with the cryptic note: 'Stefan Heym wird am 10. April fünfundsiebzig

Jahre alt' ('Stefan Heym celebrates his seventy-fifth birthday on 10 April').

26 See 'Revolutionen werden für die Freiheit gemacht', collected in *Einmischung*. See especially p. 124.

27 Demonstration in the 'Berliner Lustgarten', 9 December 1989. Included in *Einmischung*, pp. 271–2.

28 'Die Schriftsteller und das Volk', p. 68.

Bibliography

PRIMARY LITERATURE

Heym has published continuously for over fifty years, in a very wide variety of newspapers and journals: the production of a comprehensive bibliography has thus been dogged by numerous problems. Many works were written in both German and English, and in the case of Heym's larger volumes the dates of first publication in each language have been provided. With the shorter pieces, however, only the date and place of first publication are noted – except on those occasions when there is a particular reason for providing both. With works published in German alone there have also been problems, for these are scattered between the Democratic and the Federal Republics, and the gap between publication sometimes stretches up to fifteen years. Here too, details of first publication alone are provided, except when there are grounds for noting both.

The many articles in *Deutsches Volksecho*, 1937–9, are not listed separately, nor are those written for the *Berliner Zeitung*, which are contained in *Im Kopf – sauber* and *Offen gesagt*. A selection of these is reprinted in *Wege und Umwege*, together with a number of other pieces from all periods of Heym's writing. Items reprinted in that volume have not been listed separately unless there are particular reasons for noting the original source. Such items are marked with an asterisk, and a double asterisk is used for items which are collected in *Einmischung*, selected pieces from the 1980s.

As indicated earlier, all German references in the text are, where possible, to the thirteen-volume *Werkausgabe* (see section 2 below).

Except where otherwise stated, references to 'Berlin' are to Berlin, former capital of the GDR.

The primary literature is arranged in five sections:

PRIMARY LITERATURE

I BOUND PUBLICATIONS AND LARGER PAMPHLETS

Nazis in USA. An Exposé of Hitler's Aims and Agents in the USA, American Committee for Anti-Nazi Literature, New York, 1 December 1938 (second edition: 10 December 1938)

Hostages, New York, 1942; *Der Fall Glasenapp*, Leipzig, 1958

Of Smiling Peace, Boston, 1944

The Crusaders, A Novel of Only Yesterday, Boston, 1948; *Kreuzfahrer von heute* [aus dem Amerikanischen unter Mitarbeit des Autors von Werner von Grünau], Leipzig, 1950. Title revised in later edition, and established as *Der bittere Lorbeer*

The Eyes of Reason, Boston, 1951; *Die Augen der Vernunft* [vom Autor revidierte Fassung von Ellen Zunk], Leipzig, 1955

Tom Sawyers großes Abenteuer. Jugendstück nach Mark Twain in sechs Bildern (with Hanuš Burger), Berlin, 1952

Goldsborough, Leipzig [English-language edition produced by Panther Books, Paul List Verlag], 1953; *Goldsborough* [vom Autor besorgte Übersetzung aus dem Amerikanischen], Leipzig, 1953

The Cannibals and other Stories, Leipzig [English-language edition produced by Panther Books, Paul List Verlag], 1957; *Die Kannibalen und andere Erzählungen* [two of the ten stories translated by Ellen Zunk, the rest by the author], Leipzig, 1953

Offene Worte. So liegen die Dinge, Sonderbeilage zur *Tribüne*, no. 172, 29 July 1953

Forschungsreise ins Herz der deutschen Arbeiterklasse. Nach Berichten 47 sowjetischer Arbeiter [Herausgeber: Freier Deutscher Gewerkschaftsbund], Berlin, n.d. [1953]

Im Kopf – sauber. Schriften zum Tage, Leipzig, 1954

Reise ins Land der unbegrenzten Möglichkeiten. Ein Bericht [Herausgeber: Freier Deutscher Gewerkschaftsbund und die Gesellschaft für Deutsch-Sowjetische Freundschaft], Berlin, 1954; note also the different title of the West German edition, *Keine Angst vor Rußlands Bären. Neugierige Fragen und offene Antworten über die Sowjetunion*, Düsseldorf, 1955

Offen gesagt. Neue Schriften zum Tage, Berlin, 1957

The Cosmic Age. A Report, New Delhi, 1959; also published under the title *A Visit to Soviet Science*, New York, 1959; *Das kosmische Zeitalter. Ein Bericht*, Berlin, 1959

Shadows and Lights. Eight short stories, London, 1963; *Schatten und Licht. Geschichten aus einem geteilten Lande* [two out of eight stories translated by Helga Zimnik, the rest by the author], Leipzig, 1960

The Lenz Papers, London, 1964; *Die Papiere des Andreas Lenz* [vom Autor durchgesehene Übersetzung von Helga Zimnik], 2 vols, Leipzig, 1963. Note also the changed title for the West German edition, *Lenz oder die Freiheit. Ein Roman um Deutschland*, Munich, 1965

Casimir und Cymbelinchen. Zwei Märchen, Berlin, n.d. [1966]

Uncertain Friend, London, 1969; *Lassalle. Ein biographischer Roman*, Munich, Esslingen, 1969. Note the later, simplified title, *Lassalle* [with minor changes in the translation], Berlin, 1974

The Queen against Defoe and Other Stories, London, 1975; *Die Schmähschrift oder Königin gegen Defoe. Erzählt nach den Aufzeichnungen eines gewissen Josiah Creech*, Zurich, 1970

The King David Report, London, 1973; New York, 1973; *Der König-David-Bericht*, Munich, 1972

Five Days in June, London, 1977; *5 Tage im Juni*, Munich, Gütersloh, Vienna, 1974

Cymbelinchen oder der Ernst des Lebens. 4 Märchen für kluge Kinder, Munich, Gütersloh, Vienna, 1975

Das Wachsmuth-Syndrom. Short Story, Berlin 1975 [previously published in *Playboy*, see below]

Erzählungen, Berlin, 1976

Die richtige Einstellung und andere Erzählungen, Munich, 1977

Erich Huckniesel und das fortgesetzte Rotkäppchen. Märchen für kluge Kinder, Berlin, 1977

Der kleine König, der ein Kind kriegen mußte und andere neue Märchen für Kinder, Munich, 1979

Collin, Munich, 1979; *Collin*, London, 1980

Wege und Umwege. Streitbare Schriften aus fünf Jahrzehnten, edited by Peter Mallwitz [Stefan Heym?], Munich, 1980; second, expanded edition, Munich 1983

Ahasver, Munich, 1981; *The Wandering Jew*, New York, 1984; London, 1985

'Atta Troll.' Versuch einer Analyse, Munich, 1983 [MA dissertation, submitted to the University of Chicago, December 1936]

Schwarzenberg, Munich, 1984

Reden an den Feind, Munich, 1986

Nachruf, Munich, 1988

Meine Cousine, die Hexe und weitere Märchen für kluge Kinder, Munich, 1989
Auf Sand gebant. Sieben Geschichten ans der unmittelbaren Vergangenheit, Munich, 1990
Einmischung. Gespräche, Reden, Essays, selected and edited by Inge Heym and Heinfried Henniger, Munich, 1990
Stalin verläßt den Raum. Politische Publizistik, edited with an afterword by Heiner Henniger, Leipzig, 1990

2 THE WERKAUSGABE

The *Werkausgabe* in fourteen volumes, published by Wilhelm Goldmann Verlag. Some of these volumes contain minor changes from the first editions. The place of publication is in all cases Munich, and the items are here listed alphabetically.

Ahasver, 1985
Die Augen der Vernunft, 1983
Der bittere Lorbeer, 1981
Collin, 1984
Der Fall Glasenapp, 1983
5 Tage im Juni, 1983
Gesammelte Erzählungen, 1984
Goldsborough, 1981
Der König-David-Bericht, 1984
Lassalle, 1981
Lenz oder die Freiheit, 1981
Märchen für kluge Kinder, 1984
Schwarzenberg, 1988
Wege und Umwege, 1985

3 PUBLICATIONS IN NEWSPAPERS, JOURNALS, AND VOLUMES EDITED BY OTHERS

'Exportgeschäft' [poem], *Chemnitzer Volksstimme*, 7 September 1931[*]
'Melancholie vom 5. Stock' [poem], collected in *Um uns die Stadt. Eine Anthologie neuer Großstadtlyrik*, edited by Robert Seitz and Heinz Zucker, Berlin, 1931, p. 151
'In Deutschland hungert keiner', *Feuilleton der SAZ*, 21 November 1931 [under the pseudonym 'Melchior Douglas']
'Ein Bürger reißt die Augen auf', *Feuilleton der SAZ*, 26 November 1931 [under the pseudonym 'Melchior Douglas']
'Stammbuchverse für einen Kriegerverein', *Feuilleton der SAZ*, 1 December 1931 [under the pseudonym 'Melchior Douglas']

'Man befiehlt Weihnachtsruhe', *Feuilleton der SAZ*, 8 December 1931 [under the pseudonym 'Melchior Douglas']

'Die Nacht der Nächte', *Feuilleton der SAZ*, 23 December 1931 [under the pseudonym 'Melchior Douglas']

'Mond und Maschinen' [poem], *Die Weltbühne*, 8 March 1932, 387 [under the pseudonym 'Melchior Douglas']

'Berliner Hofmusik' [reportage], *Berlin am Morgen*, 24 July 1932 [signed 'F—g']*

'Hinter Karstadt' [poem], *Die Weltbühne*, 2 August 1932, 176

'Vierzehnjährige Mädchen' [poem], *Die Weltbühne*, 2 August 1932 176

'Auch eine Tragik' [poem], *Die Weltbühne*, 27 September 1932, 485

'Auftakt' [poem], *Die Weltbühne*, 8 November 1932, 702

'Nacht am Wedding' [poem], *Die Weltbühne*, 31 January 1933, 188

'Wie spricht der Hund' [poem], *Neue Deutsche Blätter*, 1, no. 3 (November 1933), 144

'Ein Brief' [poem], *Neue Deutsche Blätter*, 1, no. 7 (March 1934), 432

'Gläubigerkonferenz' [poem], *Die neue Weltbühne*, no. 15, 12 April 1934, p. 460

'Monolog des Schwerindustriellen' [poem], *Die neue Weltbühne*, no. 20, 17 May 1934, 630

'Späße der Feldpolizei' [report], *Die neue Weltbühne*, no. 24, 14 June 1934, 758–9

'Thälmann' [poem], *Neue Deutsche Blätter*, 1, no. 10 (July 1934), 601

'Galgenlied' [poem], *Die neue Weltbühne*, no. 27, 5 July 1934, 850

'Die Unschuldigen' [poem], *Die neue Weltbühne*, no. 31, 2 August 1934, 968

'Rückkehr?' [poem], *Die neue Weltbühne*, no. 33, 16 August 1934, 1038

'Die angestochene Pestbeule' [poem], *Die neue Weltbühne*, no. 38, 20 September 1934, 1025

'Gekränktes Volk' [poem], *Die neue Weltbühne*, no. 42, 18 October 1934, 1337–8

'Kämpfende Schriftsteller' [political gloss], *Die neue Weltbühne*, no. 46, 15 November 1934, 1466–7 [signed 'St. H.']

'Deutsches Seemannslied' [poem] *Die neue Weltbühne*, no. 47, 22 November 1934, 1487

'König Kapitalist' [review] *Die neue Weltbühne*, no. 51, 20 December 1934, 1625–6

'Schuschnigg contra Schuschnigg' [political report] *Die neue Weltbühne*, no. 2, 10 January 1935, 58–9 [signed 'St. H.']

'Rechtfertigung' [poem], *Die neue Weltbühne*, no. 3, 17 January 1935, 91

'Prospekt' [poem], *Neue Deutsche Blätter*, 2, no. 4 (February 1935), 252–3

'Der Unbekannte' [poem], *Die neue Weltbühne*, no. 6, 7 February 1935, 181

'Der internationale Vorsitzende' [political gloss], *Die neue Weltbühne*, no. 7, 14 February 1935, 217–18

'Leben, Leid und Tod des Hitlerspießers' [poem], *Die Sammlung* 2, no. 6 (February 1935), 292–93

'Der Kampf mit dem Drachen' [poem], *Die neue Weltbühne*, no. 10, 7 March 1935, 315

'Der falsche Louis' [review], *Neue Deutsche Blätter*, 2, no. 5 (June 1935), 314–18

'Heine heute' [poem], *Die neue Weltbühne*, no. 35, 29 August 1935, 1111

'Ruhige Diskussion' [poem], *Die neue Weltbühne*, no. 41, 10 October 1935, 1288–9

'Jahrgang 1913' [poem], *Die neue Weltbühne*, no. 50, 12 December 1935, 1587

'Ich aber ging über die Grenze ... '*; 'Deutsche Legende'; 'Deutscher Zuchthausmarsch'; 'Deutscher Brief' [poems], in *Verse der Emigration*, edited by Heinz Wielek, Karlsbad, 1935, pp. 7–8; 21; 21–2; 74

'Das gestohlene Lied' [review], *Das Wort*, 1, no. 2 (February 1936), 93–6 [signed 'S. H.']

'Bei reichen Leuten' [poem], *Die neue Weltbühne*, no. 16, 16 April 1936, 503

'Youth in Hitler's Reich', *Nation*, no. 142, 27 June 1936, 836–40

'Roosevelt' [political gloss], *Die neue Weltbühne*, no. 37, 10 September 1936, 1164–5

'Das Hängen von Owensboro' [poem], *Das Wort* 2, no. 1 (January 1937), 39–42

'Sturmführer Kaleike über Franco' [poem], *Die neue Weltbühne*, no. 6, 4 February 1937, 175

'Gestern–Heute–Morgen. Deutschamerikanisches Festspiel', *Das Wort* 2, no. 3 (March 1937), 35–45

'Spanien. Dem Andenken Hans Beimlers: "In Toledo"; "Sturmführer Kaleicke"; "Das Opfer"; "Internationale Brigade" [four poems], *Das Wort*, 2, nos. 4–5 (April–May 1937), 86–8

'Kleine deutsche Chronik. "USA"' [cultural report], *Das Wort*, 3, no. 8 (August 1938), 144–6

'Fünf Jahre Bücherverbrennung', *Internationale Literatur* [Moscow], no. 5 (1938), 26

'Kleine deutsche Chronik. "USA"' [cultural report], *Das Wort*, 3, no. 12 (December 1938), 141–3

'Kleine deutsche Chronik. "USA"' [cultural report], *Das Wort*, 4, no. 1 (January 1939), 134–8

'Amerikanische Bücher deutscher Autoren' [review of translations], *Das Wort*, 4, no. 2 (February 1939), 107–10

'Behind the German lines', *New Republic*, 20 September 1939, 180–1

'What's to become of Germany?', *New Masses*, 14 November 1939, 9–10

'Janoshik tells a Christmas story', *Chicago Sun*, 6 December 1942

'My favourite war story', *Look*, 8, no. 2, 25 January 1944, 16, 18

'I am only a little man', *New York Times Magazine*, 10 September 1944, 44–5

'The Germans hear a new master's voice', *New York Times Magazine*, 3 December 1944, 11, 52–4

'But the Hitler legend isn't dead', *New York Times Magazine*, 20 January 1946, 42

'Souvenir for Chen Wang', *Mainstream*, no. 1, (1947), 217–24

'Occupation. How was a young recruit supposed to understand an inscrutable Fräulein like Clara?', *Salute*, 2, no. 10 (October 1947), 14–15, 48–9

'It happens to me', *Tomorrow*, 8, no. 1 (September 1948), 13–17 [extract from *The Crusaders*]

'Ein Sturm muß sich in der Welt erheben', *Berliner Zeitung*, 10 June 1953, 3

'Gedanken zum 17. Juni', *Berliner Zeitung*, 21 June 1953, 3

'Für Ethel und Julius Rosenberg' [poem], *Neues Deutschland*, 23 June 1953, 4

'Gedanken nach dem 17. Juni', *Berliner Zeitung*, 24 June 1953, 3

'Ein Dummer findet sich immer', *Berliner Zeitung*, 28 June 1953, 3

'Das große Geschäft geht weiter', *Berliner Zeitung*, 5 July 1953, 3

'Die kleinen Angestellten', *Neues Deutschland*, 7 July 1953, 1

'Großmut', *Vorwärts*, 13 July 1953, 1

'Um die Sauberkeit im Kopf', *Berliner Zeitung*, 15 July 1953, 4

'Das Volk will echten Realismus', *Berliner Zeitung*, 29 July 1953, 3 [*]

'Gespräch über Literatur', *Tägliche Rundschau*, 20 August 1954, 4

'Es ist alles ganz anders', *Berliner Zeitung*, 5 September 1953, 3

'A matter of course', *New Times* [Moscow], 6 November 1954, 27–31

'Die große Tat war Frieden', *Tägliche Rundschau*, 7 November 1954, 1, 7

'A proud young world', *News. A Soviet Review of World Events*, 21, 1 November 1954, 10–12

'Warnung aus Moskau', *Tägliche Rundschau*, 7 December 1954, 3

'Heute im Kreml beginnt es', (Zum II. Allunionskongreß der sowjetischen Schriftsteller'), *Tägliche Rundschau*, 15 December 1954, 1

'Sowjetbücher verändern den Menschen', *Tägliche Rundschau*, 18 December 1954, 1–2

'Sowjetliteratur – eine Kraftquelle der Völker', *Tägliche Rundschau*, 20
    December 1954, 2
'Modernste Waffen wertlos ohne überzeugte Menschen', *Tägliche
    Rundschau*, 21 December 1954, 1–2
'Das Wort der deutschen Schriftsteller', *Tägliche Rundschau*, 24
    December 1954, 1–2
'Sowjetische Bücher – die Stimme des Sowjetvolkes!', *Tägliche Rund-
    schau*, 25 December 1954, 1–2
'Kinder ohne Tränen', *Tägliche Rundschau*, 7 January 1955, 5
'Gorki schrieb jeden Tag', *Tägliche Rundschau*, 21 January 1955, 5
'Das Wunder an der Warnow', *Theorie und Praxis der Pressearbeit*
    (1955/56), 51–66
'Dubna eröffnet das kosmische Zeitalter', *Wissen und Leben*, no. 1
    (1959), 26–32
'Silvesterabend 1999', *Neue Zeit* 17, no. 1 (January 1959), 20–3
'Berliner Gefühle', *Neue Zeit*, 17, no. 23 (June 1959), 10–11
'Station am Wege. Skizzen aus Jonas' Tagebuch', *Wochenpost*, 9
    January 1960, 7, 20
'Station am Wege. Skizzen aus Jonas' Tagebuch. 1. Fortsetzung',
    Wochenpost, 16 January 1960, 7, 20
'Literatur im Zeitalter der Wissenschaft', *Literatur im Zeitalter der
    Wissenschaft*, edited by Deutsches PEN-Zentrum Ost und West,
    Berlin n.d. [1959], 35–42
'Gesicht eines alten Arbeiters', *Wochenpost*, 17 September 1960, 1
'Hand, Hirn, Mensch', *Magazin*, December 1960, 24–8
'Der tolle Heartfield', *Wochenpost*, 17 June 1961, 14, 17
'Verantwortung', *Wochenpost*, 23 September 1961, 4–5
'The shape of the future', *The Worker*, 15 October 1961, 6
'Ferien im Bürgerkrieg. Sechsteilige Reportagen über Zypern',
    Wochenpost, December 1964–February 1965
'I arrive at socialism by train', *Nation*, 11 October 1965, 228–30
'Aus finsteren Jahren. Thomas Mann im *Deutschen Volksecho*, *Sinn und
    Form*, Sonderheft Thomas Mann (1965), 336–40
'Stalin verläßt den Raum', *Die Zeit*, 5 February 1965; *Les Temps
    Modernes*, no. 230 (July 1965), 153–6
'Die Langeweile von Minsk', *Kulturni Zivot*, 20 August 1965, 2; first
    German publication *Die Zeit*, 29 October 1965
'In höherem Auftrag', *Neue Deutsche Literatur*, 13, no. 11 (1965),
    96–104
'Die richtige Einstellung', in *Nachrichten aus Deutschland*, edited by
    Hildegard Brenner, Reinbek, 1967, pp. 35–43; 'The proper
    approach', in *Cross-Section*, Anthology of the PEN Centre,
    German Democratic Republic, edited (on behalf of the Presidium

of the PEN Centre German Democratic Republic) by Wieland
Herzfelde and Günther Cwojdrak, Leipzig, 1970, pp. 91–9
'"Rebellen, auch wenn es ihnen gut geht". Aus dem Roman *Liebe und
Tod eines Volkshelden*' [initial title for *Lassalle*], *Neue Deutsche Hefte*,
   14, no. 114 (1967), 8–21
'Schwester Margot', *Die Zeit*, 13 October 1972, 25–6
'The tender little buds of East Germany', *New York Times*, 24 May
   1973, 45
'Wie *Der Fall Glasenapp* entstand, in *Eröffnungen. Schriftsteller über ihr
   Erstlingswerk*, edited by Gerhard Schneider, Berlin and Weimar,
   1974, pp. 81–90
'Das Wachsmuth-Syndrom', *Playboy*, 2, no. 2 (February 1973),
   135–43
'Letter from East Germany', *New York Times Magazine*, 23 March
   1975, 34, 36, 38, 40, 42, 44
'Circus', *Cavalier*, August 1975, 45–6, 50, 74
'A month of good news', *New Statesman*, 4 February 1977, 148–9; 'Je
   voller der Mund, desto leerer die Sprüche', *stern*, 10 February
   1977
'Aus der Wekstatt des Autors. Drei *Collin*-Anfänge', *Saarbrücker
   Zeitung*, 30 March 1979, 8
'Mit den Schwachen solidarisch. Über Karl-Heinz Jakobs', *Der
   Spiegel*, 33 no. 18, 30 April 1979, 40
'Willkür und Verleumdung herrschen hier', *Saarbrücker Zeitung*, 23/4
   June 1979
'Das Messer an der Kehle', *Frankfurter Allgemeine Zeitung*, 26 April
   1979; reprinted in *Der Spiegel*, 34, no. 44 (1980), 58[*]
'Rede vor dem Ausschluß aus dem Schriftstellerverband', *Frankfurter
   Allgemeine Zeitung*, 22 June 1979, 25[*]
'Zwei Friedensbewegungen. Rede anläßlich des europäischen Schrift-
   stellertreffens in den Haag', *Frankfurter Rundschau*, 26 May 1982
'"Ich wünschte, daß unser Treffen Vertrauen gibt", Diskussionsbei-
   träge der "Berliner Begegnung zur Friedensförderung", Teil IV',
   Die Zeit, 22 January 1982, 14
'Die Wunde der Teilung eitert weiter', *Der Spiegel*, 37, no. 45 (1983),
   58–72
'"Nachdenken über Deutschland". Stefan Heym und Günter Grass
   diskutierten am 21. November 1984 in Brüssel' [Goethe-Institut
   pamphlet], Berlin, n.d. [1984]
'Lieber grüne als weiße Männerchen', *Zeitmagazin*, 29 November
   1985, 8
'Das Tischchen', *Kursbuch*, no. 86 (1986), 1–4
[memoirs] *Der Spiegel*, 42, no. 33 (1988), 100–111

[memoirs] *Der Spiegel*, 42, no. 34 (1988), 98–116
[memoirs] *Der Spiegel*, 42, no. 35 (1988), 108–23
'Deutsch-Deutsche Geschichtsstunde', *stern*, 27 April 1989, 56, 58, 64
'Ist die DDR noch zu retten? Aus dem real existierenden muß ein wirkliches System werden', *Die Zeit*, 13 October 1989, 5** (under title 'Neue Hoffnung für die DDR')
'Zwischenbericht', *Der Spiegel*, 43 no. 43 (1989), 41–4
'Hurra für den Pöbel', *Der Spiegel*, 43, no. 45, (1989), 30–1
'Aschermittwoch in der DDR', *Der Spiegel*, 43, no. 49 (1989), 55–8; reprinted in *Junge Welt*, 4 December 1989, 3**

4 PUBLICATIONS EDITED BY STEFAN HEYM

Deutsches Volksecho, New York, 20 February 1937 to 16 September 1939 (weekly)
König Leopolds Selbstgespräch. Eine Verteidigung seiner Herrschaft im Kongo (translated from the original by Mark Twain, *King Leopold's Soliloquy*, together with a foreword on Twain), Berlin, 1961
Auskunft. Neue Prosa aus der DDR, Munich, 1974
Auskunft 2. Neueste Prosa aus der DDR, Munich, 1978

5 INTERVIEWS

This list is far from exhaustive, and seeks only to identify the most important pieces or those which were significant in shaping this study. Owing to the considerable number of formal interviews Heym has held over the years, I have not been able to gain access to all of them. Items are listed chronologically, with the name of the interviewer featured first. Where the interview was given a particular title, this has also been supplied. As in the above section, items included in *Wege und Umwege* and in *Einmischung* are not listed separately unless there is a particular reason for doing so. The same use of asterisks applies here, with a single asterisk for items featured in the former, a double asterisk for those in the latter.

Die Wochenpost, 'Joe Jones und die unbeglichene Rechnung. *Wochenpost*-Gespräch mit Stefan Heym', *Die Wochenpost*, 14 May 1960, 4–5
Anon., 'Stefan Heym answers questions', *Outlook*, 1970, no. 4, 6–7
Bruck, Werner, '"Wir gehen noch nicht vor Freude über Bord." DDR-Autor Heym zur Annäherung zwischen Ost und West', *Kölner Stadt-Anzeiger*, 18/19 December 1971, 10
Reif, Adalbert, 'Auf beiden Seiten ist der 17. Juni umgelogen worden', *Deutsches Allgemeines Sonntagsblatt*, 8 April 1973, 6; reprinted in *druck und papier*; *Konkret*; *Nationalzeitung* (Basel)

Moskin, J. Robert, 'The creator and the commissars. An encounter with Stefan Heym, an independent man who walks the East German tightrope', *Intellectual Digest*, March 1973, 25–7; reprinted as an appendix to *The Queen Against Defoe*, pp. 115–26

Bilke, Jörg, and Konrad Franke, 'Gespräch mit Stefan Heym', *europäische ideen*, 1974, no. 4, 11–16

Mytze, A., 'DDR-Schriftsteller stellen sich vor: Gespräche mit Stefan Heym und Wilhelm Girnus', *Deutschland-Archiv*, 6 (1974), 600–12

Corino, Karl, '"Heilige Kühe aus Ost und West". Gespräch mit dem DDR-Autor Stefan Heym', *Stuttgarter Zeitung*, 18 October 1974, 10

Nater, Timothy, 'People must feel free', *Newsweek*, 25 July 1977, 60; reprinted in German translation in *Deutschland-Archiv*, 10 (1977), 1115–16

Pleitgen, Fritz, 'Nein, nein, ich bleibe dabei', *Frankfurter Rundschau*, 13 April 1978, 4

Mudrich, Heinz, '"...obwohl ich nicht persona grata bin." Arbeitsauskünfte eines Autors, den die SED nicht zum DDR-Schriftstellerkongreß zugelassen hat', *Saarbrücker Zeitung*, 31 May 1978, 'Feuilleton', 1

Böhme, Erich, and Wolfgang Bickerich, '"Warum kein Sozialismus mit zwei Parteien?" Der DDR-Schriftsteller Stefan Heym über Abgrenzung und Sozialismus', *Der Spiegel*, 34, no. 44 (1980), 54–67

Panskus, Hartmann, '"Gelitten und nicht mehr." Stefan Heym gibt Auskunft über seinen *Ahasver*-Roman', *Börsenblatt für den deutschen Buchhandel* (1981), 1581–4[*]

Wolfschütz, Hans, 'Diskussion mit dem Teufel. "Der ewige Konflikt – das ist ja das Hoffnungsvolle"', 'Die Zeit zur Buchmesse', supplement to *Die Zeit*, 16 October 1981, 2

de Waijer-Wilke, Marieluise, and Ed Rybarczyk, 'Gespräch mit Stefan Heym', *Deutsche Bücher*, 12 (1982), 86–100

Der Spiegel, '"Plötzlich hebt sich der Boden." Der DDR-Schriftsteller Stefan Heym über die Friedensbewegung in Ost und West", *Der Spiegel*, 36, no. 22 (1982), 94–100[*]

Wolfschütz, Hans, 'Gespräch mit Stefan Heym', *GDR Monitor*, 8 (Winter 1982/3), 1–14

Jens, Tilman, and Peter Pragal, 'Die DDR ist gepflastert mit Tabus', *stern*, 29 March 1984, 230

Mense, Thomas, and Hellmuth Opitz, 'Ich bin ein Romancier, der sehr oft in Schwierigkeiten gerät', *Tips*, 1984, no. 5, 8–9

Grass, Günter, and Karel Hemmerechts, '"Nachdenken über Deutschland." Stefan Heym und Günter Grass diskutierten am 21. November 1984 in Brüssel' [Goethe-Institut pamphlet], Berlin, n.d. [1984][**]

Grass, Günter, 'In einem Land zu leben, das sich selbst nicht definieren kann. Nachdenken über die deutsche Frage', *Frankfurter Rundschau*, 6 and 7 September 1985

Reitze, Paul F., (Part 1) 'Wenn sie nur auf das Bajonett setzen, dann brauchen Sie die Mauer', *Die Welt*, 28 September 1987; (Part 2) 'Stefan Heym: "Ich mag Kerle, die so tapfer sind wie Robinsons Vater"', *Die Welt*, 30 September 1987, 6

David, Fred, 'Diese Form des Sozialismus ist am Ende', *profil*, 28 August 1989, 26–7

Konitzer, Michael-A., 'Der arme Herr Honecker ...', *Wiener*, 16 September 1989, 3–5

Panecke, Volker, '"Deutschland als Gulliver?" Stefan Heym im Gespräch', *Horizont-International*, no. 18 (1990), 14–16

SECONDARY LITERATURE

The following list contains all items mentioned in the course of this study, together with a selection of material which proved particularly valuable in providing background information.

Abusch, Alexander, 'Zu einigen Fragen der Literatur und Kunst', *Neues Deutschland*, 27 July 1956; reprinted in Schubbe, *Dokumente*, pp. 440–5

'Demokratisierung der Kultur', *Sonntag*, 1957, no. 9, 'Beilage'; reprinted in Schubbe, *Dokumente*, pp. 455–60

Anderson, George K., *The Legend of the Wandering Jew*, second, revised edition, Providence, 1970

Anon., 'Birth of a spectre', *Times Literary Supplement*, 2 May 1964, 269

Beiträge zu einer Biographie. Eine Freundesgabe für Stefan Heym zum 60. Geburtstag am 10. April 1973, Munich, 1973

'Der Ostberliner Aufstand – aus der Sicht eines DDR-Autors', *Neue Zürcher Zeitung*, 9/10 November 1974, 65

'Unser Schweigen wird lauter sein', *Die Welt*, 2 August 1979, 3

'Erstickender Ring', *Der Spiegel*, 33, no. 7, (1979), 181–2

'Aus der Werkstatt des Autors: drei *Collin*-Anfänge', *Saarbrücker Zeitung*, 30 March 1979, 8

Badstübner, Rolf, et al., *DDR. Werden und Wachsen: Zur Geschichte der Deutschen Demokratischen Republik*, Berlin, 1974

Baring, Arnulf, *Uprising in East Germany: 17 June 1953*, Ithaca and London, 1972

Bartram, Graham, and Anthony Waine (editors), *Culture and Society in the GDR*, Dundee, 1984

Becker, Jurek, '*Ahasver*. Der ewige Jude gibt keine Ruhe', *Der Spiegel*, 2 November 1981, 240–6

Berger, Uwe, and Günther Deicke, *Lyrik der DDR*, Berlin and Weimar, 1970

Bessie, Alvah, 'The captains and the kings remain', *The Nation*, 218, 19 January 1974, 88–90

Biermann, Wolf, 'Die Stasi-Ballade', in *Für meine Genossen*, [West] Berlin, 1972, pp. 69–71

'Tapferfeige Intellektuelle. Literaturkritischer Brief über Stefan Heyms Roman *Collin* an Robert Havemann', *Die Zeit*, 30 March 1979, 41–2

Bilke, Jörg B., 'Stefan Heym und der 17. Juni 1953', *Frankfurter Hefte*, 30 (1975), 71–3

'Stefan Heym: *Ahasver*', *Neue Deutsche Hefte*, 28 (1981), 827–31

Binder, David, 'I'll write, publish what I like', *International Herald Tribune*, 17 April 1970, 7

Blomster, W. V., 'Stefan Heym: *Die Schmähschrift oder Königin gegen Defoe*', *Books Abroad*, 45 (1971), 690–1

Bock, Stephan, 'Der 17. Juni in der Literatur der DDR. Eine Bibliographie (1953–1979)', *Jahrbuch zur Literatur in der DDR*, 1 (1980), 141–59

'Eine große Hoffnung – Stefan Heym, der Publizist', in *Literatur Gesellschaft Nation. Materielle und ideelle Rahmenbedingungen der frühen DDR-Literatur (1946–1956)*, Stuttgart, 1980, pp. 187–202

Böll, Heinrich, 'Der Lorbeer ist immer noch bitter', *Der Spiegel*, 26, no. 39 (1972), 158, 160

Bölling, Klaus, 'Kleine Schritte statt großer Sprünge: Klaus Bölling über Stefan Heyms *Schwarzenberg*', *Der Spiegel*, 38, no. 34 (1984), 34–6

Brandes, Ute, 'Dokument und Fiktion. Stefan Heym *5 Tage im Juni*', in *Zitat und Montage in der neueren DDR-Prosa*, Frankfurt am Main, Bern, New York, 1984, pp. 128–47

Brandt, Sabine, 'Ein Ferment der Zersetzung. Stefan Heym oder die unbezwingbare Galligkeit', *Die Zeit*, 10 July 1970, 28

'Ende des Rundlaufs um den heißen Brei', *Frankfurter Allgemeine Zeitung*, 1 March 1979, 21

Brettschneider, Werner, *Zwischen literarischer Autonomie und Staatsdienst: Die Literatur in der DDR*, second, revised edition, [West] Berlin, 1974

Carr, E. H., *What is History?*, London, 1961

Cazden, Robert, *German Exile Literatur in American 1933–50. A History of the Free German Press and Book Trade*, Chicago, 1970

Childs, David, *The GDR. Moscow's German Ally*, second, revised edition, London, 1988

Christian, R. F., *Tolstoy. A Critical Introduction*, Cambridge, 1969

Claudius, Eduard, *Menschen an unsrer Seite*, Berlin, 1951
Conze, W., 'Die deutsche Geschichtswissenschaft seit 1945. Bedingungen und Ergebnisse', *Historische Zeitschrift*, 225, no. 1 (August 1977), 1–28
Cowley, Malcolm, 'Stefan Heym: *The Crusaders*', *New Republic*, 27 September 1948, 33–4
de Bruyn, Günter, *Preisverleihung*, Halle, 1972
Deutscher Schriftstellerverband der Deutschen Demokratischen Republik, *VI. Deutscher Schriftstellerkongress vom 28. bis 30. Mai 1969: Protokoll*, Berlin [1969]
Dorman, M., 'The state versus the writer: recent developments in Stefan Heym's struggle against the GDR's "Kulturpolitik"', *Modern Languages* 62, no. 3 (September 1981), 144–52
Dornberg, Stefan, *Kurze Geschichte der DDR*, Berlin, 1964
Droge, Klara, 'Stefan Heym: *Nachruf*, *Neue Deutsche Hefte*, 36 (1989), 127–30
Dube, Inge D. 'Das Amerika-Bild Stefan Heyms', doctoral dissertation, Northwestern University, 1986 (University Microfilms International No. NHG86–21779)
Ecker, H.-P., *Poetisierung als Kritik. Stefan Heyms Neugestaltung der Erzählung vom Ewigen Juden*, Tübingen, 1987
Ebert, Günter, 'Zauber und Verfall. Zum biografischen Roman *Lassalle* von Stefan Heym', *Freie Erde*, 13 April 1974
Emmerich, Wolfgang, *Kleine Literaturgeschichte der DDR*, second revised edition, Frankfurt am Main, 1989
Endler, Adolf, and Karl Mickel, *In diesem besseren Land*, Halle, 1966
Enright, D. J. 'Beer, onions, and damnation', *New York Review*, 26 April 1984, 45–6
Ernst, Otto, 'Stefan Heyms Auseinandersetzung mit Faschismus, Militarismus und Kapitalismus – dargestellt an den Gestalten seiner Romane', doctoral dissertation, University of Jena, 1965
Feuchtwanger, Lion, *Der Tag wird kommen*, Stockholm, 1945
Fink, Dieter, 'Der einzig wahre und so fort ... Rezension zu *Der König-David-Bericht*', *Forum*, 2 March 1974, 10
Fisher, Rodney, 'Stefan Heyms *Ahasver*: Der ewige Jude als Sinnbild der Kontroverse', in *Kontroversen, alte und neue. Akten des VII. Internationalen Germanisten-Kongresses*, vol. 5, edited by Albrecht Schöne, Tübingen, 1986, pp. 220–4
'Stefan Heym's *Ahasver*: structure and principles', *Seminar*, 22 (1986), 231–54
Fogg, Derek, 'Exodus from a promised land. The Biermann affair', in *The Writer and Society in the GDR*, edited by Ian Wallace, Dundee, 1984, pp. 134–51

Fricke, Karl W., and Klaus Sauter, 'Das Stalinismus-Tabu durch-
brochen: Stefan Heym, *Collin*', *Deutschland Archiv*, 12 (1979),
522–5

Fricke, Karl W., *Opposition und Widerstand in der DDR. Ein politischer
Report*, Cologne, 1984

Funke, Christoph, 'Abenteuer im letzten Jahr. Stefan Heyms Roman
Lassalle', *Der Morgen*, 23 March 1974, 2

Graves, Peter, 'Authority, the State and the individual: Stefan
Heym's novel *Collin*', *Forum for Modern Language Studies*, 23
(1987), 341–50

Greiner, Bernhard, *Von der Allegorie zur Idylle: Die Literatur der Arbeitswelt in der DDR*, Heidelberg, 1974

Haase, Horst, et al. (editors), *Geschichte der deutschen Literatur*, vol. 11,
'Literatur der Deutschen Demokratischen Republik', Berlin,
1977

Habe, Hans, 'Abschied von Stefan Heym', *Kontakte*, 3, no. 6 (June
1953), 10–11

Hager, Kurt, 'Parteilichkeit und Volksverbundenheit unserer Literatur und Kunst. Rede auf der Beratung des Politbüros des Zentralkomitees und des Präsidiums des Ministerrats mit Schriftstellern und Künstlern am 23.3.1963', *Neues Deutschland*, 30
March 1963; reprinted in Schubbe, *Dokumente*, pp. 859–79

'Kurt Hager beantwortete Fragen der Illustrierten *stern*', *Deutschland Archiv*, 20 (1987), 655–60

'Probleme der Kulturpolitik vor dem XI. Parteitag der SED. Rede
im Vorstand des Schriftstellerverbandes der DDR, 26 September 1985', *Neue Deutsche Literatur*, 34, no. 1 (January 1986), 5–27

Hanke, Irma, *Alltag und Politik. Zur politischen Kultur einer unpolitischen
Gesellschaft. Eine Untersuchung zur erzählenden Gegenwartsliteratur der
DDR in den 70er Jahren*, Opladen 1987

Havemann, Robert, 'Ja, ich hatte unrecht. Warum ich Stalinist war
und Anti-Stalinist wurde', *Die Zeit*, 7 May 1965

Fragen Antworten Fragen. Aus der Biographie eines deutschen Marxisten,
Munich, 1970

Hein, Christoph, *Der fremde Freund*, Berlin, 1982

Hilscher, Eberhard, *Die Weltzeituhr. Roman einer Epoche*, Berlin,
1983

Hohendahl, Peter U. and Patricia Herminghouse (editors), *Literatur
und Literaturtheorie in der DDR*, Frankfurt am Main, 1976

Literatur der DDR in den siebziger Jahren, Frankfurt am Main, 1983

Höller, Marina, 'Stefan Heym als zweisprachiger Schriftsteller', MA
dissertation, University of Bonn, 1984

Honnef, Theo, '"Wir haben schon wieder weiße Flecke." Die

Anfangsjahre der DDR in Werken Loests, Heyms und Heins', *German Life & Letters*, 44, no. 2 (January 1991), 143–64

Honecker, Erich, 'Wirklichkeitsnähe, Volksverbundenheit und Parteilichkeit' [Bericht des ZK and den VIII. Parteitag, 15. Juni 1971], in *Protokoll der Verhandlungen des VIII. Parteitages der SED*, Berlin, 1971; key section reproduced as the following item:

'Inhaltliche Tiefe und meisterhafte Gestaltung', *Neue Deutsche Literatur*, 19, no. 8 (August 1971), 3–6

'Hauptaufgabe umfaßt auch weitere Erhöhung des kulturellen Niveaus' [Schlußwort auf der 4. Tagung des ZK der SED], *Neues Deutschland*, 18 December 1971

Höpcke, Klaus, 'Tatkräftiges Handeln für den Sozialismus bewirken', *Neues Deutschland*, 13 June 1984, 4

Hutchinson, Peter, 'History and political literature: the interpretation of the "Day of German Unity" in the literature of East and West', *Modern Language Review*, 76 (1981), 367–82

'Problems of socialist historiography: the example of Stefan Heym's *The King David Report*', *Modern Language Review*, 81 (1986), 131–8

'Using the "Self-Translator" as a model: the translations of Stefan Heym', *Modern Languages*, 57 (1986), 31–9

Institut für Marxismus–Leninismus beim Zentralkomitee der SED, *Geschichte der deutschen Arbeiterbewegung in acht Bänden*, vol. 7, Berlin, 1966

Jackson, Joseph Henry, 'Here is that "big" book on the war you have been waiting for – war from Normandy to the Occupation', *San Francisco Chronicle*, 12 September 1948, 22, 24

Jäger, Manfred, *Sozialliteraten. Funktion und Selbstverständnis der Schriftsteller in der DDR*, Düsseldorf, 1973

Kultur und Politik in der DDR. Ein historischer Abriß, Cologne, 1982

'Wieder gefragt: Der positive Held. Höpckes Griff in die Mottenkiste der 50er Jahre', *Deutschland Archiv*, 17 (1984), 794–6

Janka, Walter, *Schwierigkeiten mit der Wahrheit*, Reinbek bei Hamburg, 1989

Jespersen, Robert C., 'Stefan Heym', in *Deutschsprachige Exilliteratur seit 1933*, vol. 2, edited by John M. Spalek and Joseph Strelka, Bern, 1989, pp. 358–72

Joho, Wolfgang, 'Licht und Schatten bei Stefan Heym', *Neue Deutsche Literatur*, 7, no. 9 (September 1961), 122–6

'Historische Aktualität', *Sonntag*, 8 March 1959, 8

'Tragikomische Ouvertüre', *Neue Deutsche Literatur* 12, no. 5 (May 1964), 129–34

Kähler, Hermann, 'Christa Wolfs Elegie', *Sinn und Form*, 21 (1969), 251–61

Kant, Hermann, *Die Aula*, Berlin, 1965
  Das Impressum, Berlin, 1972
  '"Von Helden, Autoren und Präsidentensorgen." Mit Hermann Kant sprach Elvira Högemann-Ledwohn', *Kürbiskern*, no. 4 (1980), 109–23
  'Wissen, wo man steht in den politischen Kämpfen unserer Zeit', [Tagung des Vorstandes des Schriftstellerverbandes der DDR], *National-Zeitung*, 1 June 1979, 7

Kleinschmid, Harald, '"Die Rache des kleinen Mannes". Zur kulturpolitischen Situation in der DDR im ersten Halbjahr 1979', *Deutschland Archiv*, 12 (1979), 673–83
  '"Das große Schweigen". Zur kulturpolitischen Situation in der DDR nach dem Ausschluß von neun Schriftstellern', *Deutschland Archiv*, 12 (1979), 899–905
  Tapferkeit und Vorsicht. Unklarheiten in der Kulturpolitik der DDR', *Deutschland Archiv*, 18 (1985), 117–19
  'Probelauf für Glasnost – Zum x. Schriftstellerkongreß der DDR', *Deutschland Archiv*, 21 (1988), 53–9

Kunze, Reiner, *Sensible Wege*, Reinbek bei Hamburg, 1969

Labroisse, Gerd, 'Der neue Luther in der DDR: Luther-Gestaltungen bei Claus Hammel, Stefan Heym, Helga Schütz und Bernd Schremmer', *Amsterdamer Beiträge zur neueren Germanistik*, 19 (1984), 239–66

Lahann, Birgit, 'Von einem, der zuviel wußte. Zu Stefan Heyms *König-David-Bericht*', *Deutsche Zeitung / Christ und Welt*, 3 November 1972, 21

Lange, H., 'Ein Bergarbeiterroman', *Zeitschrift für Anglistik und Amerikanistik*, 2 (1954), 358–64

Lauckner, Nancy A., 'Stefan Heym's revolutionary Wandering Jew. A warning and a hope for the future', *Studies in GDR Culture and Society*, vol. 4, Selected Papers from the Ninth New Hampshire Symposium on the German Democratic Republic, edited by Margy Gerber et al., pp. 65–78

Liersch, Werner, 'Sturz und Aufstieg', *Neue Deutsche Literatur*, 37, no. 2 (February 1989), 136–41

Loest, Erich, 'Elfenbeinturm und rote Fahne', *Börsenblatt für den deutschen Buchhandel*, 120, no. 27 (4 July 1953), 548–9
  Es geht seinen Gang oder Mühen in unserer Ebene, Halle, 1978
  Der vierte Zensor. Vom Entstehen und Sterben eines Romans in der DDR, Cologne, 1984
  'Was wäre gewesen, wenn ... Stefan Heym Roman *Schwarzenberg* –

Ein politischer Roman als Denkspiel', *Die Zeit*, 23 March 1984, 52

Lübbe, Peter, *Dokumente zur Kunst-, Literatur- und Kulturpolitik der SED 1975–1980*, Stuttgart, 1984

Lusset, Félix, 'A propos du livre de Arnulf Baring – Le 17 juin 1953: Les évènements des 16 et 17 juin 1953 en Allemagne de L'Est', *Allemagne d'Aujourdhui*, 2 (1966), 60–6, and 5 (1966), 56–64

Ludz, P. C., *Parteielite im Wandel*, Cologne and Opladen, 1968
  The German Democratic Republic from the Sixties to the Seventies. A Socio-Political Analysis, Harvard, 1970

Mallinckrodt, Anita, 'Environmental dialogue in the GDR. The literary challenge to the sanctity of "progress"', *GDR Monitor*, 16 (Winter 1986/87), 1–26

Merseburger, Peter, *Grenzgänger. Innenansichten der anderen deutschen Republik*, Munich, 1988

Milfull, John, 'Die Literatur der DDR', *Geschichte der deutschen Literatur vom 18. Jahrhundert bis zur Gegenwart*, vol. 3 part 2, edited by V. Žmegač, Königstein, 1984, pp. 591–694

Moeller, Hans-Bernard, 'Stefan Heym: Das Wagnis der literarischen Exilantentugenden und -versuchungen in alter und neuer Welt', *Deutsche Studien*, 13 (1975), 403–10

Mohr, Heinrich, 'Der 17. Juni als Thema der Literatur in der DDR', in *Die deutsche Teilung im Spiegel der Literatur: Beiträge zur Literatur und Germanistik der DDR*, edited by Karl Lamers, Stuttgart, 1978, pp. 43–84
  'Produktive Sehnsucht. Struktur, Thematik und politische Relevanz von Christa Wolfs *Nachdenken über Christa T.*', *Basis*, 2 (1974), 191–233

Morgner, Irmtraud, *Leben und Abenteuer der Trobadora Beatriz nach Zeugnissen ihrer Spielfrau Laura*, Berlin, 1974

Morris, George, 'Coaltown, Pa., on strike', *The Worker*, 11 July 1954, 8, 14

Mudrich, Heinz, 'DDR-Dokument als spannende Story – Wie und wo *Collin* entstand', *Saarbrücker Zeitung*, 30 March 1979, 8

Müller, Wolfgang, *Dichter-Helden in der DDR-Literatur der siebziger Jahre*, New York, 1989

Neubert, Werner, 'Reports über Geschichte. Stefan Heym: *Der König-David-Bericht*', *Neue Deutsche Literatur*, 22, no. 4 (April 1974), 153–5
  'Der Sinn für das Wesentliche: Stefan Heym, *Lassalle*', *Neue Deutsche Literatur*, 22, no. 8 (1974), 140–2

Neumann, Oskar, 'Der Wohnsitz ist die Botschaft', *Kürbiskern*, no. 3 (1979), 141–6

Nowak, B. 'Eine Stadt als Beweis. Stefan Heyms Roman *Goldsborough* – ein wahres Bild der Vereinigten Staaten', *Berliner Zeitung*, 31 July 1954, 3

Nye, Robert, 'Truth and power', *The Guardian*, 2 August 1973, 7

Pawlik, Peter, 'Pallawatsch. Stefan Heyms Roman *Ahasver*', *Die Zeit zur Buchmesse* [supplement to *Die Zeit*], 16 October 1981, 2

Pender, Malcolm, 'Stefan Heym', in *The Writer and Society in the GDR*, edited by Ian Wallace, Tayport, 1984, pp. 34–51

'Popularising socialism: the case of Stefan Heym', *Socialism and the Literary Imagination. Essays on East German Writers*, edited by Martin Kane, New York, Oxford, 1991, pp. 61–75

Pernkopf, Johannes, *Der 17. Juni in der Literatur der beiden deutschen Staaten*, Stuttgart, 1982

Petr, Pavel, 'Stefan Heym and the Concept of Misunderstanding', *AUMLA. Journal of the Australasian Universities Language and Literature Association*, 'Special DDR Number', 48 (November 1977), 212–21

Picard, Max, *Hitler in uns selbst*, Erlenbach, 1946

Pike, David, *German Writers in Soviet Exile, 1933–45*, North Carolina, 1982

Plant, Richard, 'A study of GI good and evil', *New York Times*, 12 September 1948, 4, 37

Plenzdorf, Ulrich, *Die neuen Leiden des jungen W.*, Rostock, 1973

Prescott, Orville, 'Books of the times', [*Hostages*], *New York Times*, 16 October 1942

'Books of the times' [*The Crusaders*], *New York Times*, 8 September 1948

Raddatz, Fritz J., 'Gruppenbild mit Genosse', *Der Spiegel* 28, no. 47 (1974), 176–9

Ratcliffe, Michael, 'Raising the Ghosts in the National Record', *The Times*, 2 August 1973, 8

'Straight between the Eyes', *The Times*, 6 January 1977, 8

Reich-Ranicki, Marcel, 'König David alias Stalin', *Zur Literatur der DDR*, Munich, 1974, 37–40; first published in *Die Zeit*, 18 August 1972, 16

Reid, J. H., *Writing without Taboos. The New East German Literature*, New York, Oxford, Munich, 1990

Reinhold, Ursula, 'Stefan Heym: *Ahasver*', *Weimarer Beiträge*, 35 (1989), 495–502

Roberts, David, 'Stefan Heym: *Der König-David-Bericht*', *AUMLA. Journal of the Australasian Universities Language and Literature Association*, 'Special DDR Number', 48 (November 1977), 201–11

Roberts, Julian, 'Crucifying Christa', *The Guardian*, 23 August 1990, 24

Rosselini, Jay, 'Der Weg zum "dritten Weg"'. Stefan Heym und sein Roman *Schwarzenberg*' *Carleton Germanic Papers*, 14 (1986), 55–67

Rüß, Gisela, *Dokumente zur Kunst-, Literatur- und Kulturpolitik der SED 1971–1974*, Stuttgart, 1976

Sander, Hans-Dietrich, *Geschichte der Schönen Literatur in der DDR*, Freiburg, 1972

Sandford, John, *The Sword and the Ploughshare. Autonomous Peace Initiatives in East Germany*, London, 1983

'The Church, the State, and the peace movement in the GDR', *GDR Monitor*, 16 (Winter 1986/7), 27–54

Schachtseik-Freitag, Norbert, 'Prosa aus zwei Jahrzehnten: Stefan Heym, "Die richtige Einstellung und andere Erzählungen"', *Deutschland Archiv*, 10 (1977), 1214–15

'Pro domo: Stefan Heym, *Wege und Umwege*', *Deutschland Archiv*, 14 (1981), 188–91

'Schwarzenberger Kolportage: Stefan Heym, *Schwarzenberg*', *Deutschland Archiv*, 17 (1984), 1332–3

Schmitt, Hans-Jürgen (editor), *Hansers Sozialgeschichte der deutschen Literatur*, vol. 11, 'Die Literatur der DDR', Munich, 1983

Schoeller, Wilfried F., 'Fünf umstrittene Tage im Juli', *Frankfurter Rundschau*, 9 October 1974

Schottlaender, Rudolf, 'Grenzen dichterischer Freiheit im Geschichtsroman', *Frankfurter Hefte*, 29 (1974), 756–60

Schubbe, Elimar, *Dokumente zur Kunst-, Literatur- und Kulturpolitik der SED*, Stuttgart, 1972

Schütz, Helga, *Julia oder Erziehung zum Chorgesang*, Berlin, 1980

Seidel, Gerhard, *Das Wort, Moskau 1936–1939. Bibliographie einer Zeitschrift*, Berlin and Weimar, 1975

Serke, Jürgen, 'Die Austreibung des Bösen', *stern*, 1 March 1979, 80–2, 86–7

Sigal, Clancy, 'Conflicts of conscience', *The Sunday Times*, 29 July 1973, 37

Simon, Horst, 'Chronist und Romancier. Zum 60. Geburtstag des Schriftstellers Stefan Heym', *Neues Deutschland*, 10 April 1973, 4

Spittmann, Ilse, and Karl W. Fricke (editors), *17. Juni 1953. Arbeiteraufstand in der DDR*, Cologne, 1982

Strauss, Herbert A., and Werner Roder, *International Biographical Dictionary of Central European Emigrés*, vol. 2, Munich, New York, London, Paris, 1983

Swaffar, Janet, '"Schließlich schreibt man immer in erster Linie für sich selbst": Ein Gespräch mit Gabriele Eckart', *Dimension*, 17 [1984], 312–43

Tate, Dennis, 'Social Realism as an Agent of Protest', *The Times Higher Educational Supplement*, 11 February 1977, 15
'Beyond "Kulturpolitik": the GDR's established authors and the challenge of the 1980s', in *The GDR in the 1980s*, edited by Ian Wallace, pp. 15–29
The East German Novel. Identity, Community, Continuity, Bath, 1984
Toper, Pawel, 'Amerikaner daheim und in fremden Ländern', *Sowjet-Literatur*, 1 (1954), 152–6
Ulbricht, W. 'Über den Charakter der Novemberrevolution. Rede in der Kommission zur Vorbereitung der Thesen über die Novemberrevolution', *Zeitschrift fur Geschichtswissenschaft*, 6 (1958), 717–29
Waldmeir, Joseph J., '*The Crusaders*: an archetype', in *American Novels of the Second World War*, The Hague, 1969, pp. 56–75
Wallace, Ian (editor), *The GDR under Honecker 1971–1981*, Dundee, 1981
'Teacher or partner? The role of the writer in the GDR', in *The Writer and Society in the GDR*, pp. 9–20
(editor), *The Writer and Society in the GDR*, Tayport, 1984
(editor), *The GDR in the 1980s*, Dundee, 1984
East Germany: The German Democratic Republic, Oxford, Santa Barbara, Denver, 1987
Walter, Hans-Albert, *Deutsche Exilliteratur 1933–50*, vol. 4, 'Exilpresse', Stuttgart, 1978
Weber, Hermann, *Die DDR 1945–1986*, Oldenburg, 1988
Weisbrod, Peter, *Literarischer Wandel in der DDR. Untersuchungen zur Entwicklung der Erzählliteratur in den siebziger Jahren*, Heidelberg, 1980
Werth, Wolfgang, 'Nachdenken über Martin W.', *Süddeutsche Zeitung*, 14 November 1974, 'Beilage', p. 2
Wessel, Harald, 'Extrem schillernde historische Gestalt. *Lassalle* – Roman von Stefan Heym', *Neues Deutschland*, 9 April 1974, 6
Wichard, Rudolf, 'Der 17. Juni im Spiegel der DDR-Literatur', *Beilage zur Wochenzeitung 'Das Parlament'*, 21 May 1983, 3–16
Wolf, Christa, *Der geteilte Himmel*, Halle, 1963
Nachdenken über Christa T., Halle, 1968
Kindheitsmuster, Berlin, 1976
Wolfe, Bertram D., *Khrushchev and Stalin's Ghost: Text, Background and Meaning of Khrushchev's Secret Report to the Twentieth Congress on the Night of February 24–25, 1956*, London, 1957
Wolfschütz, Hans, 'Stefan Heym', in *Kritisches Lexikon zur deutschsprachigen Gegenwartsliteratur*, edited by H. L. Arnold, Munich, 1978ff. Second, revised entry, 1986

Woods, Roger, *Opposition in the GDR under Honecker, 1971–85*, Basingstoke, 1986

Zachau, Reinhard K., 'Stefan Heym in Amerika. Eine Untersuchung zu Stefan Heyms Entwicklung im amerikanischen Exil 1933–1952', doctoral dissertation, University of Pittsburgh, 1978 (University Microfilms International no. 7902783)

'Stefan Heym als Herausgeber des kommunistischen *Deutschen Volksecho* (New York, 1937–1939)', in *Das Exilerlebnis*, edited by Donald G. Daviau and L. M. Fischer, Columbia, South Carolina, 1982

Stefan Heym, Munich, 1982

Zehm, Günter, 'Schreib, wie's die Macht befiehlt', *Die Welt*, 7 September 1972, 'Beilage, "Die Welt des Buches"', 2

'Der schwarze Tag des Stefan Heym', *Die Welt*, 23 October 1974, 23

Zimmermann, Hartmut, et al. (editors), *DDR Handbuch*, third, revised edition, Cologne, 1985

Zimmermann, Werner, 'Ein sehr guter zweiter Mann', in *Deutsche Prosadichtungen unseres Jahrhunderts. Interpretationen II*, sixth, revised edition, Dusseldorf, 1985, pp. 332–42

Index